Praise for the Books by George Guthridge

THE KIDS FROM NOWHERE

"This is a delightful visit to a small island in the Bering Sea without having to travel. The landscapes and seascapes are beautifully painted by an outsider, a non-Eskimo teacher, who learns to cherish and respect the culture of his students and the small village in which they live. It is a heart-wrenching story of a group of seemingly uneducable students who, with the coaching of their teacher . . . learn to love learning."
>—Jean M. Auel, best-selling author of *The Clan of the Cave Bear, The Valley of Horses, The Mammoth Hunters, The Plains of Passage, The Shelters of Stone*

"Hilarious, powerful. . . . *The Kids from Nowhere* is proof that people anywhere can accomplish amazing feats when given educational tools and instruction that fit their way of life and thinking. George Guthridge's poignant book is about hope rekindled in the icy north, and how a teacher learned to move from 'teaching' students to 'reaching' them. Read this book and discover how young people truly can learn commitment to a cause that, they come to realize, is much, much bigger than they ever initially imagined."
>—Greg Mortenson, builder of schools in Pakistan and Afghanistan and coauthor of *New York Times* best seller *Three Cups of Tea: One Man's Mission to Fight Terrorism and Build Nations . . . One School at a Time*

"Beautifully written, *The Kids from Nowhere* is a victorious account of one teacher's journey with his Eskimo students from the edge of nowhere to the brink of endless promise."
>—Janet Berliner, media consultant and coauthor of *Artifact*

"Struggle is not unusual in the Arctic, but the struggle for intellectual accomplishment and personal integrity takes a new twist in this compelling and engaging narrative. . . . Guthridge's writing is immaculate and heartfelt as he skillfully explores village life, educational practice, and the desire to succeed."
>—James Ruppert Ph.D., coeditor of *Our Voices: Native Stories of Alaska and the Yukon*

"We often talk about problems facing education. Guthridge offers solid solutions."
>—Professors John Creed and Susan Andrews, coeditors, *Authentic Alaska: Voices of its Native Authors*

"What a remarkable achievement!"
>—Grace Corrigan (mother of Christa McAuliffe)

THE BLOODLETTER

"Guthridge is a master of succinct language and wordplay. . . . It is an unforgettable book."
>—*Bay Times*

"George Guthridge, presently best known for his fine short fiction, [has written] one humdinger of a western historical novel."
>—*Locus*

"Razor-sharp portrait of men *and* women of the Old West. Fast action, slick humor, dead-on historical accuracy. Guthridge can *write*."
>—Steve Perry, author of *The Man Who Never Missed*

the kids *from*

nowhere

The Story Behind the
Arctic Educational Miracle

George Guthridge

ALASKA NORTHWEST BOOKS®
Anchorage ▪ Portland

Text © 2006 by George Guthridge

Photo credits:
Front cover, page 137 © 2006 by Elizabeth Manfred, DCCED, State of Alaska
Front cover inset, page 6, courtesy of State of Alaska, DCCED, Division of Community
   Advocacy
Pages 13, 79 © 2006 by Lyle Schwartz
Page 203 © 2006 by John Wensley
Back cover, reprinted with permission, © 1984, *The Gazette,* Cedar Rapids, Iowa

LIBRARY OF CONGRESS CATALOGING-IN-PUBLICATION DATA
Guthridge, George.
  The kids from nowhere : the story behind the Arctic educational miracle / by George
Guthridge.
    p. cm.
  ISBN-13: 978-0-88240-651-0 (softbound) 1. Yupik children—Education—Alaska—
Gambell. 2. Yupik children—Alaska—Gambell—Social conditions. 3. Yupik Eskimos—
Alaska—Gambell—Social life and customs. 4. Bilingual education—Alaska—Gambell.
5. Academic achievement—Alaska—Gambell. 6. Gambell (Alaska)—Social life and
customs. I. Title.

  E99.E7G87 2006
  372.9164'34—dc22   2006021590

Alaska Northwest Books®
An imprint of Graphic Arts Center Publishing Company
P.O. Box 10306
Portland, OR 97296-0306
(503) 226-2402 • www.gacpc.com

President: Charles M. Hopkins
General Manager: Douglas A. Pfeiffer
Associate Publisher, Alaska Northwest Books: Sara Juday
Editorial Staff: Timothy W. Frew, Kathy Howard, Jean Andrews, Jean Bond-Slaughter
Editor: Ellen Wheat
Cover Design: Elizabeth Watson
Interior Design: Andrea Boven Nelson
Production Coordinator: Susan Dupere

Printed in the United States of America

for

Shannon Boolowon
1985–1999

and

Christa McAuliffe
1948–1986

▲ A New Village house with polar bear hides.
Courtesy of State of Alaska, DCCED, Division of
Community Advocacy.

acknowledgments

I would like to thank all those who helped with this story, especially my co-coach, Bruce Currie; my family, especially Mary; the students who became like a second family; and all of the other wonderful people of Gambell on Saint Lawrence Island. In particular I would like to thank my daughters, Gretchen and Meredith, for recounting and often revealing what were sometimes painful memories; and Merle Apassingok for helping me with information about the culture and with recalling details of my years on the island.

I also would like to thank the staff at Alaska Northwest Books, especially Tim Frew, Sara Juday, and Ellen Wheat; my agent, Laurie Harper, for her contractual help; Robert Fleck, for his publishing advice; and Janet Berliner—my friend and coauthor of most of my previous books—for her invaluable assistance with editing and other textual matters.

Thanks also go to those who directly contributed to the teams' quest: Bruce Boolowon, David Bowling, Robert Carlson, Edward Gonion, George Harper, Dean Lambe, Donald Lofland, Mary Rubadeau, Lyle and Diane Schwartz, and Richard Palmiter and the other scientists at the University of Washington.

Finally, I would like to thank Bering Straits School District, Best Western Hotels, and Alaska Airlines for their financial support in making the kids' trip possible. And to all those who help run the Future Problem Solving Program: may you continue to enrich the lives of our young people.

a note about language and factual accuracy

The word *Eskimo* has always been slang and is currently considered demeaning by many Native peoples who inhabit the circumpolar North. At the time I lived on Saint Lawrence Island, however, the people of Gambell referred to themselves by that term. I have chosen to use the word for historical accuracy.

The events of this book are true. In telling the story, however, I have rearranged factual and chronological elements, and several characters are composites. A number of identities, events, and names have been altered to protect privacy. In some cases, refinements of teaching techniques that began in Gambell but that actually occurred later also have been incorporated into the story.

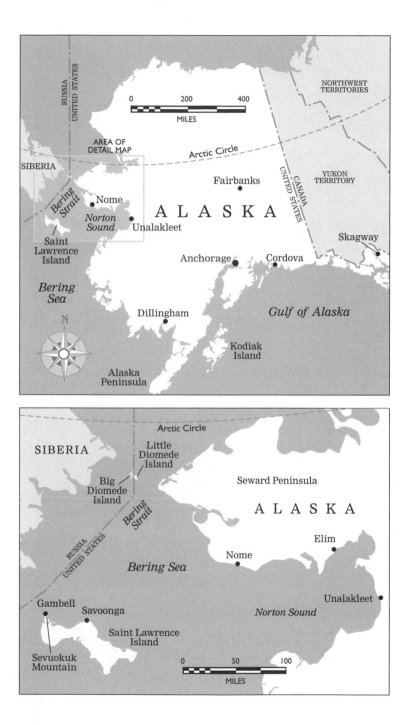

Top map

RUSSIA / UNITED STATES

NORTHWEST TERRITORIES

0   200   400
MILES

SIBERIA

AREA OF DETAIL MAP

Arctic Circle

CANADA / UNITED STATES

YUKON TERRITORY

Fairbanks

A L A S K A

Bering Strait

Nome

Norton Sound

Unalakleet

Skagway

Saint Lawrence Island

Anchorage

Cordova

Bering Sea

N

Dillingham

Gulf of Alaska

Kodiak Island

Alaska Peninsula

Bottom map

Arctic Circle

SIBERIA

Little Diomede Island

Big Diomede Island

Seward Peninsula

A L A S K A

Bering Strait

RUSSIA / UNITED STATES

Elim

Nome

Bering Sea

Unalakleet

Gambell

Savoonga

Norton Sound

Saint Lawrence Island

Sevuokuk Mountain

0   50   100
MILES

prologue

Time, the Eskimos taught me, cannot be measured by clocks or calendars. Life's benchmarks, I came to realize, are luck and love, the migration of whales, the changing of weather. In that tiny Siberian Yupik school on Saint Lawrence Island, which teeters on the edge of the world, time took on what for me was an even deeper dimension: the trials and the successes of teaching. I went there with no intention of remaining a teacher, and returned a butterfly—an insect integral to Eskimo culture—that dreams of bringing every flower to fruition.

How can I tell you how much I learned from those students, and how deeply I still love them after all these years? For I am one of the luckiest teachers alive: I bore witness to what was called an educational miracle. I watched ten teenagers, some of whom previous teachers had called "uneducable," achieve the seemingly impossible.

Those students are grown now, with children of their own, yet I will always think of them as my kids, my challenges—for is not the greatest challenge for many of us teachers the realization that our families are not in the cloister of our homes but in the chaos of the classroom? Each night we take home our students' problems and their papers, the memories of smiles and the sound of laughter and of groans over homework assigned or forgotten. Each year we recall less of the faces and more of what those faces meant to us.

It has been over two decades since "the Kids from Nowhere," as they came to call themselves one cold night while an ancestral aurora danced above us, made educational history. It seems longer, it seems shorter, it seems in some ways that time has stood still since last I stood on that hill on Saint Lawrence Island.

part 1

◄ Part of the Old Village. The house on the right is one of the few newer ones in the area.

Photo by Lyle Schwartz.

1

August 15, 1982, dawns in fog. As the small plane drones westward from Nome, my wife and two daughters strain for a glimpse of Saint Lawrence Island. Even now in my dreams I can see them waiting for a first look at the land that we are determined will be our home for several years. Mary will teach in the elementary school, and I will teach social studies and other classes "as needed" to the high school's forty-one ninth- through twelfth-grade students, in a building a mile away.

Seated behind the pilot, Meredith, age ten, seems resolute. Living among Saint Lawrence Island Yupik Eskimos, she has decided, will be an adventure. She reached that conclusion, as I am painfully aware, mostly to please me: always the daddy's girl.

Gretchen, impetuous, age six, cradles her Barbie in the crook of her arm and sits with both hands on the window, nose against the glass. Image of a prisoner, I morosely realize. "Are we almost there, Mom?" she asks for the dozenth time. "Are we at the end of the earth?"

"Just about," Mary tells her, and gives me a dark look.

I keep my gaze on the glass, barely noticing the cobalt blue waves. Trying to get under the fog, the pilot is flying so low that the waves seem to lick at the fuselage. I stare at my reflection. It haunts me, for it reminds me that I have a history of bad decision making. Then the fog falls away as if the hand of God has rolled it back, and tundra appears, an expanse of chocolate and golden-brown ending in low, treeless mountains. The pilot banks around a headland, its boulders dwarfing the plane. As he brings the wings level, he turns and, pushing his unkempt hair from his eyes and straightening his ratty flying jacket, announces in an Ed McMahon impersonation, "H-eee-re's Gambell!"

Below us, emerging through ground fog, are six huge oil tanks, a couple of large buildings, and about seventy houses. Many are shacks, others the boxy packaged HUD homes that, built for Indian reservations in the Southwest, were sent north in response to Bobby Kennedy's remark that rural Alaska is the nation's worst Appalachia. The houses protrude like molars from a gravel spit flanked on one side by the sea's white-capped wavelets and on the other by a rocky-shored lake. There are no roads, though trails run through the gravel and out onto the tundra. At the edge of the village, a blacktopped runway lines a narrow isthmus between the lake and the sea.

Mary grips my hand and, leaning close, fear in her eyes, whispers, "You said that teaching Eskimos will be romantic. This better be romantic, George."

Before I can reply, if indeed there is a comeback to such a remark, Meredith shrieks with delight and points down past the plane.

"Whales, Mom!"

Two behemoths have surfaced, spouting. In rhythmic syncopation, they arc back into the ocean, their enormous flukes slipping splashless beneath the sea. It's as if Nature is giving us a sampling of the raw power of the world that awaits us.

"Bowheads," the pilot says. "Heading south. Where you'll wish you were, come winter."

He banks again and drops the Piper Navajo abruptly to the runway, bumping down with one wheel and slowly lowering the other because of the crosswinds. He brings the plane to a halt, opens his window-door, and slides with an acrobat's ease onto the wing. When he opens the main door and puts down the stairs, we emerge into gusting wind.

Though I am from Washington state and thus accustomed to greenery, the grass surrounding the lake is the greenest I have ever seen: so suffused with color it startles me. But this is a world of contrasts—for hulked halfway up the mountain is an ice ridge, striated with black lines. Protected by the boulders above it, the ice is unmelted at the end of summer.

Nine or ten boys and young men on ATV three-wheelers crest the slope next to the runway and roar onto the tarmac. They ride single file, a couple pulling wheelies and all forming a line, facing us like a row of mechanical cavalry. After gunning their engines, they sit silently, baseball caps on backward, faces like stones.

I do not want to wave, do not want to seem as if I see myself as an arriving dignitary, but I smile and wave just the same.

Not acknowledging me, the young males roar off down the slope, a couple heading back to the village, the others peeling off toward the tundra. There is arctic stillness. No birds, no cars, no clocks—only the shush of the wind and the soft slap of waves against the black gravel beach.

Watching the young men disappear, the pilot extends a hand. "Luck to you," he says. "You'll need it."

He climbs into the Navajo, and the plane taxis away as if it is eager to depart.

Minutes later another three-wheeler—this one driven by Jones, an oily faced, roly-poly man who turns out to be the school janitor—comes sputtering from the village, pulling a cart. "Welcome to three-wheeler capital of the world!" He grins—nearly toothless.

We pile on, along with our possessions, spill off once, and plow through gravel. We pass by the HUD homes and enter what Jones tells us is Old Village, where our house is: a tiny weather-beaten shack made of dunnage lumber from ships half a century before. The place turns out to be labyrinthed with the boxes of clothing, school supplies, and canned goods we had shipped. It is also so low-ceilinged that, despite being only 5 feet 7 inches, I can easily place my palm on the ceiling. There is no plumbing—Jones shows us where to store the filled honey-bucket bags so they will freeze before we take them to the dump.

Mary puts a hand lovingly on the large, old oil stove.

"At least it *looks* warm," she says.

"We Eskimos don't live in no igloos," Jones reassures her. "Not without central heating, anyway."

Chuckling at his joke, Jones exits, and Gretchen instantly pipes up: "We want to meet some Eskimo kids!"

Mary sighs but bends and buttons Gretchen's coat against the August chill. We could use the girls' help unpacking boxes, but it's been a difficult month, leaving friends and familiar places. They need a respite.

"Just remember what your father said," Mary tells her.

"No talking about home," Meredith says in semisarcastic rote. "They might not think we want to be here."

"And being best isn't important here," Gretchen adds, also from rote. "They're non . . . noncompelative."

"Non*competitive,*" Mary corrects. "At least that's what last year's principal said at the interview."

"He said Eskimos are possessive," Gretchen says.

"*Passive,*" Mary says. "He said, 'passive.'"

Meredith looks troubled. "You promised," she says to both of us from the door. "Only five years here."

"And then we'll have enough money to live like princes!" Gretchen says.

"Prin*cesses,*" Meredith says. "Don't you know anything?"

They shut the door and, as I hear them exit the arctic entryway—the shallow covered entrance that helps keep out the cold—I sit down on the house's only chair, a metal folding chair with "Gambell Schools" stenciled on it. As I watch them tread through the gravel toward the school playground we passed on the ride here, depression pervades me, so strong it feels tangible. I have fought depression since college over a decade before, a seemingly losing battle. Now it fills up the house.

I had been a professor, then after receiving tenure I resigned to teach high school, quit that to edit a science magazine, quit that to be a full-time writer. But I had missed the classroom. I was about to accept another college position when I saw an ad for teaching in Alaska. We were deeply in debt. Teaching in Alaska would pay three times what the college job would.

"Maybe moving here wasn't such a good idea," I say, to the window.

"Stick to a decision," Mary says, already stacking soup in a cupboard. "For once."

Though I should be helping her, I head outside, following the girls without their knowing.

The girls' first encounter with an Eskimo other than Jones involves an ancient, bowlegged woman no taller than a child, who steps out from behind a house, sunlight glinting from the crescent-shaped knife she holds. Her face is recessed into a parka hood paisley'd with flowers; striped tattoos run from her mouth to her chin.

She spits tobacco and, an abrupt grin revealing a single tooth, opens her arms in greeting. "*Quyakamken!*" With a sweep of her arm, she indicates that the girls are to follow her. She totters around the corner of the house.

There, strips of red, raw walrus meat dangle from a wooden rack crusted with blood and gristle. She pulls down a strip of black walrus jerky and, expertly working her *ulaaq,* slices off a section, motions as if to eat, and hands it to Meredith. The girls eye one another fearfully, but sample the jerky, kowtowing, I am certain from my vantage point amid the shadows of the next house, to my insistence that they keep an open mind regarding whatever the village offers.

"Kinda chewy," Gretchen says, her smile a rictus.

Meredith's smile is more genuine. "Kinda like taffy," she tells the woman, who grins despite obviously not understanding the girls' words. She sets her knife down on the bloodstained table, kneels, and opens her arms. The girls step into her embrace. *"Quyakamken,"* she repeats in a softly guttural voice. *"Quyakamken."*

Only months later will we learn the meaning.

"Bless you."

She pats the girls on their behinds and sends them on their way, to the playground, with its broken teeter-totter, disconnected swings, and lopsided merry-go-round. Meredith struggles to push as Gretchen rides.

Two boys and a girl, all about Meredith's age, appear between the houses. They have on tennis shoes and jeans, the boys in T-shirts, the girl wearing a *qiipaghaq*—a short, pleated dress—above her jeans. They move forward hesitantly. Shy and respectful, just as last year's principal said. I am glad that we asked so many questions at the interview, and for the first time I am confident of our move here.

This will be a good place for the girls, I decide; a learning experience without equal, for even by Eskimo standards, the islanders are unique. Our frenzied pre-trip reading informed us that besides the Indians and Aleuts in Alaska, there are four Eskimo groups, each with its own language. The largest group—about 17,000—are the Central Yup'ik of Southwest Alaska. Up north, with a population of 11,000, are the Iñupiat—called Inuit in Canada. The next smallest group are the Sugpiag (or Alutiiq) of Kodiak Island and part of the Alaska Peninsula. Comprising by far the smallest group, just over 1,000 strong, are the Siberian Yupik of Saint Lawrence Island.

Gretchen climbs off the merry-go-round, and the girls approach the Eskimo kids hand-in-hand, unsure of themselves. Meredith manages a smile.

The Eskimos scoop up gravel and charge, faces suddenly filled with wrath. "White trash! White trash! Go back where you belong!"

Gravel peppers the girls, who drop to their knees and cover their heads, cowering before the onslaught. I step from the shadows. The kids race away, one of the boys—having found a large rock—glancing back at me with a look between leering and loathing as he flips the rock aside.

2

The village site of Gambell, named for two missionaries who drowned at the turn of the nineteenth century, has been inhabited by Natives for at least 2,300 years. During that time, the men periodically donned baleen armor to fight off Siberians who came to raid food caches and abduct women.

American whalers were the next enemy. They devastated the bowhead population and so seduced the islanders with alcohol and unkept promises of foodstuffs that three-fourths of the population of several thousand starved to death one spring.

Next came the Gambells and other missionaries, who brought hope and Jesus during the years that the island was ravaged by measles, mumps, and influenza. They insisted that the islanders stop their heathen dancing beneath the moon and not speak their Native language at school, lest the missionaries wash their mouths out with soap.

Teachers were among the latest arrivals, here for adventure or classroom experience, or like us, for the money and the lure of the aurora which, we would sadly discover, we would rarely see.

Minutes after I usher the girls back from the rock-throwing incident, there is a knock at the door, and Mr. Dan, the new principal, bows through into the house. "Come visit?" It is a ritual—a knock and someone entering before we answer the door—we will come to know only too well. Until recent times, there weren't enough houses to go around, so children and young adults slept or warmed themselves wherever there was space. Since everyone considered any house their home, no one knocked. Privacy was a privilege that ran counter to common sense.

Mr. Dan removes his jacket and tennis shoes. A Central Yup'ik Eskimo from a mainland village, he is so thin that the outline of his backbone shows through his shirt.

"Daniel Dan," he says. "Welcome to the island on the edge of forever." He smiles as we shake hands and seems so professional and genuinely gregarious that, despite being shaken by the rock-throwing incident, I warm to him instantly. Then his smile turns to a sense of concern as he looks into the bedroom—it has no door, and the curtain is pulled back. Meredith is on the bed, facing the wall, softly whimpering. Gretchen is in Mary's arms, crying as Mary wipes her face and head with a damp cloth. "Little problem with homesickness?" he asks.

Mary rises and crosses her arms, her face hard. "Little problem with kids throwing rocks at our girls." Gretchen moves behind her, hiding, arms around Mary's waist.

"I hope this isn't indicative of things to come," I inform Mr. Dan.

"You weren't told at the interview?" he asks.

"Told what," Mary says, her voice edged with ice.

"I'll find out who the perpetrators were," he says, obviously avoiding the subject he just brought up, "and take away some of their gym time."

"That's it?" she asks. "Their gym time?"

Back then we did not understand the severity of the punishment.

"What weren't we told at the interview?" I ask him.

He gives smiles all around, a hand raised as if to say we'll discuss it later, and, retreating to the door, slips into his shoes and jacket. "There's a potlatch tonight at the city building, in the teachers' honor. The mayor said it'll start at, 'oh seven maybe six.' Come at nine. You'll still be early." He grins. "Welcome to Eskimo time."

We arrive at the city building at ten and, by the time the Eskimos begin drifting in an hour later, we have put our anger behind us. Just kids and territoriality, Mary and I assure each other. As a boy, I had thrown rocks at the new kid in the neighborhood, but soon we were lifelong friends.

Most of the Eskimos sit silently on folding chairs that line the walls. A few give hugs and make quiet conversation with the returning teachers. Three of the elementary teachers are back, plus the shop teacher, who is the first teacher in the high school's six-year existence to return a second year. But for the most part, the Eskimos and teachers do not mingle.

I take a seat at the end of the row of older men. They stare forward, some with their weight resting on walking sticks. They do not seem purposely to ignore me, for they are not speaking among themselves, either. Their eyes are deep and bright, but otherwise their tawny faces are set in repose. They appear attuned to everything in the room though absorbed in nothing or no one in particular.

I then realize that there seems to be no social urge that they *should* speak. From them I will come to understand that silence is valued—integral to a culture in which calling attention to oneself is frowned on, quiet is mandatory during hunting, and orality is so highly regarded that among the elders it is used sparingly. No one is compelled to fill up silences with empty words.

"Ice cream!" Gretchen announces, spooning from a serving bowl. "With candy in it!"

"*Agutaq,*" Jones tells her, busy filling his dish with meats. "Eskimo ice cream. With berries. Good, all right!"

Gretchen takes a mouthful—and makes a face. "Crisco!"

Bowl in hand, she hurries into a corner, and I can see her spitting. Years later, we will relish Eskimo ice cream, but only that from mainland villages. Here, where resources are few, it consists of reindeer fat mixed with lard and the local, tiny, hard, often bitter berries.

Two elders rise and retrieve drums from the arctic entryway. Made of stretched walrus stomach, the Yupik drum looks like a giant tambourine with a handle. I assume that all attention will turn to the elders, but the party continues unabated as the two use spritz bottles to wet the drums. Though clearly the elders are deferred to, there is no sense of their being ostracized by too little care—or too much care. They are not fawned over and catered to, treated like children, as I often saw with elderly back home in Washington. Here, they are treated as men.

They begin drumming and singing.

Their voices are deep and yet lilting, an odd, stirring mix of bass and cacophony. Three teenage girls wearing the traditional Eskimo dress with jeans underneath step into the center of the room and begin to dance, bland-faced, their feet not moving. Except for their arms and hands, which move like those of reluctant hula dancers, their dancing is but a small swaying between knees and shoulders—gentle, conservative.

They perform two dances with no applause between, and then more young women join them. Soon the dancers are urging teachers to come dance. Mary and the girls and Mr. and Mrs. Dan and their little daughters join them. I shake my head. I have always been shy about doing anything in public unless I'm completely prepared.

When the dance ends, the center of the room empties. The elderly woman who gave Meredith and Gretchen the walrus jerky hobbles forward. A hush as still as that during prayer pervades the room. The faces of the drummers do not change, but there appears a deepening in their eyes, a look of anticipation.

The woman has the rolling gait of someone used to moving across wind-hardened snow, certainly not a dancer's grace, yet it immediately becomes apparent that her ability is much stronger than that of the young women and girls.

She keeps her feet stationary, as the younger women did, but where their bodies seemed to move as separate parts, the arms and hands not totally in flow with the torso, everything about her dancing is in concert. Where they swayed, she *writhes,* an undulating at once graceful and exquisitely tortured, the dance of an eel with the soul of an Eskimo angel and the sensuality of the human spirit.

The drumming intensifies, and though her face stays calm, her motions quicken. Now she is gyrating, energy seeming to course from her feet and emanate from her hands, which *express* rather than merely being *expressive.* Her hands tell a story I cannot understand; yet they entrance me. My eyes water in awe. Such beauty! I had minored in modern dance in college—it seemed an artistic extension of my high school interest in wrestling—but I could not dance like that if I practiced a hundred years. Everything about her bespeaks *Eskimo.* It is a dance not of self but of soul.

The drums pound faster, my heart pounds faster, and faster and faster she moves, the men's voices rising in crescendo, all eyes in the audience seeming to gleam . . . and it is done. The dance has ended, the energy goes out of her, and she is again an elderly woman who hobbles off into the crowd. No applause, but there is an appreciative, collective sigh. People start meandering from the city building. It is past midnight. Outside, the world is deep in dusk.

I smile inwardly, and a rhyme forms in my consciousness, a rhyme that is to prove a litany in the months ahead.

Come what may, we're here to stay.

3

I spend the rest of the weekend organizing my classroom.

Except it isn't a classroom. It is the library. Except it isn't that, either. The "library" is two sets of tall metal shelving crowded with books other places discarded. Flanking me are ancient textbooks, scientific tomes meaningless to anyone but specialists, and dozens of remaindered romance novels, their covers torn off to indicate that the stores returned them to publishers. All sent here, I figure, for tax reasons.

What little classroom remains is crammed with ten typing desks, each with an IBM typewriter, for a dozen students taking social studies. Unless everyone sits and clacks all period, there will be no way for the kids to take notes, much less open a book without laying it across the machine. The only answer is to put two kids at a table, facing the wall in the only available corner, and have the others put the typewriters under the desks and sit with their feet on them.

Worse, the principal's office window looks into my classroom, giving him an unsubtle control of what I do there. Behind the bookshelves is the secretary's nook—with a telephone which, I will discover to my endless irritation, will ring almost all day—and a photocopier that will often get used during class time.

On Monday, the first day of school, we have our first storm. I trudge the mile to the high school through the deep gravel, into 40-knot winds and driving rain and sleet, to find many kids already there, playing with the typewriters. Their feet are in water, the storm having beaten under the door. I frantically pull plugs and mop like a madman as the students sit bemused.

"You're a new teacher," a girl says without looking up from her typewriter. Slender and pretty except for a bad complexion, she has the top of the typewriter open and is playing with the ribbon cartridge, clearly intrigued. "You got a name?"

"George." It is custom, we learned at the interview, to use first names. Only the principal is referred to by last name. "Yours?"

"Londa."

I check my roll book, discover that she's a sophomore—this first class, geography, is for ninth and tenth graders—and realize that I've forgotten to take roll.

A muscular student—Marshall, I will later discover—sits toward the rear of the room. He has his feet up on the desk, up on the typewriter, one arm around a basketball, and his face turned toward the ceiling in a look of studied nonchalance. He wears a tank top, a garment he will don whenever the temperature is above 10 degrees.

"George, the janitor," he says.

"Gonna stay all year?" Londa asks, in a neutral voice. "Or quit early."

"Bet he leaves by Christmas," Marshall says. He spins the basketball on an index finger.

"I'm not a quitter," I tell him, loud enough so everyone will hear, and keep mopping.

"Coming back next year?" Londa asks.

"High school teachers never come back," Marshall says.

"Keenan came back," Londa tells him.

"He's not a real teacher," Marshall says. "He's a shop teacher."

As I stick the mop in the corner I feel another of my debilitating sinus headaches coming on. "I plan to stay at least five years."

Marshall brings the basketball down to his forehead. "No one's that stupid."

A boy I will come to know as Boone has been standing in the corner, watching everything. He has the chiseled features of a Greek god and the easy grace of a gifted athlete. He sits down, eyeing me with interest. Unlike the rest, he has shown no desire to play with the typewriters.

A straggly haired boy has his T-shirt pulled up and is fondling a nipple. "Five . . . years!" He belches the words, swallowing a huge breath in between.

Lobert, I decide from my roll book. To help me remember his name I think of him as "Lobe," as in "Lacking in frontal."

Two boys in the chairs in the corner giggle and put their heads together as if they need to snuggle to control their mirth. "Chip and Dale," I decide, and much to my delight later find out that one really is named Dale.

Marshall starts tossing up the basketball and catching it.

"Put the ball down," I tell him.

"Why?"

"This isn't basketball practice. It's social studies."

"School's for basketball," he says.

"Put the ball under the desk," I tell him. "Put your typewriter under your desk too." When I see him glare I add, trying to defuse his temper, "Everyone put the machines under the desks."

The anger leaves Marshall's face as the other students start moving their machines. At last he acquiesces and places his typewriter below the desk as well.

"Are you gonna give us straight As?" Londa asks. "That's what our teacher did last year."

"He only give me Bs," Lobert says. His typewriter under his desk, he has returned to fondling his nipple. "Cause I punch him out." He grins a lopsided grin. "After that he *pay* me to be good."

I gather my chalk and blackboard compass for our first lesson, on Earth's position in space. "This year, you get what you earn."

"That's what they all say, at first," Marshall remarks.

I ignore him. "We'll start with the solar system. On average, Earth is 93 million miles from the sun." I inscribe circles on the board and indicate the distance with a dual-ended arrow. "Lobert," I ask, hoping to embarrass him into paying attention and not playing with his chest, "How many miles is the Earth from the sun?"

He gulps another breath, and belches, "Ninety-three million!"

Chip and Dale giggle and put their arms around each other. Lobert looks around the room for approval. The others ignore him, as do I.

"We call that average distance from the Earth to the sun an 'astronomical unit,'" I tell everyone. "Okay, what's an astronomical unit?"

Lobert waves a hand in front of my face. "Average distance from the Earth to the sun!"

His turnabout astonishes me. He even has his T-shirt down, though he continues to pinch the nipple through the cloth.

"So if the average distance from the earth to the sun is 93 million miles, and an astronomical unit is the average distance from the Earth to the sun," I ask everyone, "then how long"—I hold out my hands as if to indicate length—"is an astronomical unit?"

"I know! I know!" Lobert frantically waves.

No one else seems willing to answer, so I defer to the kid with the nipple.

"April!" he announces.

"April?" I ask.

He cocks his head sideways like that of a curious bird. "It isn't?" His grin broadens with confidence. "February!" he says. Realizing that isn't right either, he adds, "Thursday! It's Thursday!"

Some of the other students groan and roll their eyes. Londa picks up the globe off its crescent base and looks at it appreciatively. "It is really true that the Earth goes around the sun?"

"That's crap," Marshall says. He leans over and slashes a large X on the globe with a black permanent marker. I grab the globe from Londa, who looks hurt that I've taken it away.

"Must you damage school property?" I ask Marshall.

"It's not *my* property," he says.

"It's your school," I tell him.

"That's what you say." He leans back in his chair. "Besides, the sun goes around the Earth. It comes up behind the mountain and goes down in the sea. Everyone knows that. This is stupid, man."

I set the globe in its rocker and take a flashlight from my desk. I turn off one light and show them the position of the sun, walking around as best I can amid the desks. Most students seem interested. Marshall stares at the ceiling. A tiny girl—Puffin, I will later discover, named after the Bering Sea's colorful bird that looks like a small toucan—has her geography book open, reading. She closes it and, without so much as a glance my way, exits the room.

"Where're you going?" I ask, rushing to the door.

She doesn't answer. Just turns the corner in the hallway and is gone.

In exasperation I return to the others. "You can't leave class without asking," I tell them.

Lobert gives me a look of disbelief. "We gotta ask to pee?"

A girl says in an incredulous voice, "We gotta ask to fart?" She rolls up a hip as if to demonstrate.

"You gotta . . . oh, never mind." My head is pounding. "Open your books. Read the first chapter."

At the interview, last year's principal said, "Sustained silent reading. Have at least forty-five minutes of sustained silent reading each day." He also said, "The kids are passive. They're just no trouble whatsoever. During hunting season there's a mystical thing that comes over the boys, and they really need to be out hunting. But they're never any problem, and the main hunting season isn't until the end of the school year."

The kids open their books. Marshall starts dribbling his basketball.

"That's not reading," I tell him, my head now a jackhammer.

Marshall flips his book shut. "This isn't about basketball. And it isn't about Eskimos. What good is it."

"It's about . . . " I start to say. But I'm not going to argue with him. I sit down at my desk, not wanting to seem the aggressor but wishing that corporal punishment were still in vogue. No, *capital* punishment. "It's reading," I tell him. "That's what it is."

"I don't like reading," he says.

I concentrate on keeping my face calm. I feel as if I'm standing on a volcano about to erupt. The other kids are eyeing us, seeing who will win this first, all-important confrontation. Lobert eases from his desk and sidles down the hall. I say nothing. Even my eyes don't speak. If there was one thing I learned in the sales school I attended during part of a summer after high school, it was that silence is a powerful weapon.

I am here for the money, I tell myself. *Maybe he'll leave. I'll get paid the same whether there are two students or two dozen.*

"Okay, I'll read." Marshall snatches up the book and climbs defiantly onto his desk. "I'll read up here. Try to stop me," he says with a snarl, "I'll throw you through the window."

"Just so you're reading," I tell him in a tone as business-like as I can muster. Secretly, though, I am shaken by the obvious depth of his anger.

To keep myself as calm as I can, I focus on wondering about how much of the text the kids understand. All speak English as a second language, and they lack the world knowledge that gives context. Few have been off the island, except perhaps to go to other villages for basketball games or wrestling. The previous principal told me that the kids possess great decoding skills in reading—that is, the ability to sound out words. "But do they know the words' meanings?" I asked. "How much do they comprehend?" He had changed the subject.

There is a scuffling near the door. I leave my desk and peer around the bookshelves. Puffin is battling with Lobert, who has one arm around her neck, another up under her T-shirt. The fight, though animated, seems as if in slow motion. There is a desperate look in her eyes, but she makes no sound.

I take hold of his shoulder and pull him off her. He balls his right hand into a fist, and his eyes narrow to slits. His hand remains fisted as he breaks into a grin.

"You go to the principal's office," I tell him, unsure what to do.

His grin broadens. "Maybe I should kill you, man."

He ambles off, and I turn my attention to Puffin, who has a hand under her T-shirt, rearranging her bra. She has the body of a ten-year-old. I feel that she should be playing with dolls, not having to deal with someone trying to paw her.

"You okay?" I ask.

She sneers at me. "What do you care."

She goes back to her desk, settles herself, and starts reading.

Thankfully, the bell rings. The kids troop out, Marshall dribbling his basketball.

"Five years?" he asks me. "You won't last five days."

An older student, wearing glasses and a cap that says "John Deere," comes down the hall to his locker. He moves with fluid athleticism but without the jive movements some of the other kids, Marshall especially, seem to have copied from black basketball players they have seen on what little TV the village has.

The older student gives Boone, my Greek-god student, a high-five, but that too seems without affect.

Marshall nods toward me. "This guy says he's staying five years."

The older student smiles, appraising me. "Maybe someone should straightjacket you and put you in a museum. What's that one called? . . . the Smithsonian?"

"Our teacher last year quit before Easter," Boone tells me. "The teacher before that lasted all year—but he showed movies all day."

"Sometimes the same one over and over, all day long," the older student says.

"Merle and I were in the same class then," Boone says. "We're cousins."

"The Dynamic Duo," Merle says.

As if on cue, Boone pretends to dribble his geography book, then flips it over his back to Merle, who enters the room, springs up and slam-dunks it on the top bookshelf.

"We had one teacher we called 'Statue,'" Merle says, retrieving the book and handing it back to Boone. "She fell on the ice and then sued the government for not scraping the sidewalks and streets we don't have."

"Statue walked a wheelchair to school over the drifts," Boone adds, "and then sat in it all day. She said our village had crippled her."

"Statue?" I ask, not making the connection.

"*Statue!*" Boone goes back as if to throw a pass. The old Statue of Liberty play. Merle circles behind Boone and then, in a movement combining football and basketball, takes the handoff and reverse-dunks the book back onto the top shelf, where it teeters.

"Come to the end of America," Merle says, with angry laughter. "Give us your inept, your incompetent, your incapacitated."

Perhaps seeing my confusion, Boone adds, "One of our teachers taught us a unit on the Statue of Liberty."

"Like maybe it would help us appreciate *America*," Merle says.

"Regardless, you've quite the vocabulary," I tell him.

The ease that characterized his body language turns to a sense of suspicion. "For an Eskimo, you mean."

"For anyone in high school," I tell him. His smile returns, and I add, "Especially someone who speaks English as a second language." I glance up at the top shelf. "That's quite a leap you have."

"Merle can Eskimo high-kick six-feet-eight," Boone says.

Perhaps 5 feet 8 inches tall, Merle jumps up and with both feet expertly knocks the book from the shelf and catches it.

"You're scheduled for my journalism class, aren't you?" I check my roll book. A special kid: sports plus scholastic ability. Athletics and academics. After Marshall and Lobert, Merle is a blessing. "Maybe you should be editor of the school paper. We might end up with the best one in western Alaska."

"Why bother?" Boone says, his earlier enthusiasm gone. "We're Eskimos. Nobody cares about us."

"I care," I tell him.

"Because we're special, right?"—his tone now one of angry sarcasm.

"Because I'm special," I tell him.

He gives me a look as though I have abruptly gone through a reappraisal. His lips remain tight, but the smile returns to his eyes. He takes the book from Merle and heads down the hall. Merle hurries after him, but stops and looks back.

"Maybe you *can* last the whole year," he tells me. *"Maybe."*

4

"My aide told me that the principal last year was knocked cold twice," Mary says that night. "She said that things got so bad that his son had to go live with relatives."

Clearly, the challenge of teaching twenty-seven first and second graders with minimal English skills has inspired the *educator* in her, but she is worried about Gretchen and Meredith. The Dans and one other teaching couple have children, but those kids are too young for school. Our girls are the only teachers' kids, and the only white kids, in the classroom. Added to that, they do not know the language or the customs.

I do not tell her that some kids kept punching me all day. Not hard, but constant enough that my upper arm is black and blue. And Dale, of the Chip and Dale gigglers, kept trying to grab my balls. I spoke to Lawrence, the science/math teacher, about the kid. Though the size of a mountain, Lawrence had the same problem with him.

"At the interview he told us that his son got along great here," Mary adds. "He lied to us, George. I think there have been a lot of lies."

The next day, the students are unresponsive, most just staring at their books. By the third day I give up trying to teach about the solar system. What use is it to teach about outer space when some of the students do not know the capital of the United States? It's as if life beyond the island has little relevance for most of them.

Since the textbook and the school district's scope and sequence emphasize non-American geography, I decide to start with Europe. I type up the names of all the European countries, on impulse including even the little ones, and for each country list the capital, other major cities, government, main religion, main products, and sometimes other incidental facts. It should take the kids a month to learn the chart, I figure.

Minutes after I hand out the paper, Puffin heads to the bathroom. As usual, she does not ask. She's such a tiny girl that half the time she is out of her desk and down the hall before I notice she's gone. I explain the chart for about five minutes, and send Londa after her. When Londa does not return, I send the girl who likes to fart, figuring she can use a bathroom break anyway. I end up pounding on the door, and the girls pour out.

"What's so interesting about the bathroom?" I ask Puffin.

She shrugs, walks back into the classroom, plops down, and opens her geography book.

"The rest of us are looking at the chart I created," I tell her.

She takes a paper from her pocket, holds it up to indicate that this is the chart, sticks it in her book and closes the cover.

"We're going over it," I tell her.

Her brows go down.

Before we arrived on the island, the superintendent gave all teachers a two-day in-service in Unalakleet, a mainland village, 250 miles away, where the district office is. The first words he said to the group were, "Whatever you've heard about me, isn't true."

Having heard nothing about him, Mary and I had no reference point, but later we learned that he was under suspicion of embezzlement, and was eventually convicted. The only useful piece of information we did learn at the in-service was that Eskimos raise their brows for "yes," lower them for "no." Brows down also indicates anger.

Puffin is in the brows down mode.

"I already know the paper," she mumbles, probably believing that I had not read her body language.

"You know it *all?*" I ask.

Her eyes remain downcast but her brows go up.

"You had this material in the past?" I ask the question less to test her than because I am worried that my lesson is a rerun of some previous year's material.

I breathe a mental sigh of relief when her brows go down.

"You learned it just now," I say, trying not to sound as if I am doubting her.

Brows up.

"Just now," I repeat. "In five or ten minutes in the bathroom."

Brows up.

"When I was in there she was brushing her hair," Londa offers, then seems to shrink down in her chair when the other kids glare at her.

I pick up the paper. "You know this whole thing."

Brows up.

What to do what to do what to do? Ignoring her and going on with the lesson will mean that others will probably follow her example and not learn the material. Questioning her further will mean embarrassing her, catching her in a lie.

I choose a third approach. I look around the room, using my eyes to make the others resume their work, kneel in front of her desk and quietly ask, "I believe you, but I need to know something. What's the capital of Germany?"

"Berlin," she mutters. "Other major cities, Munich, Frankfort, Stuttgart, Dresden. Main products . . ." She rattles off everything about Germany.

"Poland," I ask.

Same result. I have to look at the list to check her accuracy. She knows it better than I do.

"Czechoslovakia."

Same result.

"Andorra."

"Fairy-tale-like principality between France and Spain, Roman Catholic, skiing, parliamentary co-princedom."

My God. Even the little countries. And even the incidentals I added.

"San Marino," Boone says, putting the paper in his book and quietly closing the cover. For an instant I think he is challenging her, but he is looking at me, not at her. It is that same, simple, appraising look that he gave me when he, Merle, and I talked about a school newspaper after class that first day. "Tourism and stamps," he says easily, with no hint of hubris. "Small republic on Italy's Mount Titano. Liechtenstein. Main products are . . ."

"Netherlands," Marshall says, flipping his basketball into the air. "Two capitals, Amsterdam and the Hague. Other major city, uh"—his confidence stumbles a moment—"Rotterdam. Main products . . ."

"Last year, Marshall wrote a pen-pal letter to someone in the Netherlands," Boone says, grinning at Marshall.

Clearly irritated by Boone's revealing that fact, Marshall throws the ball up again. "The teacher made me."

"He wrote that we live underground and eat blubber all the time," Boone says, laughing, "and that it's midnight up here six months a year."

Lobert, as usual grinning his lopsided grin, starts waving his list, which looks crumpled. "Paris!" he says. "Main product, Warsaw!" When I shake my head, he tries to flatten out the paper across his desk. "Penguins?" he asks. "Is it penguins?"

What worries me is that his answers are starting to sound strangely reasonable, in a world rapidly going mad.

That afternoon we have our first high school faculty meeting. Six teachers, three aides, and Mr. Dan sit around the tables in the lunch room/home economics room while basketballs in the gym next door thud against the walls.

Keenan, the shop teacher and boys' basketball coach, looks comfortable and self-assured in his jeans with the knees ripped out. Sally, a skinny redhead, is the English teacher and Keenan's girlfriend. Since the district does not allow unmarried persons to live together in teacher housing, rumor has it that they have signed and notarized a marriage agreement they intend to tear up at year's end.

Across the table from me is Lawrence, the science/math teacher and wrestling coach, his fair-haired features consistent with a body that exudes the quiet, confident power and values of his upbringing on an Iowa farm. Beside him and nearly as big, is Gerald, the special ed teacher. He has thick jowls and a high forehead, and looks implacable—arms crossed, shoulders back, within the room yet seemingly aloof from all of its proceedings.

Lars, the short, plump, curly haired home economics teacher and former chef, enters with a plate of steaming Eskimo fry bread, which looks like maple bars but without the icing. He sets the plate in front of Mr. Dan, who snatches one up and, moving it back and forth between his hands to keep from burning himself, takes a bite and uses the bread as a kind of blunt-ended pointer that he waves toward Gerald.

"I think George has a good point here."

Gerald shifts forward and glowers at me. Though dark complexioned, his face reddens in splotches beneath his wiry, salt-and-pepper beard. The congeniality with which the meeting began dissipates.

"I don't like what he's hinting at," he says with a snarl.

His brows bear down as he watches me. Taken aback I sit back, wanting suddenly to distance myself from him as much as possible.

"I just said that some of the brighter kids could use your help," I tell him, in the most neutral voice I can manage. "Puffin, for instance. I'm no psychologist, but I've seen a lot of smart kids over the years. I think there's genius there. She has a phenomenal memory."

"Puffin the Muffin," Keenan says, in an obvious attempt to break the animosity that pervades the room.

Gerald tilts back in his chair and again crosses his arms, a look of triumph on his face. "Nothing but rote memory."

"Who said anything about rote?" I ask.

"Rote," he says. "Memorizing lists. A monkey could do that."

"What about Merle and Boone?" I ask. "I looked up their records. They've been certified as gifted and talented."

"By Alaskan standards," Gerald says. His look of triumph is a smirk, for I'm in his territory now. He knows that I'm unfamiliar with the complexities of special education, which includes gifted and talented, more commonly known as G/T. "To be G/T up here, you only need to be two years above grade level. Big deal."

"Unless I'm mistaken, we *are* in Alaska." I look around the room, pretending to see it for the first time. "And they *are* G/T. And you *are* the special ed teacher."

Gerald tips his chair forward, hard. "I . . . don't . . . have . . . time."

"In the afternoon you have three students," I remind him. "And a full-time aide."

Gerald wags a finger at me. "Don't you criticize my schedule. You used to teach college, for God's sake. I was special ed for most of my life, coming up through school the hard way. Now I teach it. What do you know about *real* teaching, Mister Elitist."

"Let's keep this professional," Mr. Dan says, eyeing each of us in turn. Then to everyone: "I think that's enough for today."

"I think there are some real brains in this school," I tell Mr. Dan as we start to rise. "And not just those three. Londa has potential. So does Marshall—if we could get past his defiance."

"Yeah, right." Gerald stands and shoves in his chair. "Let's get these village kids ready for Harvard."

5

I hang back after the other teachers leave the room. "What was all that about?" I ask Mr. Dan, whom I've come to admire.

"I'm not sure what Gerald's agenda is. I've gotten the impression that he would decertify them all if he could."

"You mean the G/T kids."

"I mean everyone eligible for special ed." He smiles grimly. "What I think he wants is an empty classroom. Welcome to the realities of teaching high school, Professor Guthridge."

We enter the gym and watch the kids play basketball. The boys are quick and agile—driving, spinning, shooting with liquid ease. Boone takes a pass from Merle, leaps, flips the ball over his head from his right hand to his left and puts in a layup off the glass. At the other end of the court, the girls are making free throw after free throw, shooting literally from the hip.

Chip and Dale, hooting and laughing, roller-skate between us and continue around the little gym, dodging players. Trying to follow them is Oleander—what the latest academic parlance calls a "special needs child"—who can run around the gym for hours, seemingly without tiring. He smiles warmly at us as he passes.

"I think Gerald believes that kids here don't need modern education," Mr. Dan continues, nearly yelling above the din. "You know, remain the Noble Savage."

We exit the gym and head down the hall to my room and his office. "It's going to take more than whale and walrus hunters and ivory carvers—and basketball players—to run villages," he says. "We need medical personnel, electrical engineers, lawyers. From among our own."

Behind us, Keenan enters the gym and blows a whistle, two shrill blasts. The sound of basketballs quickly diminishes. Chip and Dale roller-skate out into the hall, spin in a circle, and, laughing, plop down in front of their lockers. Keenan guides Oleander into the hallway, his hands on Oleander's shoulders. I sense a trust there. Keenan clearly likes the boy rather than considering him a nuisance to be endured, as I sometimes witnessed in similar situations with coaches when I was in high school. Oleander stands beside Chip, who stuffs his skates into his locker, puts on his tennis shoes, and then helps Oleander, who is his brother, into a jacket. All three run out the door, Chip holding Oleander's hand.

When we enter my classroom, Mr. Dan walks to the window behind the secretary's desk and looks out across the lake. A cargo plane is on the runway, with people unloading boxes and piling them high onto their three-wheelers and carts.

"We want modern technology just like everyone else," he says wistfully. "But half the people outside rural Alaska want to change us as they see fit, half want to preserve us in amber, and half don't understand us at all."

"You've got three halves there," I say, trying to lighten his mood.

"My point exactly. Sometimes I think everything's stacked against us. Then I tell myself, 'Stop being so pessimistic.' There's too much pessimism in villages as it is."

His voice trails off, and I sense that he's been talking more to himself than to me. He gives me a poignant smile and goes into his office. "Something I want to show you," he says. Opening his file cabinet, he rummages through the folders and draws out a transcript, which he lays out on his desk. "This was a student—dropped out now—who was here two years ago." With an index finger he indicates the GPA: 4.0. Straight As.

He runs his finger down the courses for me to see. Whale hunting, Walrus Hunting, Ivory Carving, Physical Education, Beadwork.

"Alaska's Department of Education has mandated that village educators should be teaching Native subjects," he says bitterly. "Is this what they meant? And how are people like you, a white man new to Alaska, supposed to teach us about our culture?" He stuffs the paper into its folder in the file. "Ridiculous."

I sit down. Mr. Dan's comments have made me even more heavyhearted than did Gerald's outburst.

"What you said about Merle and some of the other kids is right," he says. "But Gerald's not going to help them. You think you can get them ready for college?"

"You think they want to go to college?"

He seats himself at his desk, across from me. "That's not for you to say, George. That's their choice." He watches me intently. "So what do you think?"

"Sure. I used to teach study skills to college freshmen."

"It'd be extra duty. And you already have the newspaper and yearbook."

Couple hours a week? I ask myself. Some sessions on study skills, squeezed in between the day's usual lessons? "Shouldn't be a problem."

He leans back in his chair and interlocks his fingers behind his head. Looking relaxed, he peers off at a point above me as if seeing a hitherto troubling situation clearly and confidently.

Suddenly he tips forward, drags out a box from beneath his desk, and thuds down a thick notebook before me. "District office wants this taught here in Gambell. It's called the Future Problem Solving Program. It's supposed to build student leadership."

"I already teach ten subjects." I look glumly at the notebook. Must be half a ream in there. "I thought you wanted me to work on study skills."

"Call this a good second choice."

I pick up the notebook. It feels even heavier than it looks. I put a hand on the notebook's vinyl finish and catch my breath, for I sense that I am about to engage in an undertaking far more difficult than I had bargained for. "Okay, so what's this all about?"

"Not sure, exactly. The district just said for me to call if I find a volunteer to teach it."

"I'm supposed to teach it, and you don't know what it is," I say in a deadpan voice.

He chuckles as though at my naiveté and leans back, hands behind his head. "As I said before, 'Welcome to the Arctic.'" With a smile, he adds, "Didn't you come to Alaska to make a difference?"

"Frankly, I came for the money."

"This, George, you do for free." His smile warms. "But cheer up. You get a trip to Anchorage for the training. Go shopping. Have a beer." After a moment he adds, "I don't think you're here for the money. Suggesting that is just your little, um . . . eccentricity. I sense that, for you, successful teaching is something deeply personal."

I don't answer. But I realize that, unconsciously, I have raised my brows.

He does not seem interested in my explaining further, nor do I really want to tell him. The money was important to me, and certainly the lure of Alaska was. But there was something else involved in my decision to come here—something I haven't even told Mary.

Five years here, I figured, would exorcise my demon-need to be standing in front of students. Then I would return to writing full-time. Hadn't I been told in graduate school that those who can, do; and those who can't, teach?

Admitting that I want to teach means admitting that I am a failure as a writer.

"Good teachers keep good records," Mr. Dan says, leaning forward. "You've only turned in one attendance report all week, and that for only one period."

Brows down.

Two weeks later I head to Anchorage for the Future Problem Solving training session, and the promise of shopping and suds. I am supposed to leave on a Friday morning, but a rainstorm has turned the runway to a sheet of ice, so the plane is delayed until Saturday afternoon. When it finally arrives in Gambell, the former principal—now an administrator at the district office in Unalakleet—is exiting the plane. Given the snow job he did on us, I expect him at least to ask how things are going, but instead he stuffs cash into my hand and says, "Overnight in Nome. Should be enough there for you to stay at the Polaris." Climbing onto the three-wheeler behind Jones, he heads toward the school.

The Polaris turns out to be world-class—depending on which world you're in. At 3 A.M. a drunk tries to break down the door, insisting that I am Maude or that I'm sleeping with her and he's come to kill us. There is no phone, and the door, which has the consistency of cardboard, doesn't lock. I push a bureau against it and look for a weapon. "I've got a gun!" I yell.

"Good!" he yells back. "I'm getting mine!" He tromps on down the hall.

I go down to the lobby. No clerk, and the pay phone is missing from the booth. There's a cab outside, the driver asleep in a sleeping bag in the backseat. I wake him, run upstairs and throw my stuff into my backpack, and head to the airport. No one is there, but the door is open. The restrooms have honey buckets instead of toilets. No paper towels, no toilet paper. The flight is delayed due to mechanical problems. I sit there for nine hours. The heat isn't working. Wind whistles through the door. I don't have a book. WELCOME TO NOME, the sign says.

Alive but exhausted, I arrive at the Anchorage Hilton, where the training is, three hours before I'm to return to Gambell. There is less than an hour left of over two days' training.

About fifty teachers are in the conference room, engaged in what is obviously a final wrap-up. A large sign tells me that Bruce Currie, from Skagway—a Southeast Alaska town that for civic pride and tourist dollars has carefully retained its Klondike gold rush buildings—is conducting the session. A rotund man with a smile that belies the earnestness in his eyes, he shows slides of previous Future Problem Solving competitions to emphasize his points. White kids look back at me from the screen as I grope in the dimness to find the table with a "Bering Straits School District" placard.

Two other teachers, Patti and Lee by their name cards, are at the table. Both are young, either right out of college or nearly so. Lee has a crewcut; Patti's hair is long, like that of a flower child from the '60s. We shake hands.

"So you're the fool who replaced me," Lee whispers.

Patti leans close. "Didn't the district tell you about the kids in Gambell?"

"Tell me what?"

"Here we have another picture of the state finals, held here in Anchorage," Bruce Currie is saying. "As I've explained earlier, each team consists of three to four kids. Only the top four to seven teams, depending on age group, make state. Each year, approximately thirty-three teams from across the U.S.A., plus Canada and Mexico, make the national finals, held in Cedar Rapids, Iowa. Combining research, creative thinking, essay writing, and verbal skills in a timed event, Future Problem Solving has been called *the* most difficult academic competition for young people."

I take notes. In the week since Mr. Dan gave me the notebook I looked in it once—for about thirty seconds. The rules were so complex that I stopped reading.

All that I know is that the program was invented eight years earlier by a professor at the University of Georgia—Dr. Paul Torrance, one of the world's renowned experts in teaching the gifted.

He had realized that gifted kids' ideas often do not fit with those of their classmates. Often ostracized by their peers and sometimes ridiculed by their teachers, the gifted shut up and shut down—their ideas and energy untapped and sometimes lost.

To help remedy that, he created this program, which is designed to enable gifted kids to bounce ideas off similar kids. Together they work as a team in a competition that will help them generate creative ideas and learn to use them in a controlled, but not controlling, environment.

Other than that, I am mired in confusion, which is worsened by my anxiety over Patti's words.

"What didn't the district tell me?" I again ask Patti, under my breath.

After looking at Lee as if asking for consent before revealing something confidential, she says, "Only teachers new to Alaska end up out at Gambell. Teachers up here will quit before they'll accept a contract out there. Most of those kids are unteachable. It's the toughest school in Alaska—the pariah of Alaskan education."

"That's how the district administrators sometimes get rid of teachers they don't want," Lee says. "They offer them a contract for the island, knowing they'll resign."

"There isn't enough money in the world to make us go back," Patti says bitterly. "Gambell's a zoo."

"It's an asylum," Lee says. "Even with the best of them. You'll see."

"I've only been there three weeks," I say, "but so far it seems okay."

"Wait until winter hits, and cabin fever sets in," Lee says. "The kids go bonkers. Teachers get beaten up out there or run over with snow-machines. Last year a kid tried to burn down the teacher housing while the teachers were asleep."

"You have kids of your own?" Patti asks.

"Two girls."

She glances at Lee, a frightened look in her eyes.

"Send them south," he tells me.

"Exactly when will the teams receive the synopsized articles?" a teacher asks Bruce Currie.

"Articles?" I whisper to Lee.

"The national office gives teams synopsized material to help get the kids started with Problem Solving," he whispers.

"There are two practice competitions, and then one to see if the kids qualify for state," Patti says, leaning close.

"As if village kids are ever going to make it to state," Lee tells me. "What a crock." He eyes me seriously. "Send your girls south," he again says.

"Your teams will have about six weeks before the competition to study the packet of synopsized articles," Bruce Currie explains to the questioner. "Of course, you and the kids are free to use any other research materials that you can find. Books, interviews with experts, other articles—whatever else is available."

"Whatever possessed you to take a job like that!" Patti asks me. "Lee and I were right out of school. We didn't know any better."

"Got it over the phone," I mutter. "I wondered why it was so easy."

Lee rolls his eyes. *Another sucker,* his body language says. "Just survive this year. Then the district will give you a good village."

"Exit interviews with the kids who made state last year indicated that the competition's topics were too negative," Bruce is saying. "Drunken driving, pollution, nuclear war . . ." He pretends to shudder. "So this year the topics will be UFOs, lasers, undersea cities, and banking."

Lee raises his hand. "Isn't that pretty unrealistic subject matter for village kids?"

"We have to go by what the national office says are kids' interests," Bruce replies.

"City kids' interests," Lee says.

I glance around at the name cards on the other tables. Fairbanks, Juneau, Anchorage, schools from the bedroom communities on the Kenai Peninsula. Bering Straits is one of the few village districts represented.

"Most of us *are* from Anchorage," a teacher tells him, in a holier-than-thou voice.

"My point exactly," Lee says.

"What a waste," Patti whispers to me. "Good thing I got some shopping done."

6

As I board the Beech 99 in Nome for the return to Gambell, the pilot proudly tells the dozen of us, "This is her virgin commercial flight. We brought her up from Seattle two days ago and thoroughly tested her. You're our first fares."

The beginning of the flight proves so beautiful that I can see the Diomedes, 200 miles away. Little Diomede is a boulder-strewn island on which was built a $10 million school for the tiny village that clings to the slope. Three miles across the ice lies Big Diomede, peopled by Soviet military. They watch their smaller neighbor carefully and, I assume, with envy.

As we round Sevuokuk, the Gambell headland, I see a patch of fog huddled on the runway. Seemingly the only fog on the Bering Sea, its welcome mocks me.

Less than twenty feet off the ground, we enter the little fogbank. The last piece of the runway appears. We have missed most of it. Instead of trying to climb, the pilot puts the plane down and immediately goes into a skid. Slicked with ice, the tarmac sends us sideways. I am looking down the wing going forward. Beyond, the tundra, softened by the week's rainstorm, is a mudhole. When we hit that, we'll flip.

"If the hair on the nape of the pilot's neck stands on end, then you're in deep doo-doo," a friend once told me.

I'm seated right behind the pilot. He's fighting the controls. I watch the nape of his neck.

We're in deep doo-doo.

"Close your eyes if you're about to crash," my friend said. "The shock could pop out your eyes, and you could bleed to death even if you survive the wreck."

I'm going to die.

A calm envelops me. I am suddenly without fear. No way will I close my eyes!

A cement truck once broadsided my car. At impact I experienced a sensation nearly identical to what I do now. The same happened during a hotel fire in Mexico. I was five floors up, with no fire escape. The excitement of the fire, rather than any fear of death, dazzled my senses. I felt an overwhelming calm, one fringed with anticipation.

Relief mixed with disappointment seizes me when the pilot gets control of the plane seconds before we hit the tundra. We plow into the mud head-on. Metal screeches. Everyone is thrown forward and then back. Passengers clutch one another, crying. Some have their hands raised to Jesus. I look outside. Fog enfolds us. The wings seem drooped. I know nothing about airplanes, but it looks like major damage. The pilot appears afraid as he asks if we're okay. Everyone nods and mumbles, the most white-faced Eskimos I will ever witness.

Minutes later Mary picks me up on the school three-wheeler, unaware of the near disaster despite the fact that the plane is off the runway. The adrenaline rush is over, and I am shaking. I decide to wait until later to tell her about the flight. "Everything all right at home?" I ask as she moves back and I climb on in front of her.

"More problems." She puts her arms around me, her head against my neck.

When she does not elaborate, I shut off the engine and turn toward her.

Slowly she breaks the story. Meredith is being hounded. Mercilessly. Whenever the teacher leaves the room, the other kids pelt her with erasers, knock her books off the desk, pull her hair, call her "white trash" and what are obviously Yupik slurs.

But there is something else—something she is not telling me. I can see it in her eyes, which are blurry with tears despite the wind.

"What is it!" I ask, unable to keep the anger from my tone.

"Maybe we should . . ." She looks down, her face strained with emotion. "Maybe we should send them back to Washington. They could stay with your sister, on the farm."

"If they go, we all go."

"That's easy for you to say."

I climb off the machine and stalk toward Mr. Dan's door, waving Mary away when she tries to follow.

She's right, and I know it. If we quit, the district will pull our certificates; we are likely to be blacklisted. I won't need the license if I return to teaching college. But Mary? She's a much better teacher than I am, yet her career would be over.

I pound on Mr. Dan's door. When he answers, the bathrobe he is wearing over his T-shirt and jeans somehow makes him look even thinner than usual.

"Last year's principal said that the only problems out here are the isolation and that the kids are docile," I tell him. "Docile? The hell."

After a long silence he points to three holes in the apartment's metal door. "Bullet holes," he says. "They weren't there before the previous principal moved in."

He invites me in and makes mixed drinks, dry-village style: 7-Up and Tang.

"Let's cut to the chase," he says. "The district wanted you and Mary, and they lied to you. Maybe they'd lie to anyone to get them here, but I know that they were especially excited when they saw your résumé." He eyes me as he drinks, assessing my reaction. "Something else you should know. There was a meeting here last spring. There was talk about shutting down the high school and sending the kids to boarding schools on the mainland. Of course, most would drop out rather than leave the island."

"So they've decided to shut us down?"

"At the end of the year—if the troubles continue. And this Future Problem Solving Program? I finally had the phone conference with the district about it, and I don't think they care how the kids do, or even if we have a team. I think that the district is just using it to paper over the problems. Should things go to hell in a handbasket out here, they want to say that they offered help to the kids, but that the kids didn't take it."

"They want the program to fail," I say, guessing his intent.

"I didn't say that."

But I can see it in his eyes.

The next day, when I introduce Switzerland to my geography class, each time I say "landlocked" I too feel landlocked, despite being on an island. When I mention that the country is famous for staying neutral during the world wars, I hear *neutered.*

"It's in neutral?" Lobert asks.

"Capital, Bern. Largest cities, Zurich, Basel, Geneva," Marshall says. He rests his head against the back of his chair and flips his basketball into the air. Like everyone except Lobert, he's bored.

I dim the lights and turn on the projector. The movies are mostly black and white, many so old that they look sepia-colored. Reel boxes with belts for easy mailing back to the State Film Center in Anchorage are stacked in the corner. I've become everything I hate. Babysitting 101: Education by the Celluloid Foot.

The film's countdown flashes. No one counts. No one turns their heads to view the upside-down numbers. No one does anything. No one comments when the title reads "Fiji, South Sea Paradise." A grainy black-and-white sea rolls in behind idyllic palm trees. Tourists as white as the sand loll on blankets and chaise lounges. I check the film box. It says "Switzerland."

"Mr. and Mrs. Johnson and their children, Billie and Bobby Sue, have journeyed all the way from Indianapolis, Indiana, to spend Christmas beneath the tropical sun," the narrator says. Suitcases beside them, the Johnsons wave beside the runway as a prop plane taxis. They are all smiles, typical 1950s family, the mom and daughter in plaid summer dresses, Billie and his dad in shorts and short-sleeved white shirts.

"Better be careful that Mr. Johnson doesn't have too much fun!" the narrator continues as Mr. Johnson ogles island girls putting leis around his neck.

The scene switches and the Johnsons head for the beach, Mr. Johnson with a beach umbrella under his arm. Quickly out of his seat, Lobert follows them, squatting as he walks, literally aping them, scratching his sides. I do not bother to stop him.

The film breaks, the end flapping against the projector. In disgust I take the tape dispenser from my desk, then decide to skip the splice and flip on the overhead. A map of Europe shows on the blackboard. Numbers I put there earlier appear within the boundaries of the transparency. The students groan but take out papers and list the countries. They know Europe by heart. Even Lobert rarely misses questions.

"Never mind," I tell them before they finish.

They look up at me.

"You already know this." I angrily start to erase the board, remembering too late that the lines are projected, not drawn.

7

"It snowed, Dad!"

I blink open my eyes. "Of course it snowed! When's it stopped snowing?"

It is late October. Though pegging Yupik "moons" to "months" creates inaccuracies, it is what the Eskimos call *Kaneghyengesi,* Moon of the Freezing Lakes. Blizzards have hit with a fury, the snow almost always blowing sideways so hard that there's a standing joke that if the snow ever drifts down, winter-wonderland style, the locals will raise a golden calf and beg forgiveness for having offended the weather gods.

Gretchen is looking at us in bed and grinning as she pulls on her ski pants. "No, I mean it really snowed!"

As soon as I am fully awake I am aware of how cold it is. My breath shows. We must be out of stove oil. I open the curtains. A white wall greets me. I open the door, step with bare feet into the arctic entryway, then open the outside door.

Another white wall.

"Where're the shovels?" I ask, impressed by the snowfall.

Mary and Meredith are pulling themselves into coats. They look at Gretchen.

"Uh oh," she says.

We left the shovels outside . . . again.

I wait until Gretchen is in her coat before grabbing her and holding her as a battering ram.

"One! . . . Two! . . . Got your mittens on?"

She shrieks with delight, pulling her hands into the mittens, which dangle on string.

"Three!"

I plow her into the white wall. She starts digging, laughing, with snow flying. Soon only her boots show.

"I'm through, Dad!"

Her feet disappear, and light comes through the hole. A moment later, she sends the shovel through. Within minutes, snow is piled in the arctic entry. To dig out when snow blocks the door, you have to shovel in.

We emerge into dazzling sunlight. Each day there is a loss of seven minutes of daylight, though like most of Alaska, the island never gets completely dark even during midwinter. But when the sun is up, it's so bright that we often have to wear sunglasses. Because the snow had blocked the windows, we had not realized what time it is. It's nearly noon.

We squint up at the enormous, spangling snow mound that covers our house, then climb drifts and view Mr. Dan's place. Though its peak is at least twenty-five feet off the ground, the duplex also is buried. He's outside, shoveling. I tell him about the oil, and he promises to phone Jones. I head back toward my house.

A snowball thuds against my back.

Gretchen screams with joy and races across the drifts. I pack a snowball—unlike with the previous blizzards, this time the snow is wet enough to stick together—and the fight is on. The females prevail: three against one. After my surrender, we start shoveling the roof, fearing that the weight of the snow might collapse it. Rather, I shovel, and the girls make a snow slide down the roof and into the arctic entryway.

I'm about halfway finished when Meredith ascends to challenge me with her shovel-sword. "En garde, Darth Vader!"

Back and forth along the ridgeline we parry as Gretchen busies herself making a snow angel. Finally the battle wanes and I collapse onto the roof, exhausted more from the laughter than from the war. After a time Meredith asks me, "Still worried about your classes?" Before I can answer she picks up the shovels and seats herself on the snow slide. "Don't *teach* them," she says. "*Reach* them. Aren't you a writer?" And away she slides.

That night, I try to sleep, try to forget the problems of my classroom, but the weak light from the oil stove in the living area flickers and the damper keeps clanking.

Why was I successful when I taught before, and here the kids openly call me *sulpak*—"fool"?

I think about Meredith's words, and my heart begins to pound.

What if, I wonder, the tools of writing *could* be translated into teaching?

"Today we'll begin with reading," I tell the geography students.

All Sunday I composed this class in my mind like a story. If fiction is a construct that looks and feels like reality, why can't the living out of a lesson plan, itself an artificiality superimposed on the process we call education, be likewise manipulated? Why can't a class period take on the trappings of fiction—characters with motivation to be analyzed and articulated in reference to some overriding problem to be solved?

Establish the protagonist's emotional problem early, I often explained to budding writers in the creative writing classes I taught in college. *The plot, which is the exterior problem, causes the emotional problem to surface.*

Faced with his exterior problem—being required to read—Marshall reveals the emotional problem by suddenly standing as if to climb again, book in hand, onto his desk.

"You don't like to read," I say.

He looks at me and holds the book down against his side, perhaps relieved by this brief reprieve from the possible agony of the printed page. "No," he says, but it's a weak reply, as if he is uncertain what greater torture might befall him, given his admission.

"What if the book were in your own language?"

Anger rises in his face. As with many students his age, he cannot read or write well in Saint Lawrence Island Yupik. His language has been in written form only a few decades, and has only lately been taught in the schools.

"Not your verbal language," I quickly explain, to calm him. "Your *real* language. The language of the land. The language of hunting."

I am aware that he already has established himself as an excellent hunter. He has killed a king polar bear, which for many Eskimo men is a lifetime ambition they never fulfill.

His eyes gleam, as though the very word "hunting" has ignited him.

"When you're out whaling or hunting walrus, don't you read the water, the wind, the ice, the tides?" I ask. "During the summer, don't you read the way the tundra grass blows? Don't you read the animals you stalk? Even the little foodstuffs the mice hoard underground, don't you find and read that too?"

The anger and tension go out of him. He looks at me incredulously.

"There are more kinds of reading than understanding words on a page," I say. "If I hunted until I was sixty I probably would never know what you already do at fifteen."

I toss my book onto the desk and open the outside door.

The wind is up. The students cover their papers to keep them from blowing away. The world map slaps the wall. It's 9 A.M., and moonless. Stars hang low in the heavens.

Marshall sits down. I avoid his eyes, lest he think that I believe I've cowed him.

I need to keep thinking as a novelist, not as a teacher, and bring my students—my readers—to an ending I have fashioned without their realizing where I'm going.

"You are not children," I begin. "You do the work of men and women. You hunt walrus and whale, you sew skins and skin boats. That is how it is outside school. This has been my mistake: I have not treated us you as men and women. I have tried to entertain you rather than educate you. But I'm not Michael Jackson, and I certainly am not Magic Johnson."

The students chuckle. They know I am a horrible at basketball.

"If you want to play, go somewhere else." I gesture toward the door. "Go out and don't come back. I'll like you whether you're here or not. I wasn't trained in how to teach children, and I'm not going to start learning now. From now on, there will only be one rule in this room. *Act your age.* It is not what I ask, it is what I expect. It is the way it will be."

There is a quiet responsiveness in their eyes. No one heads for the door.

"How many of you plan to be teachers?" I ask.

Smirks come, as I anticipated, and I know that we are moving toward the story's climax. Everything hinges on the next moments.

No one raises a hand, even though Londa and Boone have privately expressed an interest in teaching.

"You are all going to be teachers," I tell them.

"No way, man!" Dale says, and Chip quickly echoes him.

"Most of you have younger brothers and sisters," I say, ignoring the outbursts. "You have nieces and nephews. You will have children some day. Some of the older high school students already do. You need to teach the children. You need to learn *how* to teach them—because you're adults."

No one speaks or moves. The clock, usually so inconsequential amid the pulse of life in the Arctic, ticks in my ears. The wind seems to flow around the students like a river.

"In hunting you don't always come back with game," I remind them, speaking quietly, relying on the truth of my words and not the timbre of my voice to carry the message. "There's no dishonor in coming back empty-handed, you all know that. But there is dishonor in going out to hunt unprepared. There is danger in that. You all know that hunters who go unprepared sometimes don't come back."

All eyes are downcast. Everyone, I am certain, knows someone who did not return from the sea or from snowstorms. There is a lot of loss in a Bering Sea village.

"From now on in my classes," I tell them, raising my eyes, "act like a child and you will be treated like a child. Come unprepared, and you'll stay after school. There will be no exceptions, because you are all adults, or you soon will be adults, and in that there are no exceptions. Every night you will have reading to do. Maybe some other homework too, but count on having reading. Every period of every day I will give a quiz. Fail the quiz because you did not do the reading, then you will stay after school and write out the assignment. Read it, or write it." They are now looking at me as if I'm insane. The earlier spell that seemed to hold them has broken. "I don't care what else you might have to do after school," I say. "Read it, or write it out. No exceptions."

Marshall blinks as if he's just now coming out of a trance. "You're not making me miss basketball. I won't stay after."

"Then you won't be allowed back in my class the next day," I tell him. "Not until you finish the work. From now on this will be a classroom, not a playroom. That doesn't mean that you won't have fun. It does mean that you will take school seriously. Or there's the door."

I fight to look calm. I have given them a business-like proposal. It's up to them to accept it or reject it. My whole year's teaching hangs on the moment. I shut my mouth and wait, careful not to single out anyone with my eyes.

The clock pounds in my ears.

Papers continue to flutter from the wind. There is one weapon that I have on my side, and that is time. There are still over 150 days to go in the school year. I will wait 150 days if I must.

I work to stay calm but without seeming aloof. I imagine glaciers moving, chunks of ice calving into the sea. Everything rides on my remaining at ease, confident and quiet.

Two minutes pass.

Finally, Boone rises from his desk and glides to the door with that athleticism of his.

My heart pulses in my throat. I don't look at him. He, and not Marshall, is the real class leader, I have come to realize. If he exits, there will be chaos in my classroom for the rest of the year.

He shuts the door, returns to his seat, and opens his book.

Marshall also opens his book.

And stays seated.

8

Blizzards blast the island, each stronger than the last. During one storm, the anemometer on the elementary school flagpole falls and freezes, the wind speed permanently registered—127 miles per hour. Snow ridges rise so high that we cannot see the next house, so wind-sculpted that they remind me of white waves about to break over us. To get to school we struggle up one drift and down the next, shouldering against the storms.

One day the snow troughs swallow Gretchen.

We exit the house into darkness—the sun does not rise now until well after 10—the wind blowing the door against the wall so hard that it hangs lopsided when I manage to close it. The cold cuts through our army coats. Good to 50 below, the salesman at Seattle's G. I. Joe store said. *Right.* In a world without wind. A temperature of 30 below with a 50-knot wind means a windchill of –150.

I help Mary take Gretchen to the elementary school, after which I face the mile hike to the high school. We trudge up the first drift, kicking into what is more ice than snow. As we reach the top, Gretchen lets go of our hands and lifts her arms in triumph.

And is gone—her coat a sail that picks her off the ground and tosses her into the trough between the drifts. "Heeeelp!" she screams. Down the wind-burnished snow she slides, her howl quickly lost beneath the wind. She tries to rise, only to go sailing into a trough where two drifts join—and out of sight.

We scramble after her—the troughs as slick as slides in a water park. A frozen water park. Mary gives up trying to stand and, diving head-first, grabs a boot. She and Gretchen crash against the ice wall, then Gretchen is in Mary's arms, crying, hood against hood. We've been lucky. Bering Sea blizzards have been known to send 100-pound backpacks sailing away like newspapers.

When I look up, I see Meredith walk by along the ridge, heading into the blizzard, head bowed, gripping her hood shut, not noticing us—an image of grim determination that will remain forever etched in my mind.

Gretchen, who also has been watching Meredith, tugs at my sleeve. When I bend down, she cups her hands and, shouting to be heard, says into the tunnel of my hood, "If we live in Gambell for a long time, will I be Eskimo when I grow up?"

The next day, despite our intention to save money, we order a snow-machine—Alaskan for "snowmobile." It's small—we can't get all the family on it at once—but the chauffeuring is a small price for being able to deliver Mary, Gretchen, and Meredith to the elementary and then drive to the high school. Each morning, as I negotiate the ever-changing white terrain in the dark, I follow the few porch lights that people leave on. By contrast, the Eskimos skirt the storms as if having a sixth sense regarding their whereabouts. Even on Halloween, when one of the worst storms hits, snowmachines with tiny children show up at our door, cat and pirate and goblin faces emerging out of the gloom. They bundle bread sacks filled with candy under their coats, climb back onto the machine, and disappear into blackness and driving ice.

As the storms grow in ferocity, I spend the nights of steadily increasing darkness in what was supposed to be our third bedroom and what is instead our food storage area. There, huddled amid the boxes, I try to figure out the Future Problem Solving process and, more to the point, how to teach it. Mr. Dan has given the other faculty a week to choose which students will be on the Problem Solving teams, so for the next several nights I pore through the huge notebook.

Because I missed the training, it will not be until the next summer, when I have three months to devote to studying the process that Dr. Torrance created, that I truly will come to understand the program. Only then will I begin to appreciate his genius. Not only did he create a program to help engage gifted children's minds, he brilliantly broke problem solving down into component parts. In so doing, he insisted that children identify the many variables that any situation involves before trying to solve any part of it. The program thus teaches a powerful cognitive tool that even many adults, overly anxious to address problems without thinking through a situation's ramifications, often never learn.

The process is theoretically simple but exacting in its applications. Each team consists of three or four students. There are three divisions, determined by grade level: fourth through sixth grade, seventh through ninth, and tenth through twelfth. The teams have the option of taking either or both of two practice tests—one in November and one just after Christmas—before competing "for real" on the state-qualifying problem in March.

Each test comes from the national office in a sealed envelope, with all Problem Solvers, regardless of age or location, receiving the same test. The FPS coach at each school proctors the test, which the teams take in their own schools either after school or on a weekend. The coach then mails in the test for scoring by evaluators at the state office. The teams with the top scores on the state-qualifying test are invited to compete in April at a state competition, which in Alaska is held in Anchorage. Teams winning the state in their respective divisions can go to nationals.

The teams have about six weeks to study the subject area that the test will involve. To make the process interesting, to stretch the kids' minds, and to help kids anticipate and ameliorate problems in an ever-changing world, the teams must study the subject and determine what changes might occur in the near future regarding that subject. If the subject is education, for example, then what is education likely to look like twenty or thirty years from now?

The test calls for each team to analyze a slightly futuristic situation, or scenario, that is usually one or two single-spaced pages in length. Of course, neither the team nor the coach has any previous knowledge of what will be asked: they only know that it will be on the stated subject area and that it will be futuristic. For example, if the subject area is education, they might be asked what problems might occur if classrooms were eliminated and all students studied from home via computer linkups.

The analysis consists of six steps. Team members are expected to confer on each step of the process, all of which must be completed on paper. The team can elect to have only one team member write up the team's ideas for each step as the team members confer, or they can divide up the writing among the team members as they proceed. Whichever the case, each team submits only one final set of answers, known as a problem booklet. After the test is finished, the coach can retype the kids' answers but in no way change them, and both the team's hand-written answers and the coach's transcribed versions are submitted.

Using no notes or books, in two hours each team must (1) identify twenty problems that can go wrong with the futuristic situation, (2) choose one identified problem, (3) solve the identified problem twenty ways, (4) choose five criteria by which to evaluate the solutions, (5) evaluate any ten of the twenty solutions and thereby identify a best solution to the problem the students stated in Step 2, and (6) write an essay.

On the example involving education, for instance, the students might decide that having all students home-schooled via computer could (Step 1) interfere with kids' sleeping patterns; lead to difficulty in interpersonal relations later in life; increase the incidence of carpal tunnel syndrome; result in older or bigger siblings monopolizing the computer and thus hindering younger, smaller siblings' learning; and so on, for a total of twenty subproblems, or difficulties, that might occur. Each subproblem, which requires from a couple of sentences to a short paragraph to explain, must have a high probability of occurring and should show research. And all twenty subproblems together must involve a variety of viewpoints, such as sociological, biological, technological, and ethical.

In Step 2, the students choose a subproblem from those they identified—one that, if solved, is likely to solve many others. That central subproblem must be stated in a particular way, using only one verb and including qualifiers so that the result becomes focused. For example, a high school team might ask, "In what ways might we reduce sibling factionalism during in-home computer instruction in order to increase learning and to help foster social interaction?"

In Step 3, the students propose twenty solutions to that central problem but without violating the qualifiers. The test evaluators would throw out a proposed solution, for instance, that reduces fighting between siblings but that is unlikely to foster social interaction.

The five criteria that the students must develop in Step 4 to assess their proposed solution might include something like: "Which solution is most cost-effective?" In Step 5, the students then use their five chosen criteria to evaluate any ten of the twenty proposed solutions. Having arrived at a best solution to their central problem by the end of Step 5, they are then ready to write an essay.

The essay for Step 6 can be written by one member of the team, or the writing can be divided among the team members. The essay must explain the chosen solution in more detail, discuss how it solves not only the identified central subproblem but also other problems that the test situation might entail, and show how the proposed solution helps better the world.

But such depth of understanding of the FSP process is months away. For now, the more I read the notebook, the more overwhelmed I feel. If I have trouble understanding the process, then how am I supposed to teach it? And as if the six-step process is not daunting enough, the bulk of the notebook also contains other specific requirements for each step, a complex scoring template, and a dizzying array of suggested teaching techniques, most of which assume that the students are highly verbal. That assumption is probably valid for many schools, but few of the Gambell students offer answers even when called on. My questions usually get answered with whatever pops into a student's mind. More often, I receive a shrug, if I am acknowledged at all.

The night before Problem Solving is to start in Gambell, I am still trying to make sense of the program's most basic rules and processes. After an hour of escalating frustration, I close the notebook and, turning off the light, stand at the room's tiny window, staring into the storm as it rages beneath the light bulb that marks the entrance to our shack.

I am certain of only one thing: I have no idea how to begin.

9

The next day the wind has reached gale force, perhaps 80 knots. As usual, school is not cancelled. I arrive at the high school to see a group of kids facing into the storm and holding their coats open. That some are dressed in light jackets and baseball caps amazes me. The windchill is −70 on what otherwise would have been an above-zero day. The kids leap high into the air and are blown backward. Marshall and Boone are on hands and knees, using the weak light of the bulb above the school doors to squint at a measuring tape stretched across the ground.

Merle, wearing a hat of bearded sealskin rather than his usual John Deere baseball cap, comes up beside me. "We're seeing how far we can fly backward." He has to yell to be heard above the wind. He points to his cousin, Boone. "We're the Wrong Brothers." He grins.

I enter the school and make my way to my classroom. No sooner do I have my coat off than Mr. Dan enters between the bookshelves and hands me a list of names.

"I've rearranged your schedule so you can teach Problem Solving as you wanted—as a class instead of as an after-school activity," he says. "These are the kids the teachers say should be participating."

I am expecting two teams—a total of eight kids. Merle, Boone, Marshall, Londa, Puffin, Meredith, a couple others. Instead, there are 38 names on the list, out of 41 students in the high school and perhaps another 35 in grades 5 through 8.

"It looks like some teachers just emptied their classes," I tell him. "And I have nine other students that period—in five other subjects!"

Mr. Dan looks around my classroom/library/business room/ secretary's nook. "We'll never be able to cram everyone in here. Home ec is free that period. You can teach Problem Solving, algebra, and reading there, and the other subjects here."

"I'm supposed to teach six subjects, including a brand-new program, in two classrooms at opposite ends of the school in the same period?"

"You'll do fine." He enters his office, shuts the door, and draws the shade down.

When sixth period arrives, three dozen faces eye me as I enter home ec. Some students lounge with their heads on an outstretched arm, some with a chin on the edge of the table, some are so slouched in their chairs that they stare directly at the ceiling. They remind me of melting clocks in a Dali painting—here to prepare for academic battle against some of the finest young minds in the state.

"Do we have to be here?" a fifth-grader whines.

"Didn't you volunteer to be here?" I ask.

"Teacher said that if we came up, he'd give us a sucker."

"It's just his extra Halloween candy," another says.

"Isn't neither! They're *big* suckers. He gave out little ones at Halloween."

"Is too his Halloween candy. You just didn't get any big ones."

The argument shifts into Yupik. Soon the two are pouting, and I'm wondering if anyone gave out Excedrin for trick-or-treat, because I could use a dozen.

"I'll be right back," I tell everyone. "Find something useful to do. Read a book, or something."

"Read a *book?*" someone asks.

"Mr. Popov told us that we were going to play games up here," a seventh grader says.

"*What* sucker?" someone says.

The conversations switch again into Yupik.

I go behind the partition that divides the classroom lengthwise and give an assignment to the two girls taking algebra. As if teaching math isn't difficult enough for me—I was the only person in the history of my university to take bonehead math pass/fail—the book consists of a series of lessons that come rolled up in a can. We spend half of our time trying to flatten out the lessons and deciding which chapter comes next.

I turn my attention to Lobert, here for independent studies in reading because of a scheduling conflict. I have dug around in the teachers' lounge/bookroom/storage attic, accessible only by a pull-down ladder, and found a fifth-grade edition of the Melville masterpiece. There are a couple dozen copies. That Eskimo whaling practices have little in common with the wholesale slaughter perpetrated by the brave boys from Nantucket was as apparently irrelevant to some previous teacher as it is to me. I am making Lobert's reading *culturally responsive,* as memos from Unalakleet tell us to do.

"Moby's Dick?" Lobert says, as he examines a booger. "I gotta read about Moby's dick?"

"Read," I tell him. *Read, or I will tear out your heart. Read, or I will hose you down outside and turn you into a statue.* "I'll be back before the bell to quiz you on the first chapter," I add pleasantly.

I step around the partitions. "I'll be right back," I tell the thirty-eight melted clocks, and dash out the door. My usual classroom is adjacent to the kitchen/home ec rooms but not connected to them. To get there means running from one end of the school to the other, and back again.

I sprint across the gym, lurch around the corner, race down the hallway to my usual classroom, and help one of my typing students with her assignment. She cannot complete the assignment on centering, I discover, because she cannot divide by two. I show her how to backspace for every two letters in a line.

I help Allana devise a business letter. An advanced office practices student, she is truly a gifted typist. I give another beginning typing student an assignment and correct the writing of the last two students who are in the journalism class, the rest having elected to try Problem Solving. I run out the door.

And run right into the opening door of the next room, as Lars steps out.

"Will you *please* take control of your classroom!" he says.

"Which one!" I ask, staggering back and holding my forehead.

"Which one? Kids have been running back and forth to the bathroom all period!"

"All period?" I point to my watch. We're only fifteen minutes into the hour.

He glowers, his arms folded, his chef's hat flopped down along the side of his face, then tosses his head, clearly having a snit, and goes back into the room. There is only one student within, working one of the elementary school crossword puzzles that Lars is so fond of handing out. Lars's aide is seated near the blackboard, reading a book. Lars sits down at his own desk and picks up his coffee.

I race across the gym and enter the home ec room. The students shift from one slouch to another.

"You'll be participating in the Future Problem Solving Program three times a week," I begin, trying to catch my breath. "You'll be divided into teams, and together you will solve problems set in the future."

"Bohr-ring," Marshall says, in an exhalation of air. He tries to roll his basketball up one arm and down the other. When it falls to the floor, the students titter with laughter, then cower beneath my glare.

If only they knew that I am thankful for the interruption. For though I now have a general idea of what Future Problem Solving is about, I have little idea of how I am supposed to teach the process and *no* idea of how to begin.

"There will be two practice problems," I say. The kids look at me blankly. Already I am aware at how confusing this must be. "Then the state problem—*if* your team makes state. The first problem will involve UFOs. The state problem will be on banking."

"White man's problems," Marshall says, just loud enough so he knows I've heard him.

There is a knock at the door, and Lars, holding his chef's hat, thrusts in his head. *"Please* control your students!"

I step into the gym. Keenan, our terrific shop teacher, is herding four students toward me, Puffin among them. As she passes, a rendition of Willie Nelson's song rings through my mind:

On the commode again,
I just gotta get on that commode again,
Having my hair done with my friends,
Yes, I gotta get on that commode again.

Two of the girls turn out not to be on my list of Problem Solvers. I can imagine the other teachers sipping coffee, smiling to themselves for having rid themselves of their charges.

I swallow my anger. "Find a seat," I tell the girls.

When I reenter the room, the other students are out of their chairs—Lobert among them.

"Sit!" I tell them.

"We aren't dogs, man," Marshall grumbles, but does as I say.

I exit the classroom, a scream forming behind my lips. Once again in the gym, in a flash of what I hope is inspiration and not insanity I yank open the door to the janitor's closet. There, in the corner, is a shovel. I snatch it up and head back across the gym.

When I again enter the classroom, I raise the shovel over my head. Kids scramble for their chairs, a couple ducking under tables. "What is this!" I demand, pointing to the implement.

"Shovel," Marshall says. "Stupid, man."

"It's a tool," I tell them. I twirl it around, then balance it on my foot, a trick I have been able to do since junior high. Flipping it back into my hand, I ask, "What's the strongest part of the body?"

"Biceps!" a student yells, coming out from under a table.

"Legs!" another says. "Everyone knows that!"

I shake my head. There is silence as the students mull the question.

"The brain," Merle says quietly.

The rest of the students look at him, and for a moment everything seems set in tableau. In that instant, he is not an obviously gifted athlete or academic but rather a respected hunter whose words are to be taken seriously.

"The brain," a younger student repeats in a voice as soft as Merle's.

"That's right," I add. "And in this program you'll sharpen that tool—by solving problems. Teams qualifying for state go to Anchorage."

The students look at one another, smiles blossoming. Adventure swims in their eyes. *Off-island? Off-island? Sell ivory carvings! See a movie! Visit a beauty salon!*

Marshall and Boone touch fists. "Shop 'til we drop," Boone says.

"But first, the practice problem," I say. "One on UFOs. Anyone know what a UFO is?"

Marshall slumps back in his chair, his aura of bored self-assurance returning. "Flying saucers—who doesn't know that!"

"Not just flying saucers," I say. "*Any* unidentified flying object—

anything in the sky that we don't immediately understand. Now, what problems might result if you saw a UFO?"

They look at me, dumbfounded.

"Can anyone think of problems?" I ask, when the silence becomes deafening.

More gawking. Even Merle is silent.

"Wouldn't people laugh if you said you had seen a UFO?" I am desperate for a response.

There is no response.

I shift gears. "What if you weren't sure you saw a whale? What problems could result?"

"We might not get it," Marshall says. Then to Boone: "This is stupid."

"Dumb," a middle school student says.

The assessment spreads like a virus.

"Do we have to come every day?"

"How come we have to walk up here from the elementary?"

"When are we going to Anchorage?"

"Bohr-ring. I'm quitting, man."

I hold up an index finger for emphasis. "Give it one month. Then quit if you want."

"Can I buy a new rifle when we're in Anchorage?" Marshall asks.

"Who said you're going to Anchorage?" I ask him.

"You did!"

"I said if you make the state finals."

"Oh, man," a younger boy says, running his hands down his face as if trying to slough off something vile.

"Stay!" I tell them, and head out the door.

"He acts like we're the dogs," I hear Marshall say, as the door is about to close. "*White Dawn,* man."

I understand the reference but do not have time to combat it. Mr. Dan has banned the film *White Dawn* from the school because the showing caused a near-riot the year before. Its depiction of an historical event involving Eskimos and whites is inaccurate; worse, it points out that, according to Eskimo belief, whites are descended from dogs having mated with immoral Eskimo women.

I return with a six-pack of Coke from the storage room. The students' eyes light up.

Ah, the power of pop.

"Here's the situation." Unsure what to do, I suddenly decide to have them brainstorm solutions for the first thing that pops into my head. "There's an . . . there's an elephant in Savoonga. You . . . you need to bring it to Gambell. How do you get it here?" I glance around the room at the faces looking at me as if I am crazy, and all the while I know that their only interest right now is pop.

But I'm on a roll, heading down a road, and backing up will be suicide. "I don't care how crazy the idea is," I tell them. "Just give me ways to get it to Gambell. Every time you give me an idea, I'll give you one back. If I don't answer in five seconds, then I'll give a pop to whoever answered last. Then it's your turn—except I'll give you ten seconds. If no one answers, the class loses a can."

"There's an elephant in Savoonga?" one student asks hopefully.

I let the scenario settle into the kids' minds. Savoonga, the other village on Saint Lawrence Island, is about thirty air miles away, across the bay. It originally was a reindeer herding camp for people from Gambell, when the animals were introduced onto the island in 1928, but the trek back and forth was so arduous—even today it involves a difficult snowmachine ride—that some families eventually elected to stay there year-round. When disease wiped out most of the herd in the early '50s, many of the herder families decided to stay in the Savoonga area. Protected by a crescent of low mountains, the area is the island's banana belt. Windchill there rarely exceeds 70 below.

"Raft the elephant across the bay!" I tell them, starting the competition.

"Boat it over!" Merle responds.

"Wait until winter, and pull it with snowmachines," I reply.

"Lure it over with hay," he says.

"Carry it below a hot air balloon," I reply, to spark their imaginations.

"Kill it, fill it with air, and float it over," Marshall says, glancing around with a haughty look when other students stare at him for his idea. "Like a seal poke," he adds.

I sense that he expects me to chastise him for his lack of humanity, but anything goes in the competition—that much I know.

"Train storks to carry it in a blanket," I say.

"Drive it over with switches," another student says.

"Drive it in a car," I tell them.

"There aren't any cars here!" someone says.

"There aren't any roads!" someone else says.

"Ten seconds!" I remind them.

"Fly it in an airplane!"

"Put it in a time machine, take it back to when there was jungle here, and it'll wander over," I say, already worried that the ideas are getting too far-fetched even for the broad comfort zone I have as a writer.

"Teach it to fetch a stick," an older boy says. When everyone looks at him, he says, "Keep throwing the stick."

"Ride it here," I say. An obvious answer.

We go on and on, students quickly running out of answers. When several begin looking frustrated, I let myself violate the five-second rule and award the first can of pop. We continue until all six cans are gone. I am relieved when the bell rings.

"Shoot around!" Marshall yells, and charges, already dribbling, into the gym.

Soon the room is empty except for Meredith and me. I feel exhausted and elated. "How do you think it went?" I ask Meredith, as I pick up *Moby Dick* from the floor.

"Do I really have to do this?" she asks, and leaves the room.

10

The next day we receive word that my best friend has committed suicide.

Raised in rural India in poverty, Om ran away from home, and against all odds—including having parents who did everything they could to keep him from getting an education beyond elementary school—he became an American professor of economics. When he went back to India to show his parents his success and his American wife, they told him, "You're nothing. You have no children—no boys."

Returning to the states, over the next three years he and his wife produced two darling sons, bought a farm, and somehow found enough money for Om's lifelong dream—buying a racehorse. The day his wife demanded a divorce and custody of the kids, Om went into the barn and hanged himself in a stall.

For two days I move like an automaton. Crossing the gym to the home ec room, I hope that a classroom filled with Problem Solvers, eager to participate if only for pop or a trip, might break the numbness. Education is enlightenment, I tell myself. Education is elation.

I check the janitor's closet for pop. The door, strangely, is unlocked. I find Lobert inside with a six-pack of Sprite in each hand. He grins his "caught in the act" grin. Wondering what transgression I will next overlook, I let the theft slide. "Get to class," I tell him, "and I better not see your face out of *Moby's Dick* the entire hour."

He runs to the room. I follow. There, instead of thirty-eight bored faces, I find six.

Merle, Boone, Londa, Puffin, and Jasmine—a very smart senior who is Boone's older sister. And Marshall, much to my surprise.

"Where are Meredith and the other elementary students?" I ask no one in particular. "And where are the middle schoolers?"

"Maybe they're hunting elephants," Merle offers, but the humor falls flat. He glances around at the other kids. They say nothing.

Stifling my exasperation, I divide the group into two teams of three, tell them that the winning team will each receive a can of pop, and hand out a problem asking how to quell public hysteria following a hypothetical UFO sighting.

"You've five minutes to solve the situation as many ways as possible." Not really knowing exactly what instructions I am supposed to give, I add, "Brainstorm with your teammates, and just jot down whatever ideas come to mind. Think of how you could stop a riot from happening." And all the while I'm thinking, *Do they know what a riot is? Do they care?*

I race across the gym. *E*, I think, *equals MC². Enlightenment equals My Classroom². Elation equals Many Cokes².* I run back, grab a six-pack from the janitor's closet, and race down the hall. If the Problem Solvers get pop, why not my other students?

I stop at Lars's door. Half a dozen students who were in Problem Solving the day before are working word-finds and crosswords while Lars sips coffee and quietly talks to his aide.

I rap on the jamb. Looking irritated at the interruption, he sets down his coffee and comes to the door. "Aren't these people supposed to be in Problem Solving?" I ask, indicating the kids in his classroom.

"They have more important things to do," he says. "I mean— *elephants*. What the hell is that all about!" He returns to his aide, his back to me.

Reaching my class, I help Allana and the other typing students, and the two remaining journalism students, who take the class every day instead of alternating between journalism and Problem Solving. Then I sprint back to home ec.

Merle and Jasmine are hunched over the problem paper, whispering in Yupik and writing furiously. Marshall is trying to balance his basketball on his forehead. Boone watches him. Puffin is gone— probably to the bathroom.

When I examine the papers, my heart sinks.

"'Have Superman solve it'? 'Ask God'? You call these answers?"

"God can do it," Boone says.

"If not, Magic Johnson can," Marshall says.

We review the testing process again. They will have two hours. First, they must identify twenty problems that could occur in whatever situation the test identifies. Then they must solve one of the problems twenty ways—all without notes or books. "And that's just two-thirds of the test," I say. "You also must assess your solutions, find a best solution, and write an essay on it."

"No problem," Marshall says, still trying to balance the ball.

"To have any hope of winning," I also remind them, "you need to come up with ideas that are way above grade level—ideas that other teams don't think of."

Marshall wads up his paper and shoots it at the wastebasket. "No problem."

"If you want a trip to the state finals, you have to earn it. With *this*." I thump my temple. "This is our chance to practice. In just two weeks, we play the first practice problem."

I give them back the hypothetical test question I devised. Marshall groans, but they get down to work. Puffin wanders in and sits looking at her teammates Boone and Marshall, not saying a word. Boone talks in Yupik to Marshall, who writes a few words, wads up his paper, shoots toward the wastebasket, and gives up.

That evening I go for a walk halfway up the mountain. The lower third of this part of the mountain is the graveyard, so I am careful to stay away from the caskets lest someone misconstrue why I'm here. I sit down between two boulders that remind me of Tikis, guarding as they do the village below and the coffins aproned with snow. In the Arctic, the ground is too hard for traditional burial, so the dead are laid to rest in caskets atop the earth, usually with rocks stacked on them to keep out animals, not always successfully. A prevalent story tells of a young islander who, considered dead, awoke from a coma to find a polar bear breaking into her coffin. The sacrilege proved her salvation: she survived the burial and the bear.

Below, the village looks tiny, like something rendered in an idyllic painting. Beyond the full moon the sky is crystalline, the stars like iridescent pebbles cast onto black ice. There is no discerning where the blue-black ocean ends and the sky begins. Sitting here, in the stillness, the wind uncommonly calm, it is easy to imagine oneself at the center of the universe.

The quietude slows my heart. The peace is truly profound. Here on the edge of forever with the wind billowing the ruff of my hood, I feel utterly and wonderfully alone. The rim of darkness, with its silver and indigo streaks of light, holds the rest of the world and all of its problems at bay. I think of the people who have been here before me. This was a favorite spot, I am aware, for hunters to watch for whales and walrus. A sense of their presence brings an overwhelming poignancy, as though their spirits ride the wind. Here, between America's Seward Peninsula and Siberia's Chukchi Peninsula, artifacts dating back a couple thousand years have marked their passing.

Earlier in the year I crossed Sevuokuk, the mountain, to Other Side—the spit's eastern edge—and watched locals dig for those artifacts, truly a village industry. In the village itself are other indications of digs, mostly from earlier times in the century, when archaeologists paid the locals twenty-five cents an hour and filled college museums with finds now worth a fortune. Old ivory sled runners, skin boat stanchions made of whalebone, dolls shamans coveted and daughters cradled, all stolen in the name of scholarship. Reputations made and relics lost: the final plight of indigenous peoples.

The most noteworthy artifacts reside in the coffins themselves. Placed on the chests of renowned hunters are ivory butterflies, wings spread and exquisitely carved. It is an honor to have such an insect alight on one's heart, perhaps meant metaphorically to carry the soul to the Eskimo afterlife. I imagine the butterfly gliding upon a July breeze, holding the hunter's spirit with the same ethereal tenacity with which the insect gathers pollen.

Snow squeaks above me, interrupting my reverie. I look up to see a figure, splashed by the moist light of the moon, threading between the boulders. Merle soon is squatting beside me, his .30-30 in the crook of his arm. He slips his hands from his mittens and massages his fingers.

"If you're up here awaiting elephants, I don't think it's left Savoonga." He grins.

"You're the one with the weapon."

He glances at the rifle in admiration. "I don't think this could bring down Dumbo. Seals, though. It's a good seal gun." He gives me a wistful look. "I shot a ribbon seal over on Other Side. But before I could bring him up with my seal hook"—an implement that looks like a bowling pin with bent spikes protruding—"a gull landed on him and started pecking out an eye. The seal's head turned up and the air came out. That broke its buoyancy, and it sank." He shakes his head in disgust. "Beaten by a bird."

I open my thermos, pour a cup, and hand it to him without asking, lest he politely decline. My drug of choice: hot chocolate, laced with raspberry syrup. He sips, smiles.

"Ice will be in soon." He gazes toward the sea. "Then winter will really be here. Though the ice comes and goes. It's not static, the way Outsiders think. Depends on the winds and current."

I stay silent, letting him talk. As usual, he teaches me more than I do him.

"In the old days my people used to dance down there by moonlight," he says, indicating a flat area at the mountain's base. "The missionaries thought we were worshipping the moon, so they stopped the dancing. Sometimes people miss the obvious. We just needed the moon for its light."

As if on cue, a whippet of snow dances up the mountain as though inviting us to join in a bone-chilling revelry only Eskimos and the Arctic can understand.

"One time," he scoops back snow and then picks up and tosses a rock, "I took a pebble from the north beach. I put it on the kitchen table, told my dad where I got it, and asked, 'Is this an Eskimo rock or a white man's rock?' He looked at it a long time, not speaking."

I imagine his father sitting at the table, studying the rock without touching it. A small, wizened man with a drawn face and sunken, haunting eyes and an infectious grin, he is an elder with over twenty-five years' experience in the classroom. People have told me that, as a teacher, he was a taskmaster and disciplinarian. When they spoke, they did so in admiration.

"Finally I picked up the pebble," Merle continues, "and closed it inside my hand. 'It's just a rock,' I told him. Dad still didn't say anything, but he nodded."

"Life is difficult here," I say. Though a non sequitur, it seems appropriate.

He laughs. "For teachers, anyway."

"For everyone."

"It's supposed to be, for us. Didn't anyone ever tell you that?" Again the laugh. Clearly he is enjoying himself. I pour him another cup. "Sometimes I think that it's like this: We used to roar like tigers, and we hunted like tigers. Then lions came along, and we said to ourselves, 'Wouldn't it be nice to be like lions?' So we roared like lions and hunted like lions. But then we realized we weren't lions. And we found out we weren't tigers anymore, either."

His words so startle me that the images seem to hang in air. An Eskimo, thinking in African metaphors? He hands back the cup, and as I recap the thermos, I have to consciously keep from looking at him in awe. I am amazed by him. In my years as a professor I met a number of brilliant young people, but never one so wise.

"Are you sure you're only sixteen?" I ask him.

He laughs, and we head down the mountain. The village awaits, like the elephant from Savoonga. "What do you want to be when you're out of school?" I ask. "Going on to college?"

"My dad wants me to be a lawyer."

Oh God, I think.

"We need someone to advise the village councils," he continues. "We have to pay so much to Anchorage attorneys."

"And what do *you* want?" I ask him.

"I want to be older," he says.

part 2

◄ Village elders enjoying a school event. Tattoos on the elders' faces indicate their husbands' successful hunts. *Photo by Lyle Schwartz.*

11

The next afternoon I group the remaining Problem Solvers into teams. The high school team consists of Merle, Londa, and Jasmine. Boone, Marshall, and Puffin, all ninth graders, are the junior high team. The elementary school team is made up of three fifth graders— Garnet, Groper, and Boone's younger sister, Summer—plus Meredith, whom Mr. Dan has bumped up to sixth grade. Having Jasmine, Boone, and Summer on the teams seems appropriate: the high school is named for their grandfather.

After racing through my routine of getting my other students started on their schoolwork, I return to tell the Problem Solving class, "Two nights ago, a young man told me not to overlook the obvious. So in this class, you're going to act like Eskimos."

His chin resting on his basketball, Marshall narrows his eyes. "We *are* Eskimos."

I grab my shovel and, picking up a chair, pretend to fend him off, lion-tamer style. Everyone laughs—even Marshall, though in a nervous, self-conscious way.

"In Problem Solving," I continue, "you're supposed to talk out the problem the test gives, then write down your ideas. But you sit like stones. At first, I thought you didn't want to compete. I had overlooked the obvious. Talking superfluously during a test goes against your training. When it comes to important things, your culture values silence."

"Because of hunting," Merle says.

"How do you solve problems when you're out whaling?" I ask.

"Nobody talks except the boat captain," Boone says, glancing toward Merle as if for approval. "We each have our own job."

Marshall gives me a look of disdain. "We *know* what to do."

"What if you didn't talk during Problem Solving, unless your team got stuck and you had to work together? What if you each had a job?"

81

My questions involve an idea sparked by my meeting with Merle. I have decided to try having the kids divide up the problems and solutions. Because the kids aren't so verbal, maybe they will be more comfortable brainstorming together just enough to make sure that they do not duplicate each others' efforts.

"A team of individuals," Merle says, seeing my point.

"Like we do in wrestling," Boone says.

"Just so I don't have to talk," Marshall says. "But I know what work is, man."

Merle leans across the table and extends a fist toward the others, as if for a team cheer. Tension so strong grips the room that, even with my pitiful understanding of the culture, it is clear that he is risking deep ridicule if the others do not respond.

He remains posed, eyes calm rather than imploring. His is a hunter's patience.

Gradually the others' brows rise. It is as if a nonverbal agreement beyond my ken has passed through the group. There is no Knute Rockne pep talk, no acquiescence to authority in the quest for glory. There is simple resolve.

"State!" he says.

I doubt if they have any chance of making the state finals, but I sense that anything less than striving for an extremely high goal will not interest Merle. Right now this is his call, and though I am certain the kids are in for a huge letdown, instead of trying to make their goal more realistic I mentally step back and let Merle take over.

Hands pile onto his fist.

"State," Londa repeats, in a kind of breathless abandon.

"State!" Merle says.

Following Merle's example, Boone chimes in with "State!" and peers at Marshall.

"Shopping!" Marshall says, grinning.

"State!" Merle repeats, and also eyes Marshall.

A change comes over Marshall. The grin vanishes, replaced by a look of resolve.

And then it occurs to me: *Merle is the boat captain, motivating his men. He is the team captain in basketball, calling the plays.*

"State!" Marshall says.

Lobert emerges from behind the partition and, tossing *Moby Dick* over his shoulder, thrusts in a hand, looking at the others, clueless about what he is agreeing to. Even my two algebra victims peer around the partition, obviously puzzled yet smiling.

"State!" the kids chant. "State, state, state!"

No classroom histrionics could have achieved what Merle has with a friendly fist. When the laughter and subsequent high-fives end, I lift my hands for quiet and, though I want the celebration to last a lifetime, I announce, "Class dismissed!"

The kids look at the clock, confused.

"Gym time!" I tell them. "You've earned it!"

"All riiightt!" They go through the door as if through a funnel.

When I enter the gym, Marshall passes a basketball to me so hard that it burns through my fingers. "Not my game," I say, running to retrieve the ball.

"Yet I'm supposed to learn yours," he says.

I set myself, ready to shoot. "Academics aren't athletics."

"I've heard that crap before." He takes the ball from me. "Like this." He demonstrates proper stance and gives me back the ball. "Square up. Balance. Breathe."

Swish!

"Hey!" I say with delight.

"Maybe I should teach *you,* man."

I run after the ball and shoot a layup rather than risk an air ball. "You teach me to play basketball, and I'll teach you to read."

"No way." He takes the ball.

An inspiration seizes me. "Teachers should be paid. I'm paid to teach you reading. So I'll pay you to teach me basketball. Ten dollars an hour."

"Fifteen. Every Saturday. Two o'clock. You're late, the deal's off."

I nod and he races downcourt, flows between two defenders, spins, and effortlessly makes a reverse layup.

Merle pleasurably mulls what *qakiqnag* means as he snowmachines toward West Cape, following the rooster tail spewing from Boone's machine. *Qakiqnag*—the urge for hunting. He wonders if whites have a similar word. The only approximation he knows is *game,* which refers to animals and shows their priorities but not the process. Theirs is sport, an undertaking without real risk. Here, he reminds himself with pride, so much rides on the man upon the snowmachine.

Each creek he crosses, crackling across its thin ice, each abrupt dip, each place where groundwater turns the trail into mud, heightens his pleasure. He has driven the route a hundred times, yet each time he concentrates on adding new information to his body of knowledge. The tundra is forever in flux. Knowing its precise topography can mean the difference between success and failure, even between life and death. Good hunters, he knows, do not live off the land but rather with it, understanding and anticipating its changes. Concentration and memorization are the keys. To feed his family he knows that he must understand the precise reason, and the likely result, of the smallest endeavors. Church, school, home, hunting: he long ago decided that they wonderfully combine to give him single-mindedness; for though he has not told his father, he knows he never will live in a law office, battling with briefs. He wants to be a man of the land.

He follows Boone down a ragged slope, muscling his machine to keep from banging the cowling into rocks. From here, the sea and slate-gray sky end in the mountains of Siberia, thirty-six miles away. Mergansers bob upon the waves and dive for fish. The water softly slaps the rocks. The vista fills him with joy. *Our* island, he thinks. He knows such thinking reflects white men's ownership concepts, but he doesn't care. How old and wizened is the land that has nurtured his people! An island once grasped by God—hence its skinny middle and its Yupik name, Sevoukok, meaning "squeezed"—a land perhaps part of the Bering Sea crossing that brought Eskimos to the New World.

Our island, he tells himself.

They park the machines in a gully, as out of sight as possible, and, keeping low, wend their way to the blind. They hope for hair seals, abundant this time of year, but will settle for late south-flying geese. They put several white plastic bags on ground barren of snow. Secured in the middle by rocks, the bags flap just enough to serve as decoys.

Neither speaks as they scan the sea, methodically starting at the horizon and moving their gaze back in tiny increments, missing nothing. A few air bubbles can mean a seal's presence, but for now the sea is devoid of possibility. He is without regret. He knows that the land and sea yield treasures when they are ready to do so. The hunter must be alert and accept the gifts.

He thinks of his girlfriend, Bunnie. Not many years from now, he has decided, he will ask his father to negotiate for her. Will his hunting, he wonders, be better during bride service, when he works for her father's family for a year? Will his prowess make Bunnie shyly smile each time he returns from the hunt? Come home empty-handed now, and his family can rely on his brothers. Hunting for Bunnie's family will impel him to hone his skills, he is certain. For the first time he truly will be hunting as an adult.

"Lost in thought? Or just lost?" Boone teases him, breaking the silence now that they know there are no seals, at least for the present. "We're out on West Cape, Merle."

"Just thinking about the reading materials that George gave us, on UFOs," Merle replies, avoiding the truth. "You get through it?"

"Didn't start. Don't intend to."

"It's pretty interesting."

Boone snorts sarcastically. "Leave school at school. We're out hunting, man."

Merle lifts the binoculars and glasses the sea. "You really think we can separate the two?"

12

A week after showing their commitment to the program, the Problem Solvers assemble on a Thursday night for their first practice problem. Only Merle seems prepared. Jasmine looks determined; Meredith, resigned. The others straggle in, none enthusiastic.

"Read the test's scenario and quickly discuss possible problems it might involve," I tell them as I pass out the sealed envelopes from the state evaluators in Juneau. "Remember, you have six steps to finish, so try to nail down the first step—identifying possible problems in the situation they give you—in no more than forty-five minutes. That will give you fifteen minutes to identify the specific problem you want to tackle and then an hour to solve it twenty ways and to write an essay on your best solution. Try to make your answers as complete as possible. If you decide, say, that 'sunspots' are a problem regarding UFO identification, then don't just write 'sunspots.' Remember, the judges cannot read your minds about what you *meant* to say. Any questions?"

Summer raises her hand. "Can I go home pretty soon?"

"Are we going to be done in time for open gym?" Marshall asks.

"Can we shoot around now?" Garnet asks. "Before open gym?"

I look around the group, nearly all of them now eager not for the test but rather for having the gym to themselves, and conclude that browbeating and begging aren't going to work. I resort to bribes. Knowing that if I promise gym time, they will just hurry through the test, I take them into the kitchen and give them the cake, cookies, popcorn, and punch that Mary made—snacks I had intended for *after* the competition. The kids head to their respective testing rooms laden with plates, popcorn sacks, and Dixie cups instead of pencils and pens.

"Don't let Puffin out of the room for anything!" I yell to Boone and Marshall as they cross the gym. "Especially not for a bathroom break!"

Once the kids are settled in the classrooms, they are to begin by reading the scenario together carefully. Each problem they then identify is worth one and a half points: half a point if the problem the students choose fits the situation, half a point if the students attack the scenario from a variety of viewpoints, such as sociologically or in terms of business rather than just in some obvious way, and half a point if they show research—a scoring rubric that also applies to the solutions that they later generate.

On both the problems and the solutions, they also can receive an additional five points per answer for original ideas: those that, in the opinion of the evaluators, are several years above grade level *and* are not duplicated by any other team in the state.

I have little hope of the students earning any points for originality. I only want them to complete the test. So it is with mental fingers crossed that, after the kids begin, I return to my classroom and open the coach's packet. I am afraid that if this first test is too difficult, the kids will just give up and go home.

I am relieved to find that the test scenario is short and realistic. The notebook warned me that the scenarios can be one or two single-spaced pages long, but this one consists of just two sentences: "A weather balloon floating over Los Angeles has been mistaken for a UFO. What problems might result?"

A paragraph then follows to help the kids with the process:

"Identify twenty problems. Then decide which of the problems you identify, if solved or resolved, might best defuse the situations that have arisen as a result of the mistaken identity. What twenty solutions might you suggest to solve the problem you chose? What five criteria might you use to assess your solutions? Assess ten of your solutions. Which is your best solution? How might you amplify it to make it more efficient and, if appropriate, more humane?"

I spend the next two hours grading papers and readying materials for the next day's classes, and then enter the classroom where the high school team is and pick up the test booklets. From the handwriting I can tell who wrote what. Londa's answers are hurried and incomplete, Jasmine's and Merle's well-reasoned and articulate. I give all three a thumbs-up.

Next, the elementary team.

I open the door to find only Meredith within, writing furiously. "Time," I say softly, wondering where the other three girls are.

Meredith angrily slams down her pencil.

"The other girls lasted about an hour, and went out the back door," she complains.

I pick up Meredith's problem booklet without looking at it, lest she become angrier. As I head to the classroom where the junior high school team is, I hear her exit, the back door slamming shut.

Marshall and Boone race for their seats as I open the door. Puffin is seated in the corner, head down, the back of her T-shirt wet, popcorn in her hair. Cake is splattered on the walls and desks, punch is slopped on the floor. Marshall and Boone concentrate on their papers, but grin at each other as Boone licks cake from his fingers.

Food fight.

"Puffin?" I ask as, too upset to say anything to the boys, I pick up their problem booklets.

She shakes her head, not speaking.

I walk over and squat beside her. Tears brim in her eyes.

"Boone was bothering," she says bitterly.

Bothering me, she means, as usual leaving off the pronoun.

"She wouldn't talk," he says when I give him my eagle eye.

"She never talks!" I say.

"But this is a competition!" he blurts.

I glance through their answers. *Let Superman solve it. Ask God for help.*

"This is the same crap you came up with ten days ago!" I tell them.

"We ran out of ideas," Marshall says.

"So instead of brainstorming more ideas, you have a food fight?"

Boone crumples his Dixie cup, tosses it at the wastebasket, and walks out the door, Marshall following.

Walking home in darkness, Meredith is thankful for the light above the elementary school as she trudges down another enormous snowdrift.

Why, she wonders, does she continue to put up with Problem Solving? For Dad?

For Dad, she concludes.

She has little interest in it. She was excited about living with Eskimos because she wanted to learn about culture. When she was in kindergarten she had heard two women speaking another language on a bus. Probably Portuguese, she has since decided. At that moment she resolved to learn other languages. Not just learn them, but *live* them. To do that, she had to understand a culture, really understand it, be one with it.

Here, with the chance to learn one of the world's rarest languages, she is studying Problem Solving, while the rest of her school day she must endure constant harassment. Kids hitting her, blackboard erasers covered with white chalk slapped against her face, her books forever being knocked off her desk. And the names—those are the most hurtful of all.

Someone tackles her from behind.

Together they roll into the next trough, the boy in a ski mask, his breath coming through the yarn. She kicks at him and frees herself, only to have someone else tackle her. Now she is on her back, snow tumbling down on her, the boys holding down her legs and outstretched arms. Terrified, she wonders if they will rape her—Mom has told her about such things—but then she hears a revving, and a snowmachine crests the mound, its light lancing through the night.

The machine comes down at her.

They're going to kill me.

She struggles and screams, to no avail. The machine is upon her—literally, the skis slamming her further into the snow. She nearly faints from the weight.

After the snowmachine passes over her, the hands release her and she lies gasping. There are frightened voices. She blinks up into light, and realizes, its sound roaring through her consciousness, that the snowmachine is again atop the snow mound, readying for a second pass. She struggles to stand, but her legs give out. The driver, also in a ski mask, revs the engine.

Another boy appears, scrambling along the drift, knee-deep in snow. Marshall! He grabs the driver and punches him. Then both boys are lost from sight, probably fighting on the other side of the drift. She gains her feet and clambers down the trough, waving Marshall away when he crests the mound and comes down to help her.

Sobbing, she staggers home, knowing that if the snow had not been soft she could have been killed, and knowing that she cannot tell anyone of the incident—for then Mom and Dad either will send Gretchen and her away, or else will resign and lose their teaching credentials.

She stumbles down the snow steps into the arctic entry. Closing the flimsy door against the wind, she leans with her shoulder against it, gasping and crying, wanting forever to shut out the world of the Eskimo.

13

Three weeks after the first practice problem, I bring a railroad to the village.

It happens like this, in the Twilight Zone that is this world of dwindling daylight: Mr. Dan arrives back from a meeting at the district office in Unalakleet and immediately calls the faculty together. The superintendent, he informs us, is losing the embezzlement battle. More importantly for our immediate concerns, the superintendent has decided that Gambell's high school will be the first small school in Western Alaska to undergo accreditation.

I blink and wonder if I'm awake. A school so troubled that it is under threat of closure, called "the pariah of Alaskan education," has been chosen by administrative intelligence to serve as the model for all other small schools in half the state.

Okay, I decide. *Produce a several-paragraph summary of the school and its mission, put it in a glassine folder, and send it on to the Superintendent Supreme. He'll spout it to the media, wave it before the state administrators in Juneau, shift the focus from embezzlement to education. End of story.*

Mr. Dan effects a grim smile. "Plan on a document of several hundred pages. We might get by with four hundred, but more likely we're looking at five or six hundred."

I glance around at the other faculty, and for once we are all of one mind. Stunned.

"The seven of us are going to write a document more than a ream long," I say.

"We'll have Fridays off to do it," Mr. Dan says.

I put my hands on the sides of my head, elbows on the table. I feel as if I need blinders to understand the superintendent's tunnel vision. "We teach kids who speak English as a second language," I say. "Kids with almost no world knowledge and with poor reading, writing, and math skills. And now, to show the quality of their education, we're going to drop one-fifth of the little time those kids are in school?"

"To complete the document on time, we'll cancel every third Thursday as well," Mr. Dan says. "But there's an upside. Your department budgets will be increased."

Our departments. Six teachers, six departments.

"Increased how much?" Keenan asks, thinking of his shop.

"Increased," Mr. Dan says.

"By how much?" I ask, jumping in.

"Increased," he says.

The last of the oil-pipeline allocations, it occurs to me. *They are blowing the wad and stumping for accreditation to make themselves look good. If they chose the district's top school, that would be Unalakleet. They would be on their own turf. They would have to work. This way, they do nothing except make demands, and if accreditation fails, they can blame the island.*

I had thought that our district administrators were stupid. Until today.

"Can I buy, say . . . a rocket ship?" I ask.

The other teachers laugh, albeit nervously.

Mr. Dan ignores them. "That would be outside your expertise," he says matter-of-factly. "You teach sophomore English and social science, not rocket science."

"Then can I buy," I ask, thinking about Problem Solving, "a railroad?"

The train the district buys me is meant to go on a foot-wide board around my room—metaphorically the perimeter of the United States: my official justification for the purchase. I envision the kids creating the deserts of the Southwest along the library shelves, the Eastern Seaboard beneath my blackboard, a Northwest logging town alongside Chip and Dale's table. There are many technical problems, and I intend to have the teams help me solve them.

The first involves the classroom doors. How can we create a perimeter without blocking entry?

I mention the problem of the doors off-handedly one day and am amazed that, after six weeks' training, the Problem Solvers' brainstorming skills have become infectious.

"Don't put the train so low," Boone says, indicating the boards we have built along two walls. "Build the train shelf higher than the door."

"Detachable bridge," Marshall says, running the engine across an imaginary expanse.

Soon Londa, Chip and Dale, Lobert, and even Puffin and the girl who likes to fart join in:

"Cut the door in half. Make everyone crawl inside."

"Put out a sign telling them to crawl."

"Cut everyone in half. Then everyone will go under the railroad anyway."

"Turn us all into midgets."

"Have some kind of hinged thing that comes down and completes the track. You know, like the countertop in a bar."

"When were *you* in a bar!"

"I see them on TV, man."

"Yeah, well, you've never been in a bar."

"Build the railroad on the floor and have everyone step over."

"Put the mountains where we have to step over. That way, if anyone steps on it, the mountains will get smashed and not the railroad."

After the bell rings and the kids exit, Gerald, the special ed teacher, enters the room to use the photocopier. He looks in disgust at the railroad project, which consists of barren boards along two walls, then peers down as if from a great height at the engine I am holding, his eyelids half-hooded below his enormous forehead.

"Trains," he says. "What kind of teacher are you! Just look at your mailbox—always messy. I wonder if you ever read your mail. And look at how you indicate you've read the accreditation flyers." He nods toward the document he's photocopying. As usual, Mr. Dan has included a paper for everyone to mark that they have read the latest district office edict in the accreditation undertaking. What began as a seven-person project has now fallen mainly on the shoulders of three—Mr. Dan; Lawrence, the science/math teacher, who is working on a master's in administration; and me, because of my writing background.

Gerald scowls. "You always put a check beside your name instead of an X in the box. Everyone else puts in nice, neat Xs. You call yourself an educator, Mr. Elitist? Get with the program."

So shocked am I over his diatribe that I just stand there looking at him. Were we in a story, I would think he needed fleshing out, made three-dimensional. Here in reality he seems more caricature than character. What could have made him so bitter, so shallow? That he had been a special ed student as a child? Was the answer so simple?

I am afraid to ask. Only a fool would pet the rabid.

Finally he's gone, leaving me alone with Lionel.

"The next practice problem," I tell the kids a week later, "is on lasers. Then in late February we play the state-qualifying problem. That's on undersea communities."

Marshall moans. "My brain's turning to blubber!"

"We don't even know how we did on the first problem," Londa says.

Barely are the words out of her mouth than Mr. Dan enters with an envelope marked "Future Problem Solving Program." I hold the envelope up to the kids and tear it open as they peer toward me and Mr. Dan looks on.

Elementary school division—our score is far below the median. High school, my greatest hope—we're barely above median. Then I look at the junior high schools, and have to look twice. Eighty-eight junior high school teams submitted booklets, and Gambell is . . . third.

My punch-cake-cookie-popcorn throwers: *third!*

My kids who *Let Jesus solve the problem.* My kids who *Let Superman solve it.*

Third!

"You see?" Marshall wags an index finger at me. "I told you we're good."

Boone raises his arms.

Touchdown.

14

The solstice comes, and afterward the welcome and inexorable climb to greater daylight. We now gain the seven minutes of daylight per day that we had lost in the months prior to the solstice. Contrary to what many people believe, most of Alaska is not dark during winter. Only above the Arctic Circle, far to the north, does the sun stay down for days—nights—on end.

In terms of latitude, Saint Lawrence Island is south of Fairbanks and Nome. In the calendar midwinter, which for Eskimos differs markedly from the seasonal one, the sun rises by midmorning and sets about five. The farther one journeys into winter on the island, the less severe the storms are, the more brilliant the sun, and the more oppressive the cold. The contrast mirrors—or shadows—the pattern that my life on the island has become, if indeed patterns and predictability in life are not merely the work of our imaginations. Certain teachers and administrators frustrate me, but the culture and Future Problem Solving are increasingly fascinating.

Perhaps because of the cold, I start writing a novel about Africa. With Mr. Dan's permission, I set up an office in the basement of his duplex, where my typing all night won't bother my family, back in our little shack. It's so cold down in the Dans' basement that I must write while wearing my coat, ski pants, and fingerless gloves. But at least it's a place where I can be alone.

I especially need to be alone the night after we get the results back on the second practice problem, on lasers. Though more of the kids have started reading the synopsized articles that come from Juneau, none of the Gambell teams placed in the mock competition. I am even more discouraged than the kids.

As I enter the duplex's hallway on my way downstairs, Mr. Dan steps from his apartment and, after commiserating with me regarding the kids' scores, asks me not to give up on Problem Solving.

I promise that I won't, though my heart is not in my promise. We step outside—he for a smoke—and soon we are slapping our gloved hands together against the cold. The ice is in, clogging the sea and building up into massive bulwarks where land and sea meet. Cold seems to wreathe the village, like an animal curling for warmth around the oil stove stacks.

"You see those houses, George?" He nods to houses a couple hundred yards away, whose lights show. "They represent a microcosm of any society. Per capita, rural Alaska has some of the highest rates of spouse abuse, child abuse, and alcoholism in the country, and the nation's highest rate of fetal alcohol syndrome. Not to mention that we rank among the world's highest rates for suicide. Or that the Arctic is becoming polluted—something to do with the magnetosphere. We aren't isolated here. It's just that we Eskimos live so far away that other people see us through rose-colored telescopes—if they see us at all."

He slips off his gloves and lights a cigarette, cupping his hands against the wind. "But that's not our biggest problem. A lot of us up North have been given too much. In my village, for instance, the whalers gave the people guns one year, then gave them *new* guns the next. My people thought that the old ones worked fine, and they had cared for them religiously, but they decided that if the whalers were bringing them new ones, there must be something wrong with the old. So they tossed the old ones out onto the tundra."

He points with his cigarette toward a falling star. There's a meteorite shower, the night alive with arcs of light.

"A few years before I came here, every family received a snowmachine. Just like that." He snaps his fingers, ends up blowing on them and putting his gloves back on. "Created by the gods in Washington, D.C. Most of the people thought that the government was wonderful. They owe it to us, people in my village said. They took so much from us, after all. But we didn't realize there were strings attached. More like nooses. We Eskimos are human—we won't turn down what's free. And like everyone else we want to deny that handouts make us reliant on the giver. We become *real* victims then, because we see ourselves as victims. Too many of us haven't learned what Zapata, the revolutionary, taught his fellow Mexicans: it's better to die standing than to live on one's knees."

He eyes me, and frowns. "What happens when the oil money runs out, or when the feds get fed up with handing out money to indigenous peoples and shut the purse? No more free lunch, no more handouts as you pass 'Go.' Meanwhile, what preparation do we give our children for what we know lies ahead? People like Gerald come here, collect their salaries, and leave thinking they've accomplished something because they pay lip service to basic skills. A little math, some rudimentary reading. What will those kids do if they end up living in a city, or if the government stops subsidizing everything? You have any idea how much it costs to heat one of those HUD houses?"

"There's always carving," I say. "I've heard that some of the people here do really well."

"You don't think there will be fluctuations in the market? You don't think that the environmentalists want to shut down the sale of Eskimo artwork? Kids like Merle—they understand the complexity. Boone does too, I think, and certainly Jasmine does. And probably Allana, the girl who's always typing? Sharp kid. It's just that she's convinced that there's nothing for her in the village except secretarial jobs, so she doesn't do anything except huddle behind that keyboard."

I realize I haven't thought of her as anything except an apprentice secretary.

"A number of years ago an elder in my village told me something really important," Dan continues. "'The problem with you kids nowadays,' he said, 'is that you don't really learn what the white man has to teach, and you don't really learn how to hunt, either. You play at both. What good is weightlifting if you don't have good, equal weights at both ends?' I've never forgotten that. I think that's why I became a principal. Why some day I'll make superintendent.

"When I was deciding whether to come here," he continues, "the district sent me out for a visit during the meetings between the administration and the parents, trying to determine whether the school should be shut down. There had been numerous assaults against teachers. It was totally out of control. 'Why do you let your kids act that way?' I asked one parent. She said, 'Because I tell them to.'

"It took me a long time to get over that. Most parents here want what all parents do: a chance for their children to lead quality lives. Others seem to think the problems will go away if the school goes away. At best, they tolerate the school. At worst?" He snorts sarcastically. "At worst they don't teach their children to lift the weight."

"There are no easy answers," I comment.

"That's right. That's why, even though at first I didn't know what we would be getting into, I've pushed you so much to teach Problem Solving. Lars is fantastic teaching home ec, but in the classroom? Word-finds and crosswords? What good is that! And Gerald, teaching sophomores to count with quarters and dimes? Isn't teaching how to *make* money more important? Much of the time you whites treat us like children, and you're shocked when we rebel because we resent it. But there's one thing we really do need to teach the kids in these schools. One thing maybe your program can help them learn."

"What's that?" I say finally.

"That there are no easy answers."

He flips the cigarette onto the hard snow and steps on it. The area is littered with butts. He's spent many an hour out here smoking and thinking, I realize.

"I sometimes get the feeling that most of you teachers think it's easier for me to work here because I'm Eskimo," he says. "It isn't any easier, George."

He walks up the short flight of stairs and into his house, leaving me out in the cold, beneath the falling stars.

15

"Your dad works at night in the duplex *basement?*" Garnet asks Meredith as the elementary school team trudges home from Problem Solving practice. Because of the mile walk, if they cannot get a ride they often make excuses to skip practice, but today all four of them are together.

"He's writing another novel," Meredith says.

"There're *ghosts* down there," Garnet says, horrified. She stops atop a snow mound and looks toward the duplex.

Groper, coming up from behind, also stops. "There aren't any real ghosts down there," she reassures Meredith.

"Are too!" Garnet insists.

"Aren't either."

"Are too!" Garnet crosses her arms, and pouts. "Ghosts of the teachers who got killed in the plane wreck."

Meredith has seen the small cross in the hallway of the elementary school. All the faculty, including the aides, dead in an instant a half-dozen years ago.

She looks at Summer, clearly the leader of the fifth graders, for an opinion. Summer shrugs and holds out her mittened hands, palms up.

"There are no ghosts in Mr. Dan's basement," Groper says with an air of finality. "The teachers' ghosts live in the school basement."

Garnet gives her a look of disdain. "If they catch you, they'll make you do homework," she tells Meredith. "And try to steal your soul."

"Only if you talk to them in Yupik," Groper says. "The ghosts want to be Eskimo."

"I don't know any Yupik," Meredith says, though secretly she has been writing down words as best she can and, after class, asking the school's Yupik instructor.

"You'd be okay, then," Groper says. She looks at Garnet and then at Summer. "Wouldn't she?"

"I wouldn't want to be caught by the ghosts no matter what," Garnet says.

"It isn't fair," Marshall says, under his breath.

Bietha, his mother, looks over at him as she stirs the stew of seal ribs and braided intestine. Like many other village women, she prefers a Coleman campstove to the electric range that came with the house. "What's not fair?"

"Nothing."

"Problem Solving?"

He sighs and nods. There is no keeping anything from her. That she seems always to know his thoughts no longer disturbs him. He finds it comforting.

"We only have three people on our team," he says, uncharacteristically feeling a need to talk. "Teams in schools that did good on the second practice problem had four. All that studying! Read this, read that! We'd have a lot less reading if we had four people."

"Reading's good for you," she says.

"Why should we have to play Problem Solving with three players? You can't play basketball with only four."

"Not even if one fouls out and there aren't more players?"

As she turns back to her cooking, he reflects on her insight. He regards her opinion highly, and not just because she is his mother. Hasn't it been said that, like her father before her, she can predict the future? To his mind, her gift for sizing up situations is as uncanny as her expertise at crabbing. Anyone could get a crab to latch onto the string weighted down by an old sparkplug, but keeping it *on* the string until it can be scooped up through the auger hole—that is the difficulty. People said she talked to the crabs as they rose: assuaging their spirits, seducing them into surfacing. Like the crabbers of old, people said.

When she turns away, he looks at her back and wishes he could tell her how proud he is of her abilities out on the ice. She spends every hour possible there, jigging for crabs and the tiny tomcod that she fries up with butter and onions. The frozen sea, she has said, is her calling.

His father emerges from the back room, using a pipe cleaner to rid his Dremel tool of ivory dust. He rarely carves, and when he does, he even more rarely sells his work. He makes his living as a hunter—seal and walrus and whale to feed his family; polar bear hides to sell for store food and heating oil. Marshall knows that his father is Alaska's best polar bear hunter, though his father will never admit it. Pride was unmanly and could violate the spirit of the animal.

"If you worried half as much about hunting as you do about those games at school, we'd all be better off," his father says, apparently having overheard the conversation.

Marshall says nothing. They have had arguments before. Ugly ones.

"You want to be a man without skills?" his father asks.

I find the Problem Solvers in a funk. The low scores on the second problem seem to have affected everyone. "Looks like it's time we studied physics," I tell them.

They protest that this isn't science class, that I'm not a science teacher, yet they dutifully follow me to the janitor's closet, where I give them each a commercial-strength garbage bag.

"We're going to conduct an experiment on slope and velocity," I say. "Grab your coats."

We go outside. Sunlight sparkles on the snow, as usual so sucked dry of moisture that it crumbles like granulated sugar in the hand. It is impossible to make a snowball or snowman, but it's great for sledding. Like sliding on ice.

But beware of the boulders.

We climb halfway up the mountain, counting our steps. I am gasping because of exhaustion that has gripped me on the walk to the mountain. Must be flu coming on, I decide, and I'm glad that tomorrow is a holiday. I plan to sleep. Haven't taken a day off since coming to the island, so it's about time.

When at last I reach the students, who are laughing at my labored climb, I indicate that students should take turns sliding down while the others calculate how long it takes to reach the bottom. How to determine slope and velocity I have no idea. Though

I once edited a science magazine, and though I love discussing science fiction with my cousin, an astrophysicist, when it comes to basic physics I am as dense as a black hole.

"You are *not* sledding," I remind them after I have caught my breath sufficiently to say more than a few words. "Mr. Dan has said it's too dangerous. You could get killed, or you could break a leg and I'd have to shoot you. It could cost me my job."

After the second run, the kids dash to school and return with pop. We sit amid the boulders and sip, everyone shivering. The temp is ten above; perfect for a picnic. Merle produces binoculars. We watch a group of hunters—including some high school boys—walk a skin boat across slush ice. Hunting is an excused absence at the school, so on good-weather days like this, many kids don't show up. How many of them actually are hunting is debatable.

"Dangerous," Boone says, nodding toward the hunters out on the ice.

Merle sneaks up behind me and, abruptly pulling down my coat collar, slaps me—hard—on the back of the neck.

He grins when I lurch around, startled. "Keeps you focused." At ten degrees, a neck-slap *hurts*. "We do it to each other out on the ice all the time."

"You fall through ice like *that,*" Marshall says, indicating the skin boat, "and you better have a hand on the boat or somebody better grab you. Get pulled under, and everyone can be right above you on the ice, and they can't get to you. *Gone.*" He gestures with his hand held flat. "Currents are really bad here." His seriousness tells me he's come close to death out on the ice. "Jones went through last night," he adds. "If Lobert hadn't been there, Jones wouldn't have shown up for work today."

Lobert was in geography this morning, grinning his usual grin. He hadn't said a word about having saved a man the night before. No one had, though I'm sure all the kids were aware of the incident. It occurs to me that no one would have mentioned the near tragedy, were it not for the giddy good nature the sledding has produced. *Not because they're hiding something from us teachers but because, for them, such events are commonplace.*

Sitting halfway up the mountain as the Problem Solvers shiver and drink Coke and, appropriately, Mountain Dew, I realize something about my teaching.

Until now I had given variety to the one English class I teach each day. Eight ways to start an essay, six ways to organize its parts, five ways to structure paragraphs. After all, isn't the maxim, "Familiarity breeds contempt"? But the result of variety has been confusion and frustration.

"Last one back to the classroom is a rotting walrus!" I tell them.

Down the mountain we slide, careening past rocks, flying over small ledges, the slick ice ironed even slicker by the previous runs. The kids easily outrace me once we reach the bottom, for my exhaustion seems to hold me even on flat ground.

I walk most of the quarter mile back to class thinking about the hunters and about what Vygotsky, the Russian pedagogical theorist, taught us educators. He said that we have placed too much emphasis on the *self* in kids. They need social actualization, not so much self-awareness, to help actualize their potential.

Didn't Eskimo training demonstrate exactly what Vygotsky proselytized? Had not generations of expert hunters passed on knowledge that minimized the danger of pushing a skin boat across slush ice? Why, as modern educators, are we so quick to teach everything anew?

Don't we love Christmas carols and the Golden Oldies? Do not our kids listen to the same songs time and again? Does not familiarity breed contentment and commitment?

Excited by the idea the hunters with the skin boat have instilled in me, I pull off my army coat as I enter the room and drop it on the floor, wipe the sweat from my forehead, and grab my chalk. No one laughs. Maybe they sense a change in me.

I draw two shorelines on the blackboard, with waves in between. "This is where we are now. This is the losing shore." I indicate the one on the left. "And this is where we want to be." I tap that shore with my chalk. "*This* is Anchorage." I look around at the expectant faces. "The central question is how do we get from here," moving my chalk, "to *here*. That's Problem Solving. Learn how to do *that*, and we'll not only get to Anchorage, we'll win there."

I let my gaze move from student to student, trying to use my eyes and body language to draw each into the question I am about to ask.

"How do we cross the ocean between those two shores?"

There is no response.

"How?" I ask.

Rather than having asked a question rhetorically and answering it myself, I wait.

"Boat," Marshall says, offhandedly.

"Ship," Meredith says.

They are off and running.

"Airplane."

"Balloon."

"Zeppelin."

"Swim."

"Ride a dolphin."

I signal for quiet.

"How about *this*," I tell them.

I pull a section of railroad track from one of the long boxes the tracks came in and place it between two tables.

"You can't build a railroad over an ocean," Marshall says.

"Aren't the British and French building the Chunnel?" I ask him.

"That goes *under* the ocean," he says.

I ignore him. "Look. Brainstorming isn't your strong suit. It goes against your culture. When you're out hunting, you don't try out an unlimited range of possibilities. You react to situations based on information passed down from your ancestors. What educators call *a priori* knowledge. Your thinking is realistic and precise. It has to be. It's a real world out on the ice, and there's very little margin for error.

"Instead of just trying this or that in Problem Solving," I go on, "let's find *one* way to do the process, and do it that way every time. A step-by-step process. Like ties in a railroad." I run an index finger down the track.

"What if the situation we're given is something we never studied?" Londa asks.

"Yeah. What if we never anticipated what they ask?" Marshall says.

"You adjust to the situation. Just like in hunting. You have learned one way to take a skin boat across slush ice, one best way, and you adjust that to fit a new situation. Some people think Eskimos don't want change. They imply that you can't handle change, that your culture is something simplistic and must be preserved like a collection of insects in amber. Your ancestors understood change. They anticipated and survived changes in weather, sea mammal migrations, animal-population die-offs. They had processes in place for handling change. Step-by-step processes that are so much part of you that you don't even realize they're there."

"So what we need to win in Problem Solving," says Jasmine, the senior with a disconcerting habit of anticipating what I am able to say, "is to figure out that step-by-step process."

Marshall crosses his arms and leans back, the picture of arrogance. "Well, what is it?"

"First, we're going to be more realistic," I say.

"No more elephants from Savoonga?" Merle asks.

"No more Savoonga elephants, no more Let Jesus solve it, no more Let Superman do it," I say, and Boone blanches. "We're going to develop a step-by-step process anyone can follow. I don't know what that is— yet." Looking at the railroad track, I sit down, already lost in thought.

"But you'll figure it out," Marshall says, with an assurance that surprises me.

Marshall's words haunt me for days. What frightens me is his absolute belief that I will develop the tools they need to succeed in Problem Solving. Do such tools exist, other than the steps outlined in the coach's notebook?

And what if the kids realize how little training I actually have in Problem Solving?

One morning there is no wind; a stunning dawn fringes the horizon in pink and orange. I decide to walk to school. Parents and kids on snowmachines wave as they pass.

As I go by the post office and start through the soft, deeper snow of the hollow behind it, I remember a conversation I had with a student at

Loras College in Dubuque, Iowa, my first teaching job. A conscientious freshman, and much older than the other students, she was researching the effects of Midwest storms on Canada geese migrations. "What exactly *is* a term paper?" she asked me one day in the library.

Given her efforts and abilities, a flippant answer would have been a disservice. So profound was her question that I stood there wondering why I had never asked the same thing of my own professors.

In one of those epiphanies that sometimes define or refine our professional skills, I intuited the answer. My mind seemed to rush down a tunnel, for the answer lay before me in the growing light at the other end—simple, immutable, and unmistakably *right*.

"At its best," I said, "it shows the relationship between two variables and attempts to explain why and to what degree that relationship exists." Seeing her confusion, I added, "In a nutshell, it tells precisely what the subject is and why that subject is true or important."

What because why.

Standing in the mushy snow, I repeat the phrase in my mind.

What because why.

Rather than being the basis of a term paper, wasn't it the basis of *all* communication?

What because why.

Suddenly I know what I have been doing wrong regarding Problem Solving.

I run toward school through the mush.

"We've been emphasizing solutions," I tell the kids, trying to control my excitement. "But when you're out hunting on the tundra or on the ice, you can't make a mistake. Right?"

The faces are no longer blank. After Marshall's assurance that I would come up with answers, the teams have been expecting this day.

"When you're hunting, it's not 'Try and try again,' like people emphasize in the cities. It's 'Be sure you're right, then go ahead.' That's what Daniel Boone, a great hunter and frontiersman, used to say. In a way, he was a lot like you. He lived life that at the time was out on the extreme. He couldn't make a mistake, not if he wanted to live.

"When you're hunting, you anticipate *problems*. That's what we're going to do from now on. Instead of spending most of the time identifying the solutions, we're going to spend most of our time identifying the problems the test's scenario gives. We'll do what you do naturally." As my enthusiasm escalates, the kids' enthusiasm grows. Their eyes are bright. Marshall, arms wrapped around his basketball, leans forward like an athlete listening to his coach's every word.

"When you're engaged in subsistence activities, you ask yourselves *what* problem might occur and *why* it's a problem," I tell them. "So repeat that: What because why!"

For a moment there is no response, and my heart skips a beat as I wait in fear.

"What because why!" I say. "Repeat it!"

I am relieved when they reply, "What because why!"

"Hit the tables when you say it!"

They slightly slap the tables. "What because why!"

"Are you wimps? Hit the tables hard!"

I slam down my hand. Pain shoots up my arm.

Whomp! "*What because why!*"

After several more swats, some hold their hands in pain. I write "what because why" on the board. "This is the basis of communication," I tell them. "Understand this, and you'll be on your way to communicating with the evaluators. Instead of trying to figure out how to begin and therefore wasting time during the tests, you'll always write, 'Blank may be a problem because of blank.' *What because why.*

"For example," I continue, in a nearly breathless excitement, "let's say that you were given a scenario about an Alaskan village, and as one of the twenty problems you isolated, you decide that finding an available water supply is a big problem. You could write, 'Drilling for water may be a problem because of permafrost.'"

On the board I label "Drilling for water" as *what* and "because of permafrost" as *why*.

"To be even more specific, you could rearrange the parts and add a new 'why,'" I tell them as I draw an arrow from the "why" to the "what." "You would end up with something like, 'Drilling for water in permafrost may be a problem because of high costs, frozen casings, and brackish water.'"

When I finish rewriting the sentence, Jasmine asks, "We would still have to prove that, wouldn't we?"

"Yes. Without notes or books," I remind her. "But look how you can work everything in, as long as you start with 'what because why.'"

I rewrite the sentence as, "Drilling for water in permafrost may be a problem, because scientists from the U.S. Geological Survey have said that it may involve high costs, frozen casings, and brackish water."

"How are we going to find out all that?" Marshall asks.

"You read," I say.

He folds his arms and lets his lips make the sound of a motorboat.

"If you want us always to write 'may be a problem' or 'may be a solution,'" Jasmine says, "won't that use up a lot of time? Couldn't we just use initials, and define them on our first page of the test?"

I give her the chalk, and after glancing around shyly, she goes to the board.

"MBAP = may be a problem."

"MBAS = may be a solution."

After she sits down, I realize that Marshall was wrong. *I* will not develop the structures we need—the steps in the process, the ties beneath our railroad of learning.

We will develop them together.

16

Today is the big day! Meredith tells herself. The state-qualifying test! After today, either her team will have earned a trip to Anchorage, and then Garnet, Groper, and Summer will *want* to go up to the high school to prepare, or they will not have made the finals and there will be no more practices.

Either way, she will not have to beg them to go to practice. Or beg someone for a ride.

Not that attendance in Problem Solving practice has been a problem these past two weeks. All they seem to talk about is the Anchorage trip. Meredith knows that the elementary kids, like those on the other teams, are mainly interested in Problem Solving because of the lure of a trip to Anchorage. That became especially clear the last time they went up for Problem Solving practice—a day so wind-free that the four of them walked instead of using the snowmachine that Garnet's father had just given her.

"I'm getting my hair permed as soon as we get to state!" Summer had said. "Mom says there's a beauty place in Penney's."

"Penney's?" Groper asked. "What's that?"

"It's where *everybody* goes in Anchorage," Summer said.

"Wow," Groper said.

"Then I'll get my hair done there too," Garnet said.

"Me too," Groper said.

"You ever have your hair done?" Garnet asked Groper.

"Sure I have," Groper said. "My mom has done it."

"That's not the same," Summer said. "It's not like having your hair done at Penney's."

The classroom clock *thunks* as the minute hand reaches nine. "Ready?" Meredith asks Garnet and Groper. Before they have a chance to answer, she swivels around so she can see Summer, who is drawing a long-haired woman in a strapless evening gown. "Ready?"

Summer keeps drawing.

Meredith looks at the other two girls.

They keep coloring.

"It's two forty-five," Meredith says. "We're supposed to go up to the high school so we can play the state qualifying problem."

The girls continue coloring.

"Dad said that we have to play the problem *today*," Meredith tells them, her impatience and anxiety growing.

"We'll play tomorrow," Groper says.

"We have to play *today*," Meredith says. "Dad has to mail in our answers tomorrow morning."

"We want to color," Garnet says.

"I'm not finished drawing my evening gown," Summer says.

"You don't want to *see* evening gowns?" Meredith asks. "At Penney's?"

"I want to finish the evening gown *now*," Summer says.

"Don't you want to get your hair done?"

"My mom can do my hair," Summer says. "Besides, I like it the way it is." She lifts her head in a haughty, diffident look. "I want to finish drawing my evening gown."

"I want to color," Garnet says.

"Me too," Groper says. "My mom can do my hair."

"What," I tell the six Problem Solvers, using a pointer to indicate the words on the board, "because . . . why."

"What . . . because . . . why," the kids repeat.

"What . . . because . . . why," I say, feeling as if I am leading them in a Hail Mary.

"What . . . because . . . why," they repeat.

Except for Boone and Marshall, who exude confidence, the kids look a bit anxious. "Remember," I say, "start with 'what' the idea is you wish to express, and then say 'why' it is true or important. Don't write, 'An undersea city might disrupt sea mammal migration routes.' That doesn't express cause and effect clearly enough. It doesn't get to the root of the problem. Instead, write something like, 'Disrupting plankton communities may be a problem because it could disturb whales' migration routes.'"

We practice fitting more sample ideas into the structure, we review the six steps of the Problem Solving process, and when I decide we can't wait for the little kids any longer, I take the teams to their respective classrooms and give them the sealed tests.

Soon the high school team—Jasmine, Merle, and Londa—have their heads together, discussing the scenario sheet they have removed from the test's manila envelope. I watch them for a moment through the door's narrow window, then go to check on the junior high team. Boone, Marshall, and Puffin are busy writing.

Still anxiously waiting for the elementary team, I call the other school, but no one picks up the phone. I grab my coach's packet, pull myself into my coat, and am at the school entrance, ready to head to the elementary school, when Mr. Dan walks in, looking dejected.

He tells me that Garnet, Groper, and Summer want to color. "I was almost pleading with them to come up and take the test, and they simply refused," he says. "I think they're afraid of failure. You want me to round them up so you can give them a pep talk?"

"You can lead a horse to water . . ." I say, deeply disappointed.

"I let Meredith leave early. She was pretty frustrated. I think she went home."

I ask him to watch the teams, and snowmachine to the house. Meredith is lying on her bed, staring at the ceiling and looking as if she is trying not to cry.

I sit on the edge of the bed. "I hear that some girls chose crayons over competition."

"Sorry I let you down, Dad."

"You didn't let me down. Don't you know how proud I am of you?"

Suddenly she is in my arms, sobbing. I feel like asking her if she wants to go back with me and serve as timekeeper, but instead I say, "We'll talk after I get home tonight?"

She nods, too upset to speak any more, and lies back down.

"We'll think of something," I say, and head back to the school. I thank Mr. Dan, and he takes off to the elementary, where he has paperwork. As if being a principal isn't hectic enough, he spends much of his time snowmachining back and forth between the schools.

After opening the coach's envelope I read and reread the test situation, which, as we guessed, involves an undersea city in the Mariana Trench, the deepest part of the Pacific Ocean. The problem is rather general. That gives the advantage to teams that come in with great ideas that will fit almost any situation, and puts us at a disadvantage. If the ideas were strong on a specific problem, I had figured, the evaluators would likely overlook weak substantiation.

I try laying another section of track on the Gambell SP&S, but cannot keep my mind on the work. I end up pacing in front of the doors of the classrooms where the teams are.

Gerald enters the hall. Too busy to work with kids after school but not too busy to shoot some hoops, he takes a basketball from his locker.

"They do well on this one," I say, "and it's on to Anchorage. They've studied aquatic plants, sea mammal migrations, even undersea volcanic vents. Think what it will do for their self-esteem if they make state."

"They're only studying for the trip. Learning should be for learning's sake." He enters the gym, and I hear the ball bounce off the rim.

Chiding myself for having spoken to him, I call time in each classroom. The kids are excited about the test. The high schoolers, deciding that the undersea city will need long-term food and oxygen sources, have proposed a best solution that involves grafting kelp to sequoia buds. They plan to grow giant seaweeds that will stretch to the ocean's surface.

The junior high team's main idea is also intriguing. Using information they read about on the energy exchange that occurs when the cold waters around Antarctica meet the warmer waters of the Indian, Pacific, and Atlantic Oceans, they have postulated a ring of undersea generators.

"Sally gave us the word 'palisades' for vocabulary in English class," Boone says proudly. "We built the idea from that."

"And you didn't even throw any cake and popcorn," I say.

"You didn't give us any," Marshall says.

"Sounds like we have a disappointed girl today," Mary tells me.

I knock on the wall, ease past the curtain into the girls' room. Meredith is just waking up.

"Think the other kids will make state?" she asks.

"They did better than I thought they would." I indicate the envelope I'm holding. The many pages the kids produced create a thick bundle. I'll have to work late into the night to type up their work for submission to the Juneau evaluators.

"But what Marshall keeps saying about the junior high team being handicapped is true," I add.

Meredith looks at me quizzically.

"The junior high team *is* at a handicap. This is the ninth year of Problem Solving and the fifth year it's been in Alaska. Some of the other junior high teams are extremely experienced. So I think we better add a member. I phoned Juneau and was told that as long as at least one student on the team took the qualifying test, coaches can switch kids as they see fit, provided that older kids do not move down to compete against younger ones. Are you up to competing on the junior high level?"

She throws her arms around my neck. "You really mean it?"

There's a squeal of delight from outside the curtain, and Gretchen bursts into the bedroom. "All right, Mere! You're going!"

"*If* the team makes it," I remind her.

"They will!" Gretchen says. "I know they will."

Meredith looks at me seriously. "I'll be ready, Dad."

I realize that she has taken her first step—a giant step—toward adult responsibilities.

"Maybe you're ready for this." I take the snowmachine key from my pocket, place it in her hand, and exit the room.

17

The next morning there's a blizzard, made even more miserable by fog. We decide that Meredith will chauffeur me to school. That way she will be able to drive up for Problem Solving in the afternoon, when we will review the kids' answers.

"She's driving in this weather?" Mary asks incredulously.

"Better than having her walk in it."

She acquiesces to my logic and starts toward the elementary school, leading Gretchen by the hand. I yank the snowmachine cord and sit behind Meredith as I show her how to work the throttle.

Just as we are about to take off, Gretchen appears out of the gray and, putting her hood close to mine, yells, "Can I ride too? Mom says it's okay. Meredith's coming right back."

When I glance up the snowbank at Mary, she shakes her head, but Gretchen squirms onto the machine, in front of Meredith, and Mary raises mittened hands in defeat. She disappears down the other side of the mound.

Meredith drives carefully around the berms to keep the machine from tipping. I have her pull up at the turquoise trailer that serves as the post office. The light is on, but the door is locked; Herbie, the postmaster, Puffin's father, has not arrived early, as I had hoped. Short and thin, he has a mischievous smile that belies his insistence on following postal regulations "to the letter." Each time I write a check, he requires two pieces of ID, though he has known me for months. That he is very bright is obvious. I can see where Puffin gets her brains.

When we reach school, I stuff the Problem Solving envelope into Meredith's coat. "Mail this on your way back," I yell into her hood. "If Herbie doesn't have the P.O. open, go there during your first break. I want this to make the mail plane. I have an accreditation meeting during my prep or I'd go to the P.O. myself."

She nods and waves good-bye as she drives away. My little girl, driving the family car for the first time—and with two teams' hopes for state riding in her coat.

Meredith drives dutifully back to the post office, going slowly in case Dad sees despite the fog. Gretchen clings to her. It is a good feeling, her sister holding onto her. It makes her feel older. She wonders what the kids back in Washington would say if they could see her now. How many of *them* have driven a snowmachine?

Herbie still has not arrived. As the girls wait in the post office's arctic entry, Meredith, ever curious, opens the envelope and scans the answers. They wait ten minutes, but Herbie still hasn't gotten there. They remount the snowmachine.

Meredith heads toward the lake rather than toward school.

"Where're you going?" Gretchen yells.

"Shortcut!" Go right past Garnet's house, Meredith has decided. Garnet is sure to see her. Then out onto the lake, drive fast, squeeze the brake, and send the snowmachine into a spin. Just like the older kids do!

So intent is she on her driving that, when her glasses ice up, she tries to clear them with her finger instead of stopping and wiping them. The result is a blur. She hadn't expected the wind to be so fierce against her face. It's not at all like riding behind Dad, her face against his back.

They pass Garnet's house, Meredith waving, and crest the berm that marks the slope down to the lake. Gretchen screams and grabs hold of Meredith's arm. "Slow down!"

Meredith reacts wrongly, giving more throttle instead of gripping the brake. They sail into the air, come crashing down on the icy hill, and they are thrown off the machine, Meredith reaching in desperation for her sister.

The envelope tumbles from Meredith's coat.

"Grab it!" Gretchen shrieks, both fighting for purchase on the ice as they scramble toward the sliding envelope. "Dad will kill us!"

The envelope blows against the berm and folds across a snow-crusted rock like a pair of wings battered by a storm. The flap opens. Pages flutter and flap free, held only by a staple.

"Go!" Gretchen cries out. "Go, go!"

One page rips away, then another and another. Instantly driven by the wind, they adhere to the berm. But how long will they stay?

Meredith reaches the berm, clutches and stuffs, clutches and stuffs. Then Gretchen is there, grabbing another page just as it tears free, and sticking the envelope inside her coat.

"We got them all?" Meredith asks.

"Next time," Gretchen hands her the envelope and paper, "I'm taking a taxi."

Two weeks later, when an envelope stamped "Future Problem Solving" arrives at school, I stare at it almost all day, fearing its news. Not until sixth period, when the Problem Solvers crowd around me, do I rip open the seal and draw out the results.

First there is a summary: "We appreciate your attempt to help your students structure their writing," the evaluators have typed, "but 'what because why' will only curtail creativity." Following that is a hand-written note saying that the junior high booklet was missing the required cover page. Why Meredith whitens when I mention that, I'm not sure.

The kids wait eagerly as I flip through the pages, looking for the scores.

High school division: thirty-eight teams participated, top four to be invited to Anchorage.

Gambell—sixth.

Londa utters a sigh of disappointment.

"Next year," Merle mutters.

Jasmine looks dejected. For her, as a senior, there will be no next year.

Junior high division: eighty-five teams participated, top seven to be invited to the finals.

Gambell—sixth.

"Yess!" Marshall says, and he and Boone high-five each other. Meredith's hands are fisted with joy, and even Puffin smiles.

"You want us to help get the team ready for state?" Jasmine asks.

"They need all the help they can get," Merle says sarcastically.

"We can handle it," Marshall says.

"There isn't any sixth place at state," I remind him. "First and second—that's it."

"No problem, man."

"The subject for state is banking," I tell him.

His bravado evaporates. "I've never been in a bank," he says.

Puffin looks up at me.

"What's a bank?" she asks.

Given its isolation, Gambell almost certainly has been the last to receive the finals notification. I therefore decide to have extra practices. And so the next night, Friday, the junior high team members drag disgruntled into my house.

We cram into the storeroom amid the floor-to-ceiling boxes of canned goods. From the tiny window we can see two hunters, rifles across their backs, snowmachining toward the orange sunset, the tundra emblazoned with dying light.

"We have to study now?" Marshall whines as he watches the snowmachiners disappear.

"You only have two weeks to prepare for state," I remind him.

"I don't want to go to Anchorage," Boone says, looking out the window. "It's hunting season."

"This is stupid," Marshall says.

"Did your ancestors give up when things got tough?" I ask them.

"Don't talk about my ancestors," Marshall says.

"Why not!"

I don't try to mask the challenge in my voice. He abruptly sits down, and I am stunned at the sudden change in him. The belligerence is gone. In its place is—what? He seems empty of animosity.

Something mystical comes over the boys, the previous principal had said.

"We're going to try and win . . . " I start to tell them.

"Some white man's trophy," Marshall interjects.

"Mr. Dan says there probably won't be any other Natives at state," Boone says.

"All the more reason to give it your best shot." Before they can protest further, I hand out sheets of paper on which I have typed up definitions about banking, taken from my college business textbook. The boys barely look at the paper. I wonder if our going is a waste of time. But they've earned the trip. There's no denying that.

When I try to review the definitions, the boys barely pay attention. They steal glances out the window, the hunters gone now, taking the boys' desire with them. I give up on the definitions and cut to banking issues.

"I need to use the honey bucket," Puffin says.

She looks up at me as if expecting me to deny her the privilege of peeing, crosses the living room, disappears into the honey-bucket closet, and yanks the curtain closed.

"How long do we have to be in Anchorage?" Marshall whines.

"The competition is three days. With travel, we'll be gone for five."

"Five!"

I might as well have told him that he will have to endure five days of having teeth filled.

Marshall slaps the paper. "What good is this!"

"Don't you think you need to know banking definitions in order to compete?"

"What good are banks," he says.

"What good are *banks?*"

"My dad says that banks are white man's things. We cash our Permanent Fund checks at the store"—referring to the money that Alaskans receive once a year for the sale of Alaskan oil.

"Where do you keep that money?" I ask him, imagining soup cans buried in the tundra, stuffed with cash and crawling with Alaska's tiny ice worms.

"What do you mean, where do we keep it!" he asks suspiciously.

I fight to keep my hackles from rising. "I'm not trying to steal your money," I say. "I'm not trying to keep you from hunting. I'm trying to prepare you to play against the smartest kids in the state."

After a moment Boone looks at me and then at Marshall.

"We'll play," Marshall says. "We'll study."

"But not today," Boone says. "We have to go. Everyone's going boating tomorrow. We've got to help get things ready." He stuffs the papers into his pocket.

"We'll start again on Monday?" I ask.

They look at one another, and nod.

"Not just during sixth period," I say. "After school, too. Here. Maybe in the evening as well."

"Okay," Boone says. He eyes Marshall.

"Okay," Marshall says.

"You think Puffin will be out of the honey-bucket room by then?" Boone asks.

We fold up the chairs and cross the little living room.

"Banking hours are over," I tell her through the curtain. "We're closing up shop."

"Simple interest," Puffin says. "Interest calculated on principal . . ."

"This time she *is* reading it," Marshall says. "She's got to be."

She pushes the page of definitions underneath the curtain.

". . . Principal earned during period is not considered during compensation," Puffin continues after a slight pause. "Compound interest—interest calculated on principal earned during period is considered during compensation. Glass-Steagall Act—forbids commercial banks to engage in investment banking."

"Really shy, but really smart," Boone says.

Gretchen bursts in from the arctic entryway. "Dad, come!"

"Watch where you're stepping!" Mary cries out, standing in the door and looking horrified at the brown stain spreading across the arctic entryway floor.

Three honey-bucket bags wait to be hauled to the dump. I had stopped putting them in the bin behind the house after spotting polar bear tracks out there.

One of the bags, not completely frozen, has broken.

"Didn't double-bag!" Boone and Marshall chime in.

Puffin appears, pulling herself into her jacket. "Yuck!" She tiptoes around the mess and exits with the boys.

"I told you to take the bags to the dump more often!" Mary says.

She exits, Gretchen and Meredith with her.

I am left alone to shovel snow into the entry, soak up the mess, and put the brown snow into bags for a late-night dump run. As I work, I contemplate shit and philosophy.

To survive in a Native village, do as the Natives do.

Always double-bag.

18

"My hands are tied," Mr. Dan says as with growing disgust I read the letter from the school district. Beyond the window of his office, the junior high team is cramming for the finals, Jasmine and Merle helping them plow through the stacks of photocopied materials on banking that I'd had the Anchorage library express mail to me. "We need you here."

"It's not fair. It's not . . . right," I tell him.

"Of course it isn't. But what can I do?"

The district has decided I cannot attend state with the kids. The accreditation documents are at deadline, and my writing skills are needed on site.

"Gerald has offered to go in your place," Mr. Dan says. "As the special ed teacher, he is nominally in charge of the program. Besides, he wants to shop."

In the end, my protests result in the district librarian's agreeing to stay with the kids throughout the program. She has school business in Anchorage. We will have a team at the finals but no coach.

The night after the kids leave, I work all night on the accreditation documents, finish up my sections of it, and the next morning become severely ill.

"The district isn't going to like this," Mary warns.

"Let them think what they think," I tell her, practicing my cough.

I phone in sick and, deciding the illness is too serious for the local clinic with its health aides, fly through nasty weather to Nome, take a taxi to the hospital, sit for two hours to see the doctor, and fly to Anchorage, where in the hotel lobby I meet with the librarian, a tiny, athletic woman who has recently climbed Mount McKinley. She commiserates with the district's usual heavy handedness, then laughs with delight as she tells me about the kids' arrival at the airport.

"Why didn't someone inform me that those kids have never been in a city?" she asks. "When Meredith and I started down the escalator to retrieve our baggage, I looked back to see the other three eyeing the thing as if it were a strange dog. They eased around it and took the stairs."

She hands me the test problem. "The moment the competition was over they went shopping," she adds. "Except for Meredith. She's in her room."

When I read the problem, I know we have studied the wrong material. The situation involves a changeover to a cashless society that has no banks. All our preparation—on banks—does not fit.

A woman who has been hired to make a video on Future Problem Solving in Alaska joins us. Since I have the only village team in the finals, she asks for my input and shows me footage of Boone and Marshall emerging from the testing room.

"And from far-off Saint Lawrence Island," she says on the film, sticking a microphone in front of Boone's face. "How do you think you did?"

"We're done." He stands blinking into the camera.

"What do you think is the competition's most exciting part?" she asks Marshall.

"Shopping."

I discuss Gambell's efforts with the program, including the fact that I have never been trained in the process, and leave the two women to continue reviewing the video while I head to Meredith's room. She is happy to see me, yet I detect a sadness. As we take the elevator to lunch, it seems as if a sign saying DAD IN TOW has been hung around her neck.

"We argued that a cashless society might lessen people's sense of community in small towns," she says as she devours a B.L.T. "We said that in small towns a bank is as important as a church. A place of business but also a gathering place. Where you can say hi to friends, besides just depositing money or getting a loan. A cashless society could take people's *center* away."

She slurps the last of her shake. "So we argued that in a cashless society there needs to be a place where people can go once a month to review hard-copy records of their transactions."

"Puffin and Marshall understood the problem?"

"Marshall seemed to understand banking better because no building was involved." She rumples up her napkin and slides from the booth, eager to shop. "We talked it through, Dad. Kid talk." Then she adds, "Marshall's really nice, Dad."

The team and I spend the next twenty-four hours enjoying the scheduled itinerary—more shopping, paintball, shopping, Chuck E. Cheese's, shopping, the Alaskan amphitheater, shopping—and dressing for the awards banquet. "All that shopping, and still we forgot something," Boone says as he and Marshall arrive at my door in suits—and tennis shoes.

We walk to the restaurant where the banquet is to be held, to find the boys from the other teams casually dressed. "They must think we're nerds," Marshall says, and he and Boone dash back to the hotel to change.

When they return they look angry.

"We phoned home," Boone says as he sits down. "They got a whale."

"Without us." Marshall plops down and crosses his arms, scowling. "They got a whale without us."

They pick at their food and clearly don't listen to the guest speaker talk about space travel—the subject, just announced, of the national competition. Despair hangs over our table as Dr. Sharon Green, Director of Alaska's Future Problem Solving Program, rises to hand out the awards.

The Skagway team, coached by Bruce Currie, whom I recognize from what little training I had, wins the high school division. Dillingham, a town in Southwest Alaska, places second.

The trophies for the junior high division come next. Meredith glances at me in hopeful anticipation. Puffin seems to stare into a realm a few inches in front of her eyes. Heads bowed, Marshall and Boone stare, disheartened, at the tablecloth.

"Junior high division, second place . . ." Dr. Green announces, "Gambell."

Meredith jumps to her feet, nearly knocking over her chair. Boone and Marshall rise reluctantly. Puffin remains seated.

"Go get your trophy," I tell her. "You earned it."

She shakes her head.

"But you have to go up."

Another shake of her head.

"Come on now, Puffin. Come *on.*"

She slowly stands and follows the others forward.

When they return, Meredith puts the trophy in the middle of the table, and everyone sits down as kids from Cordova, a fishing town in Southcentral Alaska, thread through the tables to receive their first place award.

With the back of his hand, Marshall knocks over our trophy.

"This made us miss our whale," he says.

With an index finger, Puffin rights the award as the boys look up at her. *"Entaqun sivunemta igamsiqaayugvikesqelluta aqhveghnun pimiinkut,"* she quietly tells them.

They lower their eyes, looking cowed.

As Dr. Green announces the elementary school second place, followed by applause and cries of joy, I find myself seated beside four kids who look like monks during the blessing of the bread.

Not until late that night does Boone give me a rough translation of Puffin's words.

"Maybe our ancestors sent the whale to thank us."

19

"They want to *what?*" Seated with the other Problem Solvers, Merle stares up at me in disbelief. "The same subject?"

He looks at Boone and it seems all they can do to keep from laughing.

The proposal's foolishness has shocked me, in a profession where stupidity often is the watchword. The administration wants a district Future Problem Solving competition between the five Bering Straits schools that have fielded teams. Great, except that the district has insisted that the subject will be banking.

The Gambell junior high and high school Problem Solvers have studied banking for over three weeks. The other teams will have kids who may have studied the subject for three hours.

"Let's stomp them," Boone says.

"Cool," Marshall says.

The kids' animosity toward the district office is understandable. They know that the district has a long history of giving the island short shrift. And they know that the Unalakleet Future Problem Solving teams will be made up of administrators' kids and that an administrator's wife is the coach.

At the end of the week, we fly to Unalakleet, a mainland village large enough to have cars. Beat-up pickups maneuver between snow-drifts, dodging snowmachiners. I have a Coke in the lobby of the rustic hotel and accept an invitation to the administrators' and teachers' housing: modern apartments with running water, blenders for mixed drinks—alcohol is legal here—gun racks and fishing-pole racks on the walls, skis outside the doors.

Gambell's junior high and senior high teams win their divisions handily, and my fifth graders place second. The booklet by Boone, Marshall, and Meredith—Puffin has decided against the trip—is especially excellent.

When we are about to leave for the airstrip, the superintendent asks to see me in his office, where he informs me that I should switch schools next year. "I'll be frank," he says. "I want you teaching my kids."

"Let me think about it," I tell him.

As we fly to the island, my bowels go on a binge, maybe from too much alcohol. We are in an old DeHaviland Otter, noisy and slow, and with no toilet. I endure agony for two hours, and say a prayer of thanks to Saint Anthony when we land.

Home, where the heart is.

Where the honey bucket is.

"The district's little golden Georgie," Gerald says to me when I run into him in the hall the next week. "I've been talking on the phone to the district office. They heard about you sucking up to the superintendent for a new job. You might have him fooled, but there are some other people there who know the truth. They say that your kids cheated, that they just wrote down memorized material. No real thinking at all."

In a way he is right. Unlike the state problem, the one at the district level was so general that little thinking was required.

"Mr. Elitist's memorization monkeys," he says as I walk away.

All day his words tighten my anger like a washcloth being wrung.

That evening I vow not to teach Problem Solving next year, and I angrily smash my fist again the chimney in our bedroom, recoiling in pain just as Mary calls from the living room, "Bietha's here for your dance instruction."

I emerge with bloodied knuckles wrapped in a T-shirt, saying that I scraped them on the bricks. Bietha—Marshall's mother and Mary's aide—smiles at me as Mary pours tea. Bietha's hands are arthritic and wrinkled despite her being in her forties. Benchmarks of a hard life.

We eat pilot bread swathed with jam, and talk about weather and whaling, and, this time, the ever-popular subject of airplane crashes.

"I used to fly as a child before there were airplanes here," Bietha says suddenly.

As we sip tea, she explains. "When I was a child, my father, a shaman, told me to climb onto his back. The next thing I know, I am on the other side of the island."

"Not the other side of the mountain," Mary emphasizes to me, apparently having heard the story before. "The other side of the island." An island larger than Delaware.

I do not scoff. Though strange phenomena often have natural explanations—we now know, for example, that some Air Force pilots who vanished in the Bermuda Triangle ran out of gas—I also am aware that there is much that science cannot explain. Dozens of experiments by top scientists of the time could not explain how the Janusists, a large religious group in eighteenth-century France, could be struck with sledgehammers and dropped from high heights onto sharpened pikes, all without ill effect. Or the story of a physician—a best friend of one of my closest friends—who returned to South Africa after medical school at Oxford, to help his people. He upset a local witch doctor, who said that a gazelle would grow in the physician's stomach. Its antlers would pierce his intestines, causing him to bleed to death. His stomach gradually enlarged for no apparent reason, and he died.

"How could I get there except fly?" Bietha says. "Those days, only boats and dog teams."

I listen with pleasure, aware that, unlike in the Western world, where our sense of history is physics-based and supposedly rational, in most of the world the natural and the supernatural are wedded. We in the West profess belief in God, yet often express or suppress bemusement when we learn that others view life as an inseparable blend of magic and the everyday.

"You remember flying?" I ask.

"I remember it only took a moment."

It is time to dance—my fourth lesson. She shows me how to dance like a hunter—strong but supple steps; arm movements that evoke power and precision. She laughs as I struggle; laughs not at me but with me, in an evening of laughter and tea and the breaking of bread.

After the dancing, we are all so giddy with the joy of human communion that Mary begs Bietha to read our tea leaves. She does so reluctantly, frowning as she swirls the dregs around in the pot, suddenly refusing to divulge what the leaves say, her emotionless expression unable to mask her fear. Abruptly standing and pulling on her coat while holding her stomach as if she is going to be ill, she starts for the door. Mary, thinking Bietha is teasing, blocks her way, coaxing and cajoling her into revealing the leaves' message.

"Just a trick I learn another place," Bietha says, "not from my culture, not a real thing," but Mary keeps pressing her, laughing, apparently not noticing that Bietha clearly is shaken. Finally Bietha says in a deep whisper, "Someone close to you will die soon."

Mary, suddenly white-faced, steps aside, and Bietha hurries away as if the prophecy has contaminated the cabin.

20

Senior prom. Rather, it's in the seniors' honor. For there are only four seniors, only three of whom are graduating, so—as is usual for the school dances—everyone from fifth grade on up is invited. The kids drift into the gym, mostly singly, a few of the older kids as couples, under an arch festooned with pink ribbons and balloons and cardboard stars twinkling with glitter. The girls are in expensive gowns they have ordered through catalogs, the boys wear white shirts and ties or school clothes. A mirrored ball we found in the attic casts dreamy diamonds around the walls. Ribbons grace the bleachers, and bows highlight the tables on which sit cakes that Lars and the home ec students have baked. "Eye of the Tiger," the kids' favorite, blares from a boom box.

I have dressed for the dance. I feel like I have the flu, but I have promised to chaperone and I do want to see the kids all dressed up. So at my daughters' urging, I have donned the crimson and white tuxedo I purchased to chaperone a dance the one year I taught high school in Washington. Everything, as they say, is perfect.

Except that no one wants to dance with Meredith, the teachers' kid, the white kid; and for me to have more than one dance with her will just make matters look worse. Mary has told me that Meredith is sure that Marshall, who is always sought-after for dancing, will dance at least one dance with her. But he is home sick, and I worry that whatever I have is contagious.

Something is wrong. Marshall can feel it.

He sits at the empty table, alone in his house, the gnawing in his stomach so strong that when he told everyone that he was not going to the dance, he thought he had the flu.

As if eating will quiet whatever is eating at him, he rises and lights the Coleman stove. Gas flickers into blue flame. The phosphorescent smell of the match wafts in his nostrils. The heat feels like he is standing too close to a bonfire, like the one on Fourth of July. Never before have his senses seemed so acute—and so disconcerting.

Feeling woozy, he sits down in his father's easy chair. Ivory dust rises, motes catching in the Coleman's tiny updraft and sailing toward the ceiling. His skin feels cold and clammy.

He is reaching for his basketball, hoping to calm himself with dribbling in the house—he can do that only if his father isn't home—when a vision seizes him. He sees himself sailing among stringy clouds. Below him is a woman hunched over a hole in the ice. She backs away, startled. Then the ice gives way and she is in the water, flailing and trying to grab onto the edge. She slips down and goes under—comes up again and fights.

In a panic, Marshall shuts off the Coleman and is out the door before he realizes he is awake. He yanks the cord of his three-wheeler and roars across the snow—as much gravel as snow here near the houses, this time of year—still feeling as if he is in a dream.

Mom! he wants to call to her.

He powers over the ridge on which the post office sits, wishing to call for help, but everyone is at the dance or in their houses or out hunting. He knows exactly where she struggles—her favorite spot, near the end of north beach. Half mile to go. He urges the machine forward, the throttle all the way open, snow spewing, the three-wheeler snaking and sliding through the late spring's soft wet snow.

The machine coughs.

One moment he is at full speed and the next the three-wheeler sputters and goes dead. Bad plug. He yanks the cord again, knows there is not time to replace the plug, and runs toward the shore—the going slow, the snow up past his knees in places, mushy as mashed potatoes. Like running in slow motion.

And all the while angry with himself for not having recognized that he did not have the flu but rather his body's response to the onset of a vision—his first.

A vision that is a nightmare.

A side door opens into the dance. A figure enters, framed by sunlight, and talks to the nearest kid. Then there is a cry like that of a wounded animal: "Come!"

Dancers and spectators spill outside. We learn what has happened as we run through the snow. Bietha has fallen through the ice! "Can you do CPR?" someone asks me.

"Think so." It's been years since I took the training in the Army, and as we run I pray I won't have to use it.

Snowmachines pass us. People are running from everywhere in the village. The sun is pearly pink above the jumbled beauty of the frozen sea, as if the world is witness to its own uncaring. There is no justice, I keep thinking.

We reach the bluff above the north beach. Below, a crowd has gathered around Lawrence, who is performing CPR on Bietha, while Marshall and several others struggle to carry her, strapped to a medical board, up the hill. I feel helpless.

Later we will view the hole where she fell through, see the bloodied ice where she tried to claw her way out.

Early deaths, Meredith knows, as she sits on the mountain and watches the tiny figures carry the casket through the village, come with frightening frequency to Bering Sea villages. People so drop like dominoes—suicide and accidents and illness; and how do you classify Russian roulette?—that villages sometimes merely seem terminals for those awaiting untimely graves.

Most accidental deaths are alcohol-related, though the island is officially "dry." Cancer also stalks the island, especially the residents of Savoonga, many of whom built fish camps from the buildings the Army abandoned on the southeast cape. No one from the government came, until too late, to tell them that the Army dumped toxic waste at the site.

Fighting tears, Meredith watches the mourners with the casket reach the base of the mountain. She looks out over the tundra, with its blanket of snow, its thousand shades of white. Why, she wonders, amid all this purity and austere beauty, is there so much pain?

She remembers having seen Marshall as he sat outside the clinic, his head down and sweatshirt hood pulled up, looking like Death while the health aides and a visiting nurse worked all night to try and save his mother. Gone was his angry bravado.

Gone too the pride she remembered from the time he took her hiking up the mountain, when he had pointed out where underground homes of the *Mayughwaaq* used to be, where the slope-dwellers, the *Iinwaaghmitt*, used to live, where the homes of the underground cache dwellers, the *Siqluwaghyagmitt,* once were. He had talked of those ancient ancestors as if they still existed, and she had witnessed a side of him she had never before seen—a side she had never seen in any of them. Until then, she had never before been able to see beyond the anger.

Or the time he took her to find clams, using an ice pick to chip them from the frozen shore. They washed in and broke on the gravel during storms, only to freeze when the tide receded, and thus, without shells, were ready to cook. He had given her his bread sack full.

She wants to hold him, comfort him, cry with him. But this day, she knows, the gulf between him and her is greater than ever. And so, after the funeral, she came to the mountain to be alone with her sorrow.

Below, the men set down the coffin. The place already has been prepared, so the casket lies flat. Here, Bietha will lie forever amid rocks. Here, there is no grass; no graveyard pleasantries. Here, on the edge of the earth, death is stripped of all façade.

She puts her head down in her mittens. Three days from now she and her family will leave for the summer. She wants to tell Marshall she loves him. Not as a boyfriend, but as a friend—as the sister, he has told her, he has never had. And as the best friend she has ever known.

She weeps.

I go up the mountain to be alone, each footfall an effort, and to find Meredith. She walks away without a word, heading home. I watch as the villagers leave the casket behind and head to their homes, and then I watch the sea. Except for the large crescent of shelf ice that took Bietha, it is a cobalt-blue expanse broken only by icebergs and by the Siberian mountains beyond, lifting into a sky cleared of clouds. It is a big world that surrounds me.

A figure treads up from below: Merle, laboring up the slope. He seems to sense when I am here; as if, here, he can talk to me without the protocol of the classroom.

"What do you think?" he asks, squatting beside me and looking over toward the coffin.

"About what."

"Dying."

"I'd like to be the exception to the rule."

His face seems without emotion, and I regret my flippancy but stupidly try to cover my faux pax with more levity.

"Actually," I say, "when I die I'd like to be cremated. I want my family to put my ashes in pepper shakers in five-star restaurants."

He points out to sea, where a bowhead has surfaced, spouting.

"Are you going after him . . . after it?" I ask.

He shakes his head. "There is a time for harvest. And one for healing."

I wish I had hot chocolate, or consolation, to offer him. I wish I had something significant to say. The light wind against my face and the silence of the moment make me wonder if I have ever said anything significant in my life. All my teaching—what value is it?

The sun, sinking, is a brilliant orange color, shaped like a kite. Before coming here, I had never seen such sunsets. It is as if God has stretched the sun as closely as possible to a cross. I now know why my students have difficulty with concepts of time. Here, during much of the winter, the sun does not rise in the east or set in the west. It ascribes an arc, often rising in the south and setting nearly in the north. The world of physics, as Bietha taught me, is not what our textbooks tell us.

For the moment, there is no time. My watch seems an anachronism, a product of a world I left behind. I would throw it away, were Merle not to think me foolish.

"I was in Anchorage a couple of months ago," he says, in a low voice choked with emotion. "I went up to Barrow with my dad for this year's IWC meeting." Perhaps seeing my confusion, he adds, "The International Whaling Commission. The boat captains meet to decide how many strikes each village gets next year."

This he need not explain. I know, because of public pressure, that maritime Eskimos are allotted a given, and small, number of harpoon strikes during whaling. The captains determine which villages receive which amount.

"We stopped in Anchorage on the way back." Tears brim in his eyes. "I was downtown, shopping. And I . . . and I saw people looking at me." He glances toward me briefly and then away, and with what seems conscious effort he blinks against his tears. "I knew what they were thinking, George. I could sense it. 'There goes another village Eskimo,' they were thinking. 'There goes another dumb village Eskimo.'"

His mouth tightens. "I know I'm smart!" He shakes his head. He appears weary, worn down by intolerance.

"What am I going to do about it," he says.

I wish he had asked his father instead of me. I doubt if I even can offer avenues for considering the question. I am just a teacher in a little school on the edge of nowhere.

"Probably not much you can do about it, in the big picture," I say, feeling it is *he* who should be advising *me*. "You're not single-handedly going to overpower prejudice. But you can stand up against it. How about a little academic one-on-one next year?"

"You mean Future Problem Solving," resolve settling into his face.

"Next time, though, Gambell can't take second. Seconds are table scraps. Some people are saying that our trophy this year was a fluke, and I can't disagree. We didn't really know what we were doing."

Chuckling, he nods.

"Next year," I tell him, "you'll have to win state, and you'll have to win big. The only way to get some people's attention is to step on their preconceptions. You won't be playing for yourself next year, Merle. You'll be playing for your people. Screw up, and you'll be giving bigots an even greater chance to smirk."

We watch the sun wane.

"Sounds more like a crusade than a competition," he says at last, and smiles wryly.

I leave him. When I look back from the bottom of the mountain, he is still sitting up there, looking out over the village and the sea, watching over his world.

part 3

◄ Coffin amid rocks on the mountain.
Photo by Elizabeth Manfred, DCCED, State of Alaska.

21

The next school year we land in Gambell in fog and sleet. The pilot, by coincidence the one who brought us here the first time, wears a white scarf like those of fighter pilots in old movies. It flutters in the wind as he lowers the Piper Navajo's stairs and with genteel aplomb gestures for us to descend, sleet beating against our faces.

Despite the wind, there is no sound. Perhaps only those of us who have lived in the Arctic can appreciate its times of profound silence. In winter the ice crackles and groans, the wind howls and even hisses. But during summer, if the gulls are gone and the sea is calm, silence lies like a shroud across the land. You hear only your heartbeat, and you fear that the world outside yourself is but a cruel ruse of the senses.

You know then that you are back at another beginning.

"Your carriage approaches," the pilot says, as a distant sputtering disturbs the stillness. The school's big three-wheeler crests the rise, the engine increasingly louder, a goggled Jones leaning into the wind, the rickety cart jouncing behind.

He shuts off the machine and extends an ash-blackened hand. "Welcome to three-wheeler capital of the world." He grins. "Welcome back." He pulls his goggles up onto his forehead. Crescents grime his cheeks. He has been cleaning someone's oil stove. Mine, I hope.

"The kids, they out at the fish camps. Mr. Dan he's here. That big Bruce too."

During the state finals, Bruce Currie, the FPS trainer, had told me that he wanted to leave Skagway. When Sally, our excellent English teacher, decided to leave Gambell, I convinced Bruce to come to sunny Saint Lawrence, island of beaches and bananas. He was not difficult to convince. He had moved to Alaska from Georgia, wanting to teach in a quiet Native village. He did not realize until too late that Skagway, once the gateway to the Klondike Gold Rush, is a Caucasian community and a major tourist attraction.

After we unpack I go to greet him. His house is so tiny and he is so large that it looks as if it were built around him. He's angrily mopping. "Someone left a bucket of filthy water under the sink," he says. "So I dumped it out—into the sink. I forgot that there's no plumbing."

I sit down and, after initial small talk, tell him, "When I was in the hospital in California this summer, I began thinking about Problem Solving."

"Hospital?" he asks.

"Just tests"—though in truth the flu-like symptoms that had seized me toward end of the year had so worsened during summer vacation that I had spent much of July in bed. "The doctor thought I might have pericarditis—water around the heart. Apparently it was just exhaustion. All work and no play."

He laughs when I tell him that I grew so tired of other patients asking me what igloo life is like that I began telling them I ate blubber with Grey Poupon. Some, grimacing, seemed to believe me.

"The doctor wanted me to quit teaching here. When I said I wouldn't, he insisted that I reduce my workload. He wrote to the district. So this year I only have five classes—and one classroom." I hold up an index finger, and Bruce chuckles. At the state competition, I had told him about my schedule.

"Something happened at the hospital that might affect our kids," I go on, shifting the conversation back to Problem Solving. "There was an ugly, leafless tree by my window. It started me thinking about how most kids play Problem Solving conservatively. They write down general ideas. They stay near the trunk, if you see my analogy. But out in the branches is where the real points are scored."

"Originality points," he says, following my reasoning.

We both know where I'm headed. Most teams write down somewhat generalized problems and solutions to the situation the test gives, to assure that they receive credit for addressing the situation, for showing memorized research, and for examining the test's scenario from multiple angles. However, to have a chance at brainstorming the advanced ideas that can earn teams five extra "originality" points per idea—ideas that are in the judges' opinion several years above grade level and that no other team in the state can also have suggested—

requires specificity and an ability to apply it to the test scenario precisely. Teams are proud, and justifiably so, if they score one or two "originals."

"What if our kids could score ten more originals than any other team?" I ask. "That's a fifty-point buffer, in case they mess up part of the test. And as you know, the test is so complicated, all teams mess up somewhere."

Bruce dumps the mop bucket outside and comes back in, shaking his head sadly. "Concentrating on originals is risky. It's too easy to come up with a great idea that doesn't fit the situation. The judges throw it out, and you've got squat."

I have thought about that. Meredith and I had discussed it endlessly, to Mary's growing irritation, on the long drive back to Seattle from Disneyland and the Southern California hospital. With Meredith seated in the front seat and Mary and Gretchen in back, Meredith and I had gone over and over the Problem Solving notebook—reviewing the rules and deciphering the complicated scoring rubric. Whenever Meredith tired, Mary would move forward and we would go over the teaching techniques that the program suggested, including inventing our own.

We were nearly back to Seattle, where we would board the plane for the flight to Alaska, when I realized how critical the concept of "originals" was to playing the game well.

It was a matter of mathematics.

"What if we train the kids only to play ideas that could possibly be originals?" I ask Bruce. "Even if only half of their ideas are accepted," I lower my voice in an effort to contain my excitement, "we could win state. Do it right, and the kids could score 225!"

"Not possible. No team anywhere, to my knowledge, has broken 220." He puts away the mop bucket, draws water from the thirty-gallon trashcan, and washes and dries his hands. "I don't think any team in Alaska has even broken 200. Most first-place teams here score below 130."

From the fridge he takes out a king crab, probably purchased from one of the locals for five bucks. "I'm sure that the Problem Solvers here are nice kids who want to win," he continues, "but ultimately they won't be able to compete with kids from Kenai and Anchorage. Remember, in most schools Problem Solving is only for the gifted."

"What if the kids are willing to put in the time to learn precise steps in doing original thinking?" I ask him. "What if they could then apply those ideas exactly to a test situation? How many hours of instruction would that take? Fifty? Sixty?"

He shrugs and lifts a brow as if to indicate that the kids here are not up to the task.

I ask, "Remember the survey at state that said Problem Solvers average ten hours of homework for the finals? We'll do ten times that. We'll out-research everyone else."

He looks at me in disbelief as he puts a pot on the stove. "You're going to get kids from a traditional Eskimo village to do a hundred hours of homework for state?"

"They'll do a hundred hours of homework for the qualifying problem. For the finals they'll do 150. We won't walk into a test and just start spilling out ideas. That goes against Eskimo training."

He frowns and does not reply, probably for fear of upsetting me.

"It's not Future Problem *Guessing,*" I add. "It's Future Problem *Solving.* Which contractor would you hire: someone who arrives at a worksite and relies on spontaneous creativity, or one who has prepared for almost every eventuality? We'll help the kids foresee every eventuality imaginable, brainstorm every situation that might be asked. Instead of a couple dozen general ideas, we'll teach the kids to brainstorm two or three *hundred* possibilities, analyze them for originality, and enter the competition with a preparation the likes of which has never been seen before."

He does not answer, so I play my hole card. I want him on my side not only because of his background in debate and his Problem Solving experience, but also because I need someone else in Gambell who believes in the program, someone off whom I can bounce ideas.

"I think many kids quit last year because they didn't see the reality of the situations I gave them," I tell him, thinking of the elephant from Savoonga. "This year I'll make Problem Solving real for them. It won't be a game anymore."

"You'll never motivate them to do that much homework."

"I don't intend to. Remember Boone? You met him at state."

"Smart kid."

"His cousin, Merle, is a senior. He'll motivate them."

"This Merle—he can do that? He can motivate them?"

"Wait until you meet him."

After a moment, Bruce says, "I don't think this will work. But these are your teams." He extends me a hand. "You call the shots. I'll help any way I can."

"We'll break 225," I tell him as we shake, and he chuckles at my idealism.

"This year, if kids take Problem Solving, I want them for at least a semester," I tell Mr. Dan. "No more dropping out just because they wake up in a bad mood."

"That's fine," he says, "for the ninth graders. I want them to have the academic foundation the program can give them. For the older kids, it has to be their choice."

We go over the list of likely prospects. Four ninth graders look promising. Alvin has low test scores but great artistic ability. "Maybe Problem Solving will help him actualize his creativity," Mr. Dan says. Bess, Kasha, and Romie have spectacular end-of-year achievement test scores. "I've been a principal in rural Alaska for eight years," he says, "and I've never before seen middle school numbers like these. We'll put those four in Problem Solving whether they like it or not. It'll be good for them."

Unlike last year, when I held Problem Solving three days per week amid my sixth-period, six-subject crush, this year it is my only sixth-period subject. This year I only have five subjects all day—geography, American history, world history, government, and Problem Solving—plus a prep period.

And I have a new classroom, which I inherited from Sally, the red-haired English teacher who took a job elsewhere and therefore is not back on the island this year. The room has a large blackboard, eight tables, and windows that face the airstrip and the afternoon sun. Whenever my students have work to do, I turn on the boom box I bought, having decided to play what the kids don't usually hear— classical, '50s rock, and quiet country western—as low-volume background music. I'm in educator's Heaven.

The previous year's Problem Solvers are the first to enter when sixth period rolls around. Merle, Boone, Marshall, Meredith, and Londa quickly get out their notebooks, ready to write. Puffin takes a chair in the corner and sits with her arms crossed, staring out the window.

The ninth graders wander in and sit at tables in the back. Kasha, last year's cheerleading captain—middle schoolers do the cheerleading, so the high school has enough players to field a girls' basketball team—looks perky, clearly eager to participate. Bess, tall and lanky, gazes at her desk. Stocky, athletic Romie seems angry. Alvin takes out a piece of paper and, as if oblivious to his surroundings, begins to draw.

After an introduction, I paraphrase the Problem Solving circular from the evaluators' office in Juneau. "This year the test scenarios will be more precise than in the past," I tell them. "That means you will have to address the situation *exactly* or be eliminated from the competition. There is also a required skit competition"—Marshall groans— "but we'll just walk through it. It doesn't affect the main score." Most of the kids sigh with relief.

"This year there also will be an individual competition, should some of you want to participate," I continue, "and a short-story competition, open to students around the world. Both of these new competitions are voluntary. Any takers?"

"Will we make it to Anchorage this year?" Kasha asks.

"We're going to be champions this year," I tell her.

"To be a champion," Boone recites from the maxim I gave the team the previous year, "you've got to think like a champion, act like a champion, and work . . ."

". . . like an Iditarod dog," Marshall interjects, altering the adage.

"The first problem," I say after the laughter subsides, "will involve prisons."

As I pass out papers on the subject, Puffin rises and sidles to the door.

"No bathroom breaks this year," I tell her.

"I'm not going to the bathroom. I'm quitting."

She exits. I give Merle the rest of the papers to hand out and hurry after her. I halt her before she enters her *sanctum sanctorum*. "The team needs you," I say.

She shrugs and tries to step around me.

"You're one of the smartest kids I've ever taught. Don't you want to compete against kids of your caliber?" She doesn't react, so I add, "I think your team will win."

Her eyes water with frustration. "You shouldn't have made me accept the trophy. You shouldn't have made me go up there in front of everyone."

Then she is gone into the bathroom. For a moment I stand looking at the door. Puffin's participation is key to the team's success. Londa prepares well but freezes up during the tests. Merle, Marshall, Boone, and Puffin are a state championship–caliber team, I had figured.

What to do? Play Meredith at the high-school level?

Though she is in seventh grade this year, she's only eleven.

Play Londa.

Discouraged, I reenter the classroom, only to encounter Romie about to exit.

"I'm quitting too," she mumbles, trying to push past without touching me.

"You can't quit."

"Puffin did."

"Puffin's a sophomore. She's already participated in Problem Solving. It's her decision if she stays. You're in here for the year. That's Mr. Dan's decision."

"*Your* decision," Romie says angrily as I head her back to her chair. She shoves her papers aside and stares defiantly out the window.

"Prisons," Merle says, and gives me his usual wry smile as he hands me the leftover papers.

22

"The good news," Mr. Dan says, at the first faculty meeting, "is that this year the district will pay teachers who coach academic teams, not just athletic ones. Battle of the Books, Math Counts, Academic Decathlon, Olympics of the Mind—coaching such things means extra pay."

"Future Problem Solving?" I ask.

"Not on the list. The district says there's no interest in it."

"Not even among the Unalakleet kids? At the district competition last year they said they wanted another crack at us."

"Their coach said that the kids don't want to play anymore."

Gerald gives me another of his feral grins and leans toward me, his huge forehead reflecting the overhead light. "Guess you're no longer the district's golden boy," he whispers.

Months later we will learn that the Unalakleet kids asked to have a team but were told that no other students in the district were interested in Problem Solving this year.

The discussion turns to the latest spin on the educational merry-go-round. This year all special ed students except Oleander will be mainstreamed. Mr. Dan informs me that, besides teaching history to Chip and Dale and Lobert, who are slow learners rather than truly being special ed, I will have two ninth-grade special needs kids, Darrel and Festus, in geography.

"Darrel the dollar man!" Lars blurts.

Wrists together as if he's handcuffed, Gerald adds, "Festus, come arrest us!"

Lawrence looks at Gerald with a studied tension I have never seen in Lawrence except on the wrestling mat. Then he looks at the shop teacher, Keenan, who is frowning, and then at me, and I realize he is thinking the same thing as I am: is this how teachers act behind closed doors?

Mr. Dan explains that the two boys will follow the same scope and sequence as the other kids, but with reduced expectations and lowered outcomes. Teaching about distant countries to Darrel and Festus seems pointless to me. Darrel will never leave the village. Festus's sense of time is so undefined that he cannot distinguish what he did yesterday from what he has heard happened in the village decades ago.

"Wouldn't Darrel and Festus be better served if they spent a big chunk of each day learning janitorial skills?" I ask. "Jones certainly could use some assistance, and when those kids graduate they would have a job waiting for them."

Mr. Dan shakes his head. "Politically incorrect. They learn what the other kids do."

After the meeting, Gerald tells me, "This year you'll have to come down from your ivory tower, Mr. Elitist. This year you'll learn what *real* teaching is."

I busy myself with Problem Solving and with lesson plans, especially those for Darrel and Festus. In my ten years of teaching I have never taught special needs kids, and at first I approach each day with trepidation. But that worry soon dissipates.

Darrel likes to blow his nose in dollar bills and give them to the unsuspecting. In some ways I appreciate his sick humor. Initially he does not show up for classes until half past the hour, but after I start giving quizzes as soon as the bell rings each period instead of waiting for everyone to be seated, as I did last year, he is usually at his desk, ready to respond.

Festus, who has a toy sheriff's badge and handcuffs someone probably bought him at Woolworth's, spends all his extra time hunting Communists. According to local lore, villagers once hid a defector from Siberia in the duplex basement. My biggest concern regarding him involves protecting him from the other kids, who pick on him mercilessly. My heart goes out to him: like him, I was always the smallest boy in class. Unlike him, I had the ability to verbally parry; and if that didn't work, I would spike my oppressor in the head with my track shoes, which I always carried, and run like the wind. When the other boys became bigger and faster, I joined wrestling, where small kids could prevail.

During lunch, which I have begun to take in my room, I endure Festus's incessant questions, few of which make sense except in his context, and most of which he will repeat the next day. We work on those geography skills I think he needs: where Nome and Anchorage are, and what they are like. I come to enjoy his company.

It also helps to know that Gerald and Lars assume I hate teaching him.

Swamped with five students, four of whom are mainstreamed into other classes for most of the day, Gerald is mandated to assist the regular classroom teachers by tutoring the special ed kids on mainstream subjects. He thus asks me for a list of the modified scope-and-sequence skills that Festus is supposed to know.

I make up the list: Locate at least forty states on a map of America. Name and locate the main cities of the West Coast states. Name Alaska's main products. Explain how and where ivory carvings are sold.

Then, angered at the district's edict concerning such kids, I skip several lines and as a joke jot down more: Name, by memory, the states in descending order of population and by entrance into the Union. Give the populations and the demographics by gender, religion, race, occupation, and age for every state. Name all state flowers in alphabetical order.

My first major mistake teaching on the island was my agreeing to compete my Problem Solving teams against the Unalakleet kids on a subject where we had an obvious advantage.

My second mistake was that note.

"You fucking elitist," Gerald says during lunch the next day, holding up the paper before me. "If this is some slam toward me or my kids . . ."

"I was referring to the scope and sequence," I tell him.

"You lying sack of shit."

He knocks his plate and silverware away with a sweep of his wrist and then crumples the paper in his fist. Then, as if realizing that he may need the paper as evidence, he smoothes it across the table-edge and holds it up. "I'm keeping this in a very safe place." He walks away.

That afternoon the Problem Solvers are unusually quiet; news of the words between Gerald and me has circulated. Eliciting a discussion is usually difficult, and today it appears impossible. This year, I have decided that whenever possible, we will not confine ourselves just to the synopsized articles. I hand out an article on prison costs and tell everyone to write a summary.

Mr. Dan appears at the door, so I put Merle in charge and head to Dan's office behind him, like an errant child. I expect to see Gerald there, the two of us having to make up like little boys, but it's just Dan and me. He indicates for me to sit down.

"I know what happened," he says.

"Everyone does except me," I reply.

"Meaning?"

"Meaning his attitude baffles me. You think I offended him in some earlier life?"

"I'd fire him if I could. If things were up to him, he would decertify all the special ed kids and spend his time hunting and fishing. I think half his problem is that he wants to go play in the woods instead of teach."

"Not any woods here," I comment acidly.

"One thing's for sure, he won't be back next year. He wouldn't have been here this year if special ed teachers weren't so hard to find." He leans forward and lifts an index finger. "But you're not without fault in this."

"It was just a joke. It won't happen again. But if he ever hits me? I'll hit him back, credential or no credential. I'll shoot him if I have to. And that's no idle threat."

He does not reply, so I exit the office, return to the classroom, and check the students' progress. Merle and Meredith are composing well-organized, insightful essays rather than summaries. Londa and Boone are discussing an idea from the article that might be useful on the first practice problem. Even Marshall has produced several sentences.

I look at the ninth graders' work. Bess and Romie have not written a word. Alvin is doodling. Kasha proudly shows me her paragraph. It is incoherent.

I dismiss everyone to the gym except the ninth graders, and stand eyeing them. "Even if you're not here to win, you're expected to work. This is for class."

"I wrote," Kasha says, angrily crossing her arms.

I try to be gentle with her. "You wrote like this last year?" I ask softly.

"Mr. Popov always liked what I wrote."

"According to your scores you should be writing a lot better than this," I tell her. To the others, I say, "Did you write last year? Or just turn in blank sheets of paper?"

Romie sends the article sliding across the table. "I don't understand this . . . stuff."

"Did you read it?"

She looks down.

"Did you try to read it?"

Despite the downcast eyes, a flicker of emotion crosses her features, and I realize that she didn't read it because she can't read it. She had straight As and scored in the mid 80s on the standardized tests, but she can't read an article from *TIME* magazine.

"According to your CAT scores, you all should be able to read this easily," I tell them, holding up the article and avoiding singling out Romie.

"You mean those end-of-year tests?" Kasha asks.

She glances toward Romie and Bess, and a look of reality dawns in their faces. Kasha's eyes go downcast.

"Mr. Popov helped us," she says.

What she is telling me is such a violation of professional ethics that I hesitate to rephrase her words. "He gave you the answers to the standardized tests?" I ask at last.

"He just came around, and if it was the wrong answer he would clear his throat."

"Or roll his eyes," Romie says.

Kasha looks up. "Was that wrong?"

I'm sure he didn't cheat because he feared for his job; he was leaving anyway.

He did it because he wanted the kids to feel good about themselves.

Would he have done the same for city kids? Or for those in his native Russia?

"Go to the gym," I tell the ninth graders. "Go play basketball."

They file out silently.

I am not about to charge back into Mr. Dan's office after my earlier stupid, angry bravado. I wait until evening, then trudge through the deep gravel to the duplex.

"Oh Jesus," he says after I tell him about the tests. He sits down and rests his forehead on the heel of his palm, as if suffering a headache.

If one class's scores are invalid, the entire school's scores will be called into question. It makes me wonder why no one in the district office spotted the anomaly. Unless no one cared to look: the scores are a basis for funding. The better the scores are compared to those of previous years, the more money that flows in from the legislature.

"I don't think Romie can read," I tell him. "Kasha certainly can't write. I have no idea what Alvin and Bess can do. They all should be in another class. They'll never handle Problem Solving. Not the way we're going to play this year."

"It's your team." There is a distant look to his eyes, and I know he isn't thinking about Problem Solving. "Do what you want."

After a moment I say, "Let's retest them first. We have to anyway."

The next day, they retake the tests. I worry that the kids will just blow off the exams, but instead they buckle down. That evening, Mr. Dan and I hand-score the language arts battery, my main area of concern.

Top students usually read well above grade level. Kasha, the eighth-grade valedictorian, reads at the seventh-grade level, as does Bess. Romie, the eighth-grade salutatorian, reads just below the fourth.

Alvin, who scored among the lowest in the class the year before and who was placed in Problem Solving because of his artistic talent, reads at second-year college.

Such are academics in the Arctic.

23

That night I leave school by eight, skip the Friday night card game, and sink into sleep. I awaken at midnight to my two alarm clocks and head out into slashing rain to the duplex to work on my novel.

A figure appears in the gloom of the little light above the next house. Londa, I realize. She has a sleeping bag under an arm, flashlight in hand. Heading to a party? Some abandoned Old Village shacks serve as sites for parties and lovers' rendezvous.

She glances around and crawls under a building.

I follow her and, feeling terribly the intruder, stoop and peer in under the house.

I find her unrolling the ratty bag amid a tiny sleeping area she has created, the sides of cardboard nailed to the ancient joists, more cardboard covering the gravel. There are two stubby candles, a wadded-up blanket, and an open backpack with a T-shirt and a bra hanging out. Balls of waxed paper and a crumpled up paper sack litter a corner.

She is living here, I realize.

As she sees me, fear shows in her face. She snaps off the flashlight, as if darkness will secure her secret, but I have seen her even darker secret. Someone has blackened her eye. And her lip is swollen.

"Londa," I say, into the darkness.

"Don't, Mr. G."—a name she sometimes calls me this year.

"You need to come out of here," I tell her.

"Why?"

"Because my butt's getting soaked," I reply as I back out.

At last she crawls out, trailing the sleeping bag, one hand on the side of her face, shielding the blackened eye. I pick up the other end of the bag for her.

"It's my sleeping bag," she says. "I didn't steal it. No matter what they say."

"I'm not interested in the bag. We need to get you someplace warm. Someplace not so wet." I start walking away. "I think Mary made some cookies. Chocolate chip."

Londa follows me, and not for the first time I thank God for chocolate chips.

When we enter the house I leave the light off in the living room and tell the girls to get back to bed; they're crowding at their bedroom curtain. Mary, without comment, gives Londa milk and cookies and a cold compress, and makes up a bed in the storeroom. Then begins a war without words. Londa shakes her head but does not resist when Mary, wise enough not to say anything that will send Londa on her way, helps her to bed. Mary turns off the storeroom lamp, leads me by the hand into our bedroom, and softly shuts the door.

"In the morning I'll tell Mr. Dan," I whisper, after explaining where I found Londa. "He'll find a home for her, if she hasn't one. There's always my office in the duplex basement."

"As cold as it gets down there?" Mary frowns at my suggestion. "She can live here with us, if necessary. We'll do whatever it takes."

I walk to my office in the duplex and sit ready to type, but instead think of Londa.

And Merle and Marshall. And Meredith. Their faces flare in the dimness, their names melodic. Romie and Bess. Kasha. Alvin. Boone. Puffin, Festus, Darrel, Lobert, Chip 'n' Dale.

They all are so alive in my classroom, while I feel so dead down here at night. Though I need the release that writing gives, the classroom seems to hold the greater stimulation and creativity, despite the successes I have had as a writer. I had entered teaching to make money while I did my "real job," writing, at night. But now teaching seems more than occupation. It is becoming an obsession—one that pays benefits I could never have known as a writer; for I have lived scenes I probably could not have dreamed up regardless of my imagination.

The electricity goes off—there is an outage in the village at least once a week—and I sit in the windowless darkness, thinking of Dale's habit of answering almost every question with "I.D.K.," his acronym for "I don't know." When I challenged him to stop the practice, he grinned and switched to "I.D.C." . . . "I don't care."

He does not realize that the harder he tries to get under my skin, the more I enjoy his efforts. Maybe it is true with all kids, but there is an essential *goodness* that shines through the students' eyes and actions. The time, for instance, that he and Chip phoned to say they were bringing me *imanat*—warm clams from the stomach of a newly killed walrus, an island delicacy that I was eager to try. Unfortunately, when the boys arrived they handed me an empty bread sack, having eaten all the clams on the way over. "We have no no-power," they sheepishly admitted.

A hand cold as death clamps around my wrist.

My pulse stands still, as if my blood has frozen. The only sound is the catching of my breath in my throat. I try to turn my hand, but whatever—whoever—has hold of me will not let go. I think of the tales of the teachers' ghosts, and sweat breaks out on my forehead.

As quickly as it occurred, the sensation is gone.

I gather my resolve and, trying to quiet my trembling, feel around for my flashlight. When I snap it on, the concrete walls look back at me from within nimbuses the flashlight casts.

I stare at the walls, too frightened to move. I'm a science fiction and horror writer, I tell myself in self-mockery, hoping to overcome my fear. Terror is supposed to go with the territory.

Still, it is a long time before I can summon the strength to open the door to the greater basement, where an old board-covered cistern lies. It is a deathtrap for lemmings that sometimes fall in, and the vessel, I have been told, much to my previous bemusement, that holds the teachers' souls.

Swathed in sweat, I rush up the stairs and head home. Londa is gone. "She said she was going outside for a cigarette," Mary tells me. "She never came back. I think she was worried that people would talk. I think she was trying to protect us."

I search for her, under the house, and in the darkness. To no avail.

In school the following Monday, she says nothing about what took place. All day I wonder if I should contact social services, even though it will likely create a greater rift between Londa and her family.

That afternoon I cancel practice and sit staring at the desk. I realize that the problems involved with academic coaching are growing beyond the classroom. It frightens me more than the ghost did.

Meredith quickly finishes her schoolwork and skims a photocopied article about prisons. This one is on recidivism. What team wouldn't think of that! What good is reading anyway! She and Marshall definitely agree about that. And if she hadn't had to skip fifth grade, she could be on the elementary team with Garnet, Groper, and Summer. They are certain to make state this year, whereas this year's ninth graders weren't going anywhere!

"CRAP," she writes, in red felt pen across the article.

And underlines it twice.

She traces around the letters and then underlines them in blue felt pen, wondering if there is a way she can quit the team without getting Dad angry. Mindlessly she writes, "CRAP = C."

An idea forms. She finishes the word: "CRAP = COMMON."

After hunting beneath her desk seat for a black marker, she writes: "COMMON = C."

Excited, she glances about the room, wanting to show someone her discovery. Finally, she tells Wymena, her teacher, that she needs to go to the high school *now*, knowing that Wymena will gladly be rid of her. Wymena has informed her that any problems Meredith has with other kids aren't her concern. "I'm not here to teach teachers' kids," she said.

Wymena gives permission with a wave of her hand and returns to reading the sports page.

Irene, one of the eighth graders, sticks out a leg, blocking Meredith's exit. Leaning back and locking her fingers behind her head, Irene says to the ceiling, *"Atagpunun aglaa uyuq laluramkaaghaq"*—Run to your daddy, White Trash.

Everyone giggles.

Meredith stops at the door and waits for the giggling to stop.

"Meghmun qetgeghi nulluqhlak," she says—Take a jump in the ocean, walrus butt.

Then she is gone, leaving the others to wonder how anyone could have learned the language so quickly. And without their knowing.

24

Meredith tells me about her idea, but asks me not to tell the others she thought of it. Knowing that I will need something visual to explain her idea to everyone else, something concrete, I send her to the shop to ask Keenan for a funnel. "Box it up," I say.

Merle hurries in as she's leaving, excited yet frustrated over information he found in an article about prisons. "It's about Joliet Prison in Illinois," he tells me. "It says that galvanic skin-resistance tests," he runs his finger along the text as he paraphrases, "indicate that people prone to violence become more violent in crowded situations." He looks at me. "Doesn't everyone get tense in crowded places? Isn't this just saying that prisons are overcrowded?"

Boone enters and drops several pages of synopsized articles onto my desk. "I read all this last night," he says, "and I didn't find any originals."

Those few who have read anything the night before start in on what has become a daily ritual: complaining about how hard it is to come up with original ideas, either from reading or from their brainstorming sessions.

This time, though, I do not have to cajole them to read more or think harder. Merle's information has given me an idea. I write "Galvanic skin-resistance tests MBAP" on the board. (Galvanic skin-resistance tests may be a problem.)

"But galvanic skin tests aren't a problem," Merle says. "Overcrowding is."

"That's right," I tell him.

Marshall crosses his arms around his basketball and slides down in his chair, as if to show that finding originals is beyond him.

"What do you call it when people go kind of nuts here during winter?" I ask. "You know, from being cooped up too long, like during blizzards?"

"Claustrophobia," Londa says.

"Cabin fever," Merle corrects.

The kids agree with me when I point out that "cabin fever" or "claustrophobia" aren't original ideas. My timing is perfect—for just then Meredith returns, box in hand. "What if I told you that this is a magic box?" I ask, holding it up. "What if I told you that this box can turn common ideas into original ones?"

"Sure," Marshall says—but his attitude is not total disbelief, for he puts the basketball on the floor and leans forward.

With a flourish I open the box and lift the funnel in triumph.

"Oh, man," Marshall says, as if I really have lost my mind this time.

"You funnel down the ideas," I say, holding the thing before them like a chalice.

"Funnel them down?" Londa asks.

"Make them smaller. General ideas are almost never original ideas," I tell them. "That's because almost everyone knows general information. Remember, for an idea to be an original it can't be duplicated by any other team—and the evaluators have to think it's a great idea. To have any hope of having original ideas, you have to be very precise."

I walk among the students, making sure that they all focus on the funnel. "You can make ideas more precise by what we call *funneling*." I turn the funnel around and peer at them through it. "In writing, it's the little things that are important, not the general ideas. The same is true for Problem Solving. You funnel down the general to the specific."

Back at the board, I point to what we've written. "Claustrophobia isn't just caused by physical walls," I tell them, running a hand over the classroom wall, "but by what is called 'territorial imperative,' the distance of comfort between individuals. That's more precise than 'overcrowding.' We're funneling down our broad concepts. We're making them more exact. Watch, I'll show you what I mean."

I suddenly stoop and then slowly bring my face very close to Marshall's. He pulls back, frowning.

"You see, the closer I get, the more uncomfortable he becomes," I tell everyone as I straighten up again. "Some people are comfortable at fairly close ranges, others need a lot of distance between them and other people to be comfortable. That's what the galvanic skin-resistance tests measured. The tests didn't measure 'overcrowding.' They showed something much more precise. They showed that violent people usually need lots of room—they have a pretty big territorial imperative."

On the board I write *Territorial imperative MBAP for prison populations*, and Londa blurts, "That's an original. I just know it is!"

"I think so too," I tell them, almost joyous as I put the chalk back in the tray.

"But isn't that just renaming ideas?" Boone asks.

"It's making them more specific," Merle says. "We started with 'cabin fever' or 'claustrophobia.' Now look what we have."

Following his lead, I run an index finger under "territorial imperative" through the board's chalk dust.

"You're turning general ideas into original ideas," I say. "Isn't that what most inventors do? Take a general idea and make something original by making something specific?"

"Cool," Marshall says.

"But don't we need a lot of those?" Londa asks. "To win, don't we need a lot of originals? I mean, how will we know what to funnel?"

Now it is time to introduce Meredith's idea.

"I am going to give you a tool so you can figure out whether your ideas are original ones," I tell them. "You'll *grade* ideas that you get from brainstorming or reading." I put on the board:

A = <u>original</u>. High probability that no other team will think of it.
B = <u>uncommon</u>. Some teams might think of it.
C = <u>common</u>. High probability that most teams will think of it.

I explain how funneling can work. The kids can brainstorm and read, and if they don't come up with any "A" ideas, they will funnel down "B" or "C" ideas to something more specific. "Until you come up with some 'A' ideas," I say.

The kids seem confused, so I draw a cartoon face on the board with a rectangle for a brain. "The human brain is made up of two parts,"

I tell them. "In the back 10 percent is where imagination lives—that is, where the original ideas are. And the front 90 percent of the brain consists of common ideas."

"The front 90 percent is crap," Marshall says. I join in the kids' laughter, amazed at how much he and Meredith are on the same wavelength.

"Unfortunately, usually we must wade through crap," I say to more laughter, pretending to step in manure and scrape it off my shoe, "to find original ideas." I put the chalk down.

"Don't worry that you're thinking of common ideas. Just keep funneling, and sooner or later you'll come up with great stuff."

To try out our new tools, we grade three of the ideas that the kids had earlier identified as possibly being prison problems:

insufficient reading materials = C
recidivism = C
emotional problems during conjugal visits = B

We decide to funnel down the last one. A little brainstorming produces: "crying when inmates and spouses must separate," "more heartache afterward," "anger over their kids' problems," and "worry over family finances." The kids like the last one best, and though they agree that it could be funneled down to problems such as "worries over taxes during conjugal visits" and "worry during conjugal visits about loss of the main wage earner's income," they decide to leave it as "worry over family finances during conjugal visits."

"Will this mean less reading?" Marshall asks hopefully.

"Probably more reading," I tell him. "You can't funnel without information."

His brows draw down.

"But couldn't we rerun 'A' ideas?" Londa asks.

Now I'm confused, so she asks me to pull up the U.S. map, behind which are listed this year's Problem Solving tests and dates:

Prison Problem, October 15
Greenhouse Effect, January 15

Famine (State-Qualifying Problem), March 1
Nuclear-Waste Disposal (State Finals), April 18
National Problem (Subject TBA), June 4

I see her point. If ideas could be applied more than once, the kids wouldn't have to start from scratch in preparing for each test.

"Territorial imperative won't work for the greenhouse effect problem," Marshall says. "No way."

"It doesn't have to work for *every* test," Londa says.

"She's right," I say. "And it would mean less reading."

"Heyyy!" Marshall pats Londa on the back, and she demurely smiles.

"Do we have to play both practice problems?" Kasha asks.

"A lot of teams skip the second practice problem," Marshall says.

"At the finals last year, some kids said they skip both practice problems," Boone adds. "They start studying for the state-qualifying problem in August."

At first I tell the kids they need the practice. But they start howling and insisting that ideas from the prison problem will work for greenhouse effect. So I relent, but with two conditions: "First, you must prove to me that you really can apply ideas from one problem to later ones. And, for the prison problem, you will need to dig up and funnel ideas. I mean, really dig and funnel, so you'll have original ideas to begin with."

After they agree to my conditions, I say, "Okay, let's see you apply 'territorial imperative' to"—I point to the board—"the state problem on nuclear waste disposal."

The kids try to convince me that people overseeing nuclear waste repositories might go crazy from cabin fever and try to blow up the canisters, but I adroitly refuse to credit anything so far-fetched. Then Meredith pipes up, and everyone quiets down.

"People don't have to go crazy," she says. "What if they were cramped, like two office workers crammed into a cubicle? Couldn't differences in territorial imperatives affect their decision-making?"

Wow, I think. Some of my fellow graduate students when I was working on an MBA wouldn't have thought of that.

"Pretty good," I say, careful not to be overly enthusiastic for fear that other kids might feel that they couldn't come up with something similar.

But they do. They're off and running. They bounce from "territorial imperative" to say that "the Peter Principle could affect decision-making." We had discussed the Peter Principle—that people in any organization rise to the level of their incompetence—a couple of weeks before, so the notion of having incompetent people in executive positions is fairly easy to explain.

Next, from ideas about conjugal visits in prisons, they question whether office workers in love would change their territorial imperative.

"Office romances . . . uh . . . affecting territorial imperatives—may be a problem?" Kasha haltingly asks, and when I smile in approval, she grins.

"*Adversely* affecting territorial imperative," Marshall says, lifting an index finger.

Merle, who has seemed lost in thought, abruptly brightens. "No. Changes in territorial imperative from office romances may adversely," he glances toward Marshall, "affect the Peter Principle."

There is a hush in the room as everyone looks at him, amazed. His ability to find the essence of ideas makes me wonder if that isn't how the Eskimo survived in such difficult conditions these thousands of years. Not by attempting to alter the environment, as the white man has tried, but by synthesizing whatever the environment gave him.

"The Peter Principle Office Romance *Syndrome,*" Boone says, giving Marshall a surreptitious grin, and adds, "may be a problem because of territorial imperative."

Later I will discover that "adversely" and "syndrome" were two of the ten vocabulary words Bruce had assigned that week in English class.

"Okay, you win," I say, and most of the kids applaud themselves. "We won't play the second practice problem."

No sooner have I spoken than I know it's a mistake. They need all the feedback they can get from the evaluators in Juneau. I hold up my hands, correcting myself.

"How about," I suggest, "you really work at the prison problem. Then, instead of skipping the practice problem on the greenhouse effect, you play it but skip the research. Just pretend it's one of our scrimmages, and concentrate on technique."

They mull the idea and most agree.

"Bess?" I ask. "That okay?"

As usual she hasn't been participating. She nods without enthusiasm.

"Romie?"

"Guess so."

"Alvin?"

Without looking up from his doodling, he says, "Less work? Sure."

I maneuver the class back to the subject of prisons. "Let's take another common prison problem. Homosexual rape." I write it on the board and discuss it as delicately as possible, but notice Romie has put her head down on her arms.

It occurs to me that she is trying to keep from crying.

"Could territorial imperative cause rape?" Kasha asks, referring to the board.

"Maybe." I kneel beside Romie.

"What's wrong?" I ask quietly.

She shakes her head, which is still down.

"Something I said?"

Her mouth puckers, and she snuffles. "They do that in prison?"

"It happens."

She lurches from the chair and runs from the room.

I look around at the others, who abruptly busy themselves with schoolwork.

Kasha leans toward me. "Her brother's in prison," she says.

25

The next morning, just before geography, Kasha smiles brightly as she hands me an essay in the hall. "It's on integration. In prisons."

I try as best as I can to read it without looking defeated. The piece might as well be about integration in Antarctica, for all the sense it makes. As before, the prose is made up of sentence fragments. At least she's consistent.

I hand it back to her. "I don't think the evaluators would understand this." I am not Gregor Popov. I will not lie to students just to make them feel good.

Her lips tighten, revealing her disappointment. "I can't think in English," she says, studying the paper. "Even when Wymena coaches us in basketball, I have to translate what she's saying into Yupik to understand what she wants."

She looks up at me with huge, innocent eyes. "You think I should quit Problem Solving?"

"You can't. You're a freshman."

"You think I should quit trying?"

There is no stubbornness in her. She isn't Romie. She simply has reached how I have always conceived of Vygotsky's famous Zone of Proximal Development: the point, the great Russian theorist postulated, beyond which a child cannot progress without assistance. And she has found that her teacher cannot help her.

"You say you translate Wymena's instructions during basketball practice?" I ask.

"Sure. I want to play better. We want to win, George."

Four of the five starters on the girls' basketball team are freshmen. Bunnie, Romie's sister, is the only upper-classperson. Not listening to the coach could mean breaking up the beginning of a four-year team. If they learn to play well, Kasha and the other freshmen girls might have a powerful team by the time they are seniors.

"Take this home tonight," I tell her, touching the paper. "Can you try writing it in Yupik? I know you speak Yupik, but do you write it?"

"Can I write it during geography?" Her eyes sparkle. "I'm ahead in the book."

"Just don't translate it. Begin over again, but this time in Yupik."

She clutches the paper to her sweatshirt and runs into the classroom to get started.

Fifteen minutes into the period, when the other ninth graders are busy calculating differences in latitude, Kasha comes to my desk and gives me a sheet of paper filled with Yupik's long words. She looks worried. "How will the evaluators understand me if I write in Yupik during the Problem Solving test?" she asks.

"You still have the English version?"

She retrieves it and hands it to me. To her dismay I tear it up and let the pieces float down toward the wastebasket. I hand her back the Yupik version.

"Don't worry about what you wrote in English," I tell her. "Go translate this."

What she hands me fifteen minutes later is clear and coherent.

I smile and extend her a hand.

Meredith and Kasha. We have two players. We need two more.

As the class exits I ask Romie to remain behind.

"I didn't mean to upset you yesterday," I tell her.

Her stubborn pout is gone. She has the worried look of someone who has realized that the world is more complex, and uglier, than she had imagined.

"I'll make a deal with you," I continue. "I want to have a special session with you and Bess. If you really participate, I'll talk Mr. Dan into letting you quit Problem Solving, should you still want to afterward. Okay?"

She looks down at her tennis shoes. "Okay."

Shifting the subject, I ask, "What do you want to do after you graduate?"

"Join the National Guard," she mumbles.

"The Guard only meets one weekend a month and a couple of weeks a year. What do you want to do the rest of the time?"

"I want to graduate . . . and join the National Guard."

She leaves the room.

The next afternoon Romie and Bess show up for the special session. I have asked Meredith to come as well; I need her as a catalyst.

And I have a secret weapon.

Rubber flies.

Ask Eskimos to stalk polar bears or steer a skin boat among towering icebergs or drive a snowmachine into the wilderness in a whiteout, and they will do so with hardly a qualm. But bugs petrify most Eskimo kids, even though insects abound in the Arctic: mosquitoes so thick they can cover a sleeper in seconds, stinging horse flies so fierce that they literally have been known to drive caribou crazy. No-see-um gnats swarm and bite with abandon, and white sox can raise yellow welts the size of grapes.

I set a six-pack of pop on my desk, and the girls lean forward eagerly. But when I dump the rubber flies out on a table, the Eskimo girls recoil so quickly that Bess nearly topples backward in her chair.

I smash one of the rubber flies, and it pops up again. Romie and Bess nervously laugh and settle into their seats.

"What can I do with these?" I ask, pounding one down with my fist.

No one answers.

I bring out two more six-packs.

"What?" I ask.

"Smash them!" Meredith yells.

"Sock them!" I scream, again pounding down with my fist.

"Squish them!" Meredith yells as I drop a fly in front of each girl.

Romie and Bess look at theirs fearfully.

"Tear off a leg!" I shout, but I can't do it—the rubber is too thick.

"Push them away?" Romie asks in a small voice, delicately shoving the fly aside.

I point to Bess.

No answer.

I point to the pop and back to Bess.

She blows the fly, and is delighted that it slides away from her. "Blow at it?" she asks.

"Bother it?" Romie asks, her face now close to the insect as she flicks it with forefinger and thumb.

"Cook it!" I yell.

"Yuck!" Romie says.

Bess sticks out her tongue as if she's going to be sick.

"Fry it!" Meredith yells. "Fry the fly!"

"Fly the fly!" I throw mine into the air.

"Throw the fly!" Romie says, and tosses hers at Bess.

"Sail the fly!" Meredith's goes flying toward Romie.

"Bam it!" Romie says, and slaps down with her hand on Bess's desk.

"Harder!" I tell all three girls as I distribute more flies.

Meredith and Romie slap down, Romie giggling. Bess puts her hand down softly on the rubber insect and instantly pulls away.

"Harder!" I scream.

Whump!

"Harder!"

Whump!!

Soon Meredith and Romie are throwing the bugs against the blackboard, stomping on them, sticking them with thumbtacks. Even Bess is laughing.

I hand each girl two cans of pop. "Now, for our next test . . . "

"That was a test?" Romie asks.

"I don't just give away pop," I tell her, and she grins. "For our next test, we're going to pretend you have a dog in your backyard."

Bess frowns, and when I ask her what's wrong she says, "We don't have backyards."

"Those are white people's things," Romie says, then perhaps remembering that Meredith and I are white, lowers her eyes.

"Okay, behind your house," I say, nonchalantly adding a third can of pop to the girls' hoard, to lighten everyone up. "The dog keeps getting off its rope. What can you do to keep it where it belongs?"

After more prodding and Pepsi, the girls are off and rolling: bigger rope, build a fence, build an electric fence, dig a ditch, dig a moat, train it, get a girl dog, cut off its legs, kill it, hire a watchdog, hire a watchcat, circle the dog with its poop, ring the area with ammonia. On and on and on, the girls laughing ever more freely. By the time they run out of ideas they are exhausted more from laughing than from the brainstorming. I award them the rest of the pop and dismiss them to the gym. Minutes later I see them on the bleachers, waiting for open gym to start, talking and laughing.

The next day, Romie shows up with a dictionary and tape recorder, and struggles to understand the readings and my lectures.

Now there are three.

"I don't know what's gotten into Romie," Wymena says at the next faculty meeting. "A week ago I couldn't get her to listen to me during basketball practice. I couldn't get any of the ninth graders to listen. 'You can coach us,' they kept saying, 'but you can't watch us play. You can't look at us.' They wouldn't guard, they wouldn't get aggressive on offense. I was beginning to think I'd made a real mistake trying to build a team around the ninth graders.

"Then last week Romie just *blossomed*. She started driving to the bucket. Even the boys have difficulty stopping her. Then Bess started in—her arms are up, she's challenging in the paint, playing like a real center." Wymena looks around at the rest of us. "We've got a team, this year."

The next day, Romie forgets to bring the paragraph she wrote in geography the morning before. There's a sleet storm, so I don't want to send her home to retrieve it, even though her house is the closest to the school. "Turn it in tomorrow," I say.

"I'll just rewrite it," she says.

"You worked on that for a half an hour yesterday," I say. "Bring it in tomorrow."

She frowns, sits down, and ten minutes later comes to my desk with the essay.

"Found it?" I ask. "Guess you didn't take it home after all."

"No, I rewrote it."

The piece seems identical to yesterday's. When I look up at her, she grins and heads out the door. "I'll prove it!" she yells happily, and within moments I see her through the window. She's pulling on her jacket as she runs home.

When she arrives back minutes later, I am amazed: the two essays don't just seem identical, they *are* identical, word for word, all the way down to the punctuation.

"You wrote this, from memory?" I ask.

"Sure. Easy. I wanted to learn it, so I wrote it out again last night." She takes another copy from her jacket to prove it.

"You wrote an essay and copied it over and knew it word for word?"

"Is that bad?"

"No, Romie." I feel like laughing. "This is good. This is very, very good."

"What is?" Kasha asks, coming forward.

I explain that Romie has just reproduced an essay she wrote the day before.

"I can do that," Kasha says offhandedly.

"You're kidding."

"Sure I can." There is not a trace of guile or boasting in her innocent look.

Four years later, when Kasha is high school valedictorian and Romie is salutatorian, they still can produce, down to the comma, essays they wrote as freshmen. They do not have Puffin's rapid recall and ability to synthesize information, but they can reproduce material verbatim.

"We have a team," I tell them. "You girls are going to be *awesome.*"

They grin at each other, and we high-five.

Every other day after school, I drive our three-wheeler—this year's present to ourselves—down to the elementary and meet with the sixth-grade Problem Solvers.

"Not coloring today?" I ask each time I meet with the girls.

"No coloring!" Groper, Garnet, and Summer boom.

"On to Anchorage?"

"Anchorage, this year!"

I love a good chorus.

At first, Meredith's grading system baffles these younger kids. They want to give every idea an A. But soon they catch on, and I'm delighted at how easily they funnel ideas down into specifics, and possible originals.

Based on Summer's interest in fashion design, "Problems with prison uniforms MBAP" becomes "Individuality issues MBAP." After we read an article about how a Navy brig reduced violence by painting cells a calming pink, that idea becomes, with my help with vocabulary, "Coordinating calming colors in uniforms with men's color needs MBAP." The girls add three or four sentences of information from the article, and we have a paragraph. A good hour's work.

"This paragraph is yours to memorize," I tell Summer, and she dutifully copies the result from the board into her notebook.

"Learn it so well," I add, "that you can apply it to any situation I give you."

When she finishes writing, I remind them, "Don't just memorize this stuff. You have to know the material . . ."

"Inside out!" they yell, as usual. "Upside down! Forward and backward!"

"You can color now," I say before I exit.

But they don't take out their crayons. As I leave, they are hunched over their notebooks, discussing the ideas in Yupik in low voices and scarfing down the chocolate chip cookies they get for superior sessions.

Learning. Earning.

26

October arrives, but instead of winter, we have a week of Indian summer. The morning of our first practice problem is without wind, the temperature a balmy forty-five. I go to school early, telling myself it is in case I have forgotten essentials—pens, paper, pop—for the evening's test, but in actuality I'm nervous and lately have been having severe insomnia. Staying home means staring at the walls.

As usual, the school breakfast consists of coffee, juice, and Lars's delicious Eskimo fry bread. Because so many Gambell families live below the poverty line, the school is a recipient of a federal program by which the kids get breakfast free, a benefit Mr. Dan extends to the teachers in the hope they will arrive early. But I rarely partake, for Lars is always there.

"Think your teams will do well this year?" he asks as he brings a steaming batch of fry bread in from the kitchen. His voice sounds affably innocent.

It catches me unawares. Or maybe it's just the smell of the bread that makes me answer without measuring my words.

"At least one team will win state," I say, reaching for a sample, outwardly calm. "If not this year, then next year."

Merle is such a team motivator, and the kids are so convinced that they not only will make state this year but will win it, that going to Anchorage and coming home without a trophy seems unlikely. In my mind the goal now seems not just possible but pure, clear, and, in a psychological sense, already attained. We just have to reach out and grasp the trophy.

Something similar had happened to me my first year of college. Though I had been a mediocre high school student, my wrestling coach had convinced me that *any* process can be broken down to a series of small, learnable steps. When some upperclassmen asked me what grades I would earn, I had said "straight As" without a moment's hesitation. I remember being shocked when they laughed. Didn't they know that I had examined the goal, found it attainable, and was simply going to figure out the many small steps I had to take to achieve it? And I did.

Lars drops two more fry breads onto my plate. "Last year's trophy was a fluke. Know what a fluke is? Tail of a whale."

He walks away, chortling. "Tail of a whale," he repeats. "Tail of a whale." At the kitchen door he halts and looks back, his face suddenly serious. "That joke you made about Festus? That list? That was goddamn criminal. And you call yourself a teacher."

He closes the door behind himself.

The fry bread tastes flat.

"Fire extinguishers!" Lawrence yells from the gym. "Grab fire extinguishers!"

I run from the home ec room. "Fire in the generator shack!" he shouts as he barrels out the main door, a fire extinguisher in each of his massive arms.

I follow him outside, only to see him strap the extinguishers to his three-wheeler and race away. Everything seems to move as an eerie scenario, people spilling from houses and driving three-wheelers toward the six enormous oil tanks.

Flames lick up the nearest tank, which dwarfs the generator shack at its base. Men are unrolling a hose toward the lake. Others hurry toward them, hauling a generator.

I get another extinguisher from the school and hustle toward the fire. Already the flames crown the tank, a stream of fire has feathered up the next tank, and flames spew from beneath a third as if someone has turned on a stove too high under a teakettle.

"Anything I can do?" I ask Merle as he takes the fire extinguisher from me and passes it to another man, who runs toward the oil tanks.

"Just thank God it's oil and not gas," he says, "or we would all be dead by now."

Soon the flames engulf the tanks. Like the other villagers, I stand there helplessly watching the winter heating source rise thousands of feet into the sky in great curls of black smoke. The men who were at the lake, working with the generator, come trudging back, looking disgusted and discouraged. A rumor filters among the crowd, and a student translates for me: the brand-new fire-fighting equipment, for which the village wrote a grant, is useless. Because each clan vied for the honor of providing this part of village security, the responsibilities were divided. The clans never convened to see if the generator's fittings matched the hose.

"Fire brigade!" someone yells, and people run home for buckets.

But there is no stopping the flames. One oil-tank lid, over a dozen feet in diameter and weighing perhaps a thousand pounds, blows off and sails over the elementary school—300 feet away—like a Frisbee. The nearest Old Village shack ignites into flame, its weathered wood like dry kindling.

I run home to empty my house of valuables and then race to the duplex to rescue my manuscript from my office. Descending the basement stairs, I can sense the *presence* there again.

Given today's situation, I wonder what the ghosts would say, had they voices.

The teams play the prison problem on Monday, the state office having granted us an extension because of the fire.

The kids are somber and cold. A storm hit over the weekend, as if aware that the village is without heat until emergency oil arrives in the small, expensive drums everyone will have to use for the rest of the winter. The temperature has plummeted. The school has no electricity except for two little emergency lights in the gym ceiling. The kids wear jackets and take the test right after school so they can use the late-afternoon sunlight.

So quiet are they that I often peek in through the little window in the doors, to make sure no one has left. All are subdued, some on the verge of tears.

No one asks for pop.

"Time," Bess softly reminds me when the two hours are up. A flip of a coin determined that Alvin would play the problem as the fourth member of the junior high team, and Bess would be timekeeper. That she is not playing seems a relief to her.

The teams wordlessly exit the building. I gather up their answers and head to the elementary, where Mr. Dan has overseen the sixth graders' exam. I am glad that Meredith has the three-wheeler. I feel like walking.

I read as I walk. Gone are the silly answers I would have expected even a week ago, and in their place is a remarkable maturity. The test scenario asks what problems might occur in a prison space station set midway between Earth and the moon. That we had never considered being asked about a prison anywhere except in America makes me even prouder of the answers.

The high schoolers' main solution involves using galvanic skin-resistance tests to identify violent offenders. The kids would then put those prisoners into mental-exercise programs that would reduce their territorial imperative. The junior high team's main idea, recognizing that a prison can only operate as efficiently as its support staff, discusses ways that staffs separated by thousands of miles might better work as a team. "The Earth staff and the one in the space-station prison are like clans," the booklet ends, "and they must work together."

It is the elementary team's main idea—the central problem that, stated in Step 2, the students have elected to solve twenty ways—that is the most astonishing. Summer is the strength of the team and, given her interest in clothing, I expected their main answer to focus on fashion. Instead, it focuses on fire. "What happens if a fire breaks out in the space station?" they ask. "Fire needs oxygen, but so do people."

That night, by candlelight, I type up the booklets on an old manual typewriter, careful not to change anything, even punctuation. The junior high and the high school's booklets are each over forty double-spaced pages long, the elementary school's nearly half that. As I work, my eyes well with tears of pride at the insights and effort the tests demonstrate. In the morning I will stuff the typed versions and the original versions into a manila envelope and mail them to the evaluators.

Gambell? I remember someone telling me. *It's an asylum out there. It's a zoo. Just survive this year, and the district will give you a good village.*

Know what a fluke is? Tail of a whale.

The hell.

27

The booklets are the initial test of the "research first, creativity second" emphasis we have tried this year, so I am hoping that at least one team does well, lest I consider abandoning the method.

Three weeks later, when I enter sixth period and show the kids the unopened letter marked "Future Problem Solving Program, Juneau, Alaska," everyone hushes and leans forward as I nervously tear open the envelope.

"Well?" Marshall asks.

"I'm reading," I tease him, my pulse racing as I see the results. "Don't rush me."

Then I announce: "Gambell high school, *first.* Gambell junior high, *first.* Gambell elementary, *first.*"

For a moment no one moves. All eye each other in astonishment. Then everyone erupts into high-fives, hooting, hugging, jumping around the room.

"Wait, there's more!" I skim an attached letter. "'We Alaska evaluators were so impressed with Gambell's high school entry,'" I read aloud, "'that we submitted it to the national evaluators to be re-scored, in case we misjudged the national criteria. The national evaluators agreed with our scoring. The Gambell high school team scored the highest in the nation.'"

The kids hoot and holler, but my blood runs cold as I read the last sentence.

I take a breath, knowing the disappointment that will follow, and read aloud:

"'As an example of excellence, we have taken the liberty of sending the Gambell high school booklet to every team in the country.'"

The celebration abruptly ends in looks of apprehension and disbelief.

"We'll never be able to use our ideas again," Merle says, summing up what I am sure all the other kids realize. "Everyone will duplicate us."

Marshall slams down a fist. "All that work! For a *practice* problem?"

"We'd have to start over," Romie says.

There is no hope in her voice.

I stifle an urge to give a pep talk, and dismiss them to play basketball, though I know that no one will feel like playing.

That day, however, is not the worst the week offers up for me.

The worst begins the next morning. Lars phones. "You live so close to the store, George, so could you pick up a loaf of Hawaiian bread? The round kind. I want it for home ec. Some is supposed to have arrived, as unlikely as that seems."

Winter's first full-blown blizzard is upon us, so Mary and I decide that Meredith won't play chauffeur. Against gale-force winds, I slide forward the back half of the snowmachine's canvas cover, so only the windshield and cowling are masked. Leaving most of the machine covered during short hops helps retain engine heat on days like this.

I stop at the store and find two elderly Eskimos in the long arctic entry, trying to shoo a husky outside. It gazes forlornly out into the storm and stands with its legs wide, weight shifted back, as if expecting to be shoved. "Go!" one man shouts, waving.

"Out!" the other says.

I give the dog my most malevolent eye.

"Aani! Suka!" —Get out and hurry up about it!

The dog dashes outside, tail between its legs.

The men look at one another, astonished, as, pleased with myself, I head into the store. "Eskimo dog," I say. "Doesn't speak English."

They are still chuckling when, bread in hand, I leave, only to find the cover of my snowmachine flapping like huge black wings, the loosened hooks banging against the machine. To keep the cover from flying away, I race forward in my clumsy bunny boots and the bulky Refrigerwear snowsuit I bought this year to replace the previous year's army jacket.

But I'm too late.

The cover rips from its last hook and goes flapping into the swirling, howling storm.

No!

I stash the bread in its grocery bag between the handlebars and the windshield, and clomp as fast as possible after the cover.

It hits the ground and slides across the wind-burnished snow.

I pounce on it spread-eagled, exhilarated by my catch.

I look up as the grocery sack flies by.

Next, the Hawaiian bread rolls past like the head of the gingerbread man.

I bundle up the snowmachine cover, which slaps my face, and leap for the bread.

"Gotcha!" I clutch it to my chest, just as the cover loosens from my grip and, unfurling like a parachute, drags me along as I fight to keep it from flying away. I slam into the side of a shack. Icicles cascade from the overhang, bouncing off my head.

But I have the snowmachine cover. I have the bread. I have beaten the blizzard. Caesar of the storm! Lawrence of Alaska!

I pull off a mitten and, holding it in my teeth, with freezing fingers unzip the Refrigerwear front and stuff the bread inside.

When I finally reach school, Lars looks askance at the mangled loaf, but seeing the fire in my eyes, says nothing.

"I wouldn't be taking that off quite yet," Mr. Dan says as I peel off my outerwear.

There have been two boxes with my name on them, he tells me, sitting on the tarmac since the night before. He suggests that I use first period, my planning period, to pick them up before someone absconds with them.

I head back into the storm, hoping that the boxes are the hydraulic weight set I ordered. Wall-mounted and capable of being folded up, it will be perfect for the tiny cabin. No more running around the gym to try to wear myself out enough so I can sleep; I'm down to a couple hours a night. I'll bulk up and buff up—maybe bring back the highs of high school wrestling, the washboard abs, the joy that made me compete and smile at the same time.

To my relief, the boxes are still beside the runway. The smaller one, three feet long and eighteen inches wide, is extremely heavy. The larger, three feet wide and seven feet long, is too big to carry on the snowmachine.

My excitement overrules reason.

I balance the larger box across the seat and place the other atop it. There is just enough room for me to squeeze my knees onto the back. By leaning over the boxes, I can drive my weightlifting set home.

Charles Atlas of the Arctic! Schwarzenegger of the snows!

Except I have forgotten the obvious.

All snowmachines have an emergency kill switch that the rider can connect to a sleeve via a short, coiled wire. If the rider falls off, the machine stops.

I have not clipped on the coil. A fact the machine probably knows.

For the first dozen yards the ride is fine, despite my cramped knees. Then I try to turn.

The bigger box slides forward against the throttle, smashing my thumb. When I pull my thumb away in pain, the machine leaps forward rather than stopping.

I am thrown off and onto the tarmac. The machine, box against throttle, roars off, sparks flying as it races down the runway.

"Damn you!" I run after it, even clumsier than before, the wind worse here than among the snowdrifts surrounding the store.

The scene is from the Keystone Cops: a teacher chasing a snowmachine driven by a weight set down a landing strip. Then an even more surreal event occurs: an airplane drones down out of the storm, wing lights ablaze like the eyes of a predator after prey.

I don't see my life flash before me. I see Cary Grant in *North by Northwest,* when the plane swoops down behind him.

I dodge off the runway, and the plane keeps coming, my machine directly in the way.

I see the headline: "Dumbbell after Dumbbells Wipes out Arctic Aircraft."

But the wings of luck are with me.

The snowmachine hits a bump, does a ninety-degree turn, the boxes teetering, and heads toward the sea. High berms line the runway, so as soon as the machine reaches those hillocks, it will stop.

The machine does not stop.

It hits the first berm, lunges into the air, slams down hard . . . and keeps going, the boxes jouncing crazily but somehow, as if by magic or miracle, staying put.

The machine, riderless except for the weight set, plows across the ice.

I barely notice the plane land with a screech of brakes and a revving of engine.

My snowmachine is headed toward the open ocean.

Bathed in sweat, I scramble across the first berm and stagger up the second. My machine and its cargo reach the lacework of cracks near the edge of the ice, about to disappear forever beneath indigo-blue waters.

How to keep this quiet on an island without secrets! Everyone is going to know.

"Problem-Solving Coach Condemns Machine to Watery Grave."

Then, as if God has wearied of His jest and has pitied the poor fool on the frozen shore, the boxes tip off onto the sea ice. The machine stops less than ten feet from the ocean's edge.

Walking slowly lest I overheat even more and risk hypothermia, I head to the maintenance shed next to the elementary school. The door, as usual, is unlocked. I find a long rope and tie a seal hook onto it, trudge back, crawl out onto the ice as far as I dare, whirl the rope around my head and, on the third try, snag one of the snowmachine runners. I back off the ice and drag the snowmachine to safety.

Next I do the truly stupid.

Rather than risk anyone's seeing my predicament, I tie the rope onto the machine, then tie the rope around my waist and crawl out to the boxes, ice crackling beneath me. I try to move the boxes, but they are too awkward to move unless I stand up. I spear one box with the seal hook and, after making sure that it has caught on part of the apparatus within, crawl back, dragging my treasure, and repeat the process with the second box.

I collapse onto the shore, pulse pounding, glad to be alive—and unseen.

When I open my eyes, the pilot stands over me.

"You okay?" He helps me up. "Jones will be here in a couple of minutes with the school snowmachine and sled. We'd have been glad to have given you a hand."

When Jones arrives, I silently thank the pilot for saying nothing to him about why my snowmachine and two large boxes are sitting next to the ocean's edge. I follow Jones and the sled to my cabin, where he drops off the boxes, and wave him away when he offers to take them inside. He heads toward the school with his cargo of food. I fumble my door key out of my snowsuit pocket.

The padlock is frozen.

I drive to the maintenance shed, locate a butane torch and matches, and return.

By the time I get the torch lit, my hands are white with cold and a dozen matches litter the snow. But at last the torch blasts, and I heat the lock. Water dribbles out. I let the lock cool and insert the key.

It doesn't work.

The lock's no good.

I roar back to the shed, swearing into the wind, grab a crowbar, return and break the hasp. Exultant, I haul the boxes inside, check my watch—fifteen minutes before my class starts—and, unable to contain my impatience, tear open the cardboard.

The main part of the weight system, to be mounted to the wall, is six feet six.

The walls are six feet two.

28

"Guthridge said this." Gerald slaps the *Nome Nugget* during the next faculty meeting. "Guthridge said that."

The success of our Problem Solvers is splashed across the second page. A subhead announces that the high school team scored the highest in the country.

"It even was on RATNET last night," Lars says, referring to rural Alaska's television station. He stands by the kitchen, stirring the contents of a bowl that he holds in the crook of his arm, and shakes his head in disgust.

"Think you could have gotten them to mention your name a few more times?" Gerald asks me as he slides the paper toward the other teachers.

"Maybe I should have used a pseudonym when they interviewed me," I tell him.

"You don't see *my* name in the paper."

"You wouldn't have time to be in the paper."

"Enough of this," Mr. Dan says. "The damage is done."

I sit fuming. Mr. Dan's seeming change of heart is disconcerting. Just how much of my phoning the press did involve ulterior motive? I wonder. The kids did not ask me to, though they reveled in the article, and a couple proudly told me that they had seen the news broadcast.

The real purpose of the publicity was not for the kids' ego. It was to light a fire under them, after the letter from the evaluators. Too, I figured our superintendent could use some favorable press. The state FPS program will pay the kids' way to Anchorage if we make the finals. But if we win the state finals, there is no funding available for going to nationals. The district will have to foot the bill, or else we can't attend.

Unable to hold back my anger, I lean toward Gerald and say in a low voice, "You brag about what a great basketball coach you were down in Seattle. How everyone called you 'Mr. Technical.' Yet what have you done here? Besides sit on your butt."

Gerald rises and makes a fist.

"I said let it go." Mr. Dan's voice is hard, his eyes like agate-eye marbles.

But I'm too angry to push away the pain this time. "You think Problem Solving's so simple?" I ask everyone. "I'll tell you what. I'll challenge four of the kids against four of you."

On Friday afternoon, the Problem Solvers take on the teachers. Unlike with the actual program, there is no preparatory research. The problem, submitted by the village council, turns out to be a real one: The council has just received word that the local Headstart Program might lose its federal funding. There is too much absenteeism among preschoolers the program serves. What can be done?

As usual, each team must identify twenty problems, decide on a central problem to examine, brainstorm twenty solutions to the central problem, analyze ten of the solutions for effectiveness, and write a final essay about what the analysis concludes is their best solution. Through the narrow window in the classroom doors, I watch Merle, Marshall, Boone, and Meredith—heads bent and backs hunched, the image of eager, serious negotiators. By contrast, Keenan, Lars, Lawrence, and Wymena—Gerald is too busy to play—spend most of the time arguing.

The next Monday, Bruce, who has scored the booklets, announces the winner.

The kids have beaten the teachers by fifty points.

Most of the teachers' solutions involve games and rewards designed to increase attendance. The kids, on the other hand, looked at possible root causes of the problem. They noted that, since Eskimo children are named for a recently deceased loved one, disciplining a child can be an affront to the dead. The result, they argued, is that children in the village are often spoiled. The team proposed a return to discipline similar to that in the old days: renew the elders' disciplinary council and reestablish the gravel ring where errant children were forced to exercise until exhausted. They also suggested developing a process in which elders, not just anyone, will award certificates to kids with excellent attendance.

"Doesn't prove anything," Wymena says after perusing the test booklets.

"You should never have let your teams stomp the Unalakleet kids," Mr. Dan tells me when we're alone. "Plus it didn't help that you turned down the superintendent's offer to teach there."

"What was I to do? Stick my nose in his ass? Is this the corporate world?"

"Whatever makes you think it isn't? Don't you know you signed away all idealism when you obtained your teaching license? Are you really so naïve? Didn't you know how political public school teaching can be?" Leaning forward, looking more like a father than a friend, he adds, "George, when it comes to most administrators, you're dealing with devils."

His words too soon prove prophetic. The Future Problem Solving Program's range of influence is wider than I had imagined. Two of the nation's top experts in teaching creative thinking in science have heard of the high school scores and want to meet me in Fairbanks, where they will guest-lecture at the university. For an entire afternoon we will exchange ideas. The National Science Foundation, which is sponsoring the experts' visit to Alaska, will pay all costs, even for my substitute.

I submit the request through Mr. Dan. An administrator with family ties to the Unalakleet coach phones back to deny the request. "We don't see what that has to do with education," he tells me.

Months later we will learn that he acted without asking the superintendent.

True to my promise to the kids, we do little research for the Greenhouse Effect practice problem. Rather, we review fundamentals. They need to know the structure behind communication so well that they will be like expert typists, unable consciously to name the location of the keys. That, I know, requires recitation.

"What are the five Ds of teaching?" I ask the kids.

"Drill, drill, drill, drill, drill!" they chant back.

"What are three Fs of real writing?"

"Focus, focus, focus!"

"What is the core of communication? Boone?"

"What because why."

"What are you going to do this weekend?"

"Hunt."

"What?"

"I'm going hunting."

"Why?"

"To get some ducks."

"Put it together with a *because*. Cause and effect. Cause and effect."

"I'm going hunting because I want to get some ducks."

"Focus!"

"I'm going duck hunting because my mother wants ducks for dinner."

"Focus farther!"

Exasperated: "I'm hunting pintails this weekend because my mother wants them for dinner with the Uponaks."

"How many elements in that sentence?"

"Three? 'I . . . hunting pintails this weekend . . . my mother wants them for dinner with the Uponaks.'"

"How many of the elements are focused?"

"Two? . . . 'hunting pintails' and 'dinner with the Uponaks'?"

"Does an off-island audience know where you live? Do they know the Uponaks? Do they care who the Uponaks are?"

He finally decides on, "I'm hunting pintails here on Saint Lawrence Island this weekend because my mother is making dinner for the family of Jettman Uponak, who helps my dad run the village store."

"What is the core of communication? Romie?"

"What because why!"

"What are you going to do this Friday night?"

"Play basketball."

"What will you do when you play basketball?"

"Score a lot of points."

"Use 'what-because-why.' "

After a couple of false starts, she says, "I want to score a lot of points against Savoonga this weekend because we want to win."

"Don't the Savoonga players already know you want to win? They're your audience. The people watching you aren't the audience. They're just spectators. Are you telling the Savoonga players anything they don't already know?"

I prod and probe, and she comes up with, "I'm going to drive the baseline at least six times during the game with Savoonga this weekend because it will open up Bunnie for a three-pointer."

"How many focused elements?"

"Two?. . . 'drive the baseline . . . the game with Savoonga this weekend' and 'open up Bunnie for a three pointer'?"

"Good, Romie! Now focus all three. Who are you? Who is the "I" in the sentence? What position do you play?"

"Point guard."

She is the top scorer in the district, an accomplishment that will propel the girls, despite their inexperience, to second place in the district tournament. And the boys will make the state finals, led by Boone's and Merle's finesse and Marshall's muscular rebounding.

"Now put your ideas together," I say, ready to write on the board.

After a couple of tries she comes up with, "The point guard, I'm going to drive the baseline during the game with Savoonga this weekend because it will open up Bunnie for a three-pointer."

"See?" I thump the board. "There's no difference between communication theory and what you do every day! No difference between writing and any other activity. Problem Solving isn't about learning to write. It's about learning to focus *any* task."

Then back to the basics: "What do all professionals have in common? Londa?"

"Precision."

"What produces precision? Bess?"

"The ability to focus."

"What do all successful hunters have in common? Merle?"

"The ability to focus."

"What is communication? Kasha?"

"The transference of information as precisely as possible."

"What is mathematics? Kasha again."

"The litmus of communication."

"What must a successful mathematician have? Bess?"

"Focus."

"What produces focus? Alvin?"

Bored: "Precision."

"What must successful artists have in order to draw or paint precisely, Alvin?"

Slumped over the table, he no longer doodles but instead effortlessly makes masterful drawings of animals. Bored by my constant questioning, he says, "Focus."

"What is more important, subject or style? Marshall?"

"Subject."

"What are the three steps to finding an original subject? Again, Marshall."

"Brainstorm for quantity not quality, grade for originality, then prioritize the 'A' ideas."

"Sounds like someone has been listening," I say. He smiles.

Then, to everyone: "Pretend that the Greenhouse Effect has occurred. Mali is a lush grassland. Your job is to identify twenty problems that may have resulted for Mali, and to solve one of those twenty ways. What must we do before we solve the problems?"

Everyone except Alvin yells, "Understand the scenario! *Then* identify the problems!"

"Okay, let's look at the problem. Where's Mali? Boone?"

"Western Africa. Sub-Sahara. Neighbors are"—after a moment's reflection—"Mauritania, Algeria, um, Niger. Cattle, I think. Moslem nation."

As usual, his memory stuns me. It has been a year since he was in geography.

"Okay," I say. "Just like when you're out hunting. Don't be like Ben Franklin, 'Try and try again.' Be Daniel Boone: 'Be sure you're right, then go ahead.'" We have gone over these ideas so many times that the kids mouth my phrases, mocking me. "Analyze. *Then* act. Let's start with a business problem."

Business is Meredith's area of responsibility on her team. For a long time her gaze goes blank. Silence seizes the room. Everyone is aware that not answering will mean more drill.

"An undersupported infrastructure may be a problem for Mali," she says, "because . . . because the industrialized world may give the country tools and technology it can't really use."

I smile inwardly at her ability to plug almost any problem into our "what, may be a problem because why" structure. She truly is becoming expert.

"Technology such as?"

Meredith lifts her head as if to speak, but with a finger against my lips I indicate that I want someone else to answer.

More awkward silence.

"Like having computers for calculating cattle production," Alvin says at last. "Pretty silly, if there's no electricity to run them."

"Good, Alvin." To the high school team: "Same scenario. Give me a religion problem."

"The Greenhouse Effect may result in adverse reactions from Moslems because . . . " Merle says, but looks stumped.

"Turn it around," I tell him. "Follow the format we've developed."

He jots down some ideas and says, "Adverse reactions from Moslems may be a problem if . . . if the Greenhouse Effect turns Mali into a grassland paradise because . . . because Moslems . . . some Moslems . . . believe that suffering is God's will."

I have no idea if his interpretation of Islam is correct, but he is deeply interested in religion, so I trust his judgment. I give him a thumbs up and dismiss the class early.

As the door shuts, I sit down, tired but satisfied, feeling that this day I have lived up to one of my beliefs. *Teaching is technique, not charisma: we are educators, not entertainers.*

29

The last day of December, all the high school kids gather in the gym, as they do once every month, for the awards assembly—for the farce.

So many faculty fear disappointing students that each kid ends up with several Certificates of Achievement. There seems to be little room for anything except success in contemporary education, as if no one fails in the real world. The trashcan outside the gym ends up with most of the certificates.

This day I type up nothing. Instead, I will give out an Oscar. To Londa.

I wish to award her dogged determination. She reads twice as much as any of her teammates—Merle, Marshall, or Boone—and spends three times longer writing up ideas. During brainstorming sessions, she appears to cower before their intellects and unintentional sexism, but she comes in each day after school to ask for more homework.

For the Oscar, I paint light bulbs golden, but each time I plug one in, it smolders and pops. I settle for a dead golden bulb with a toilet paper roll base wrapped in aluminum foil. I record thirty seconds of Beethoven and arm myself with the largest flashlight I can find, to wave when Londa comes forward to accept her trophy, blushing and waving to the audience of forty kids seated on three bleachers.

She does not show up.

"Is Londa ill?" I ask around. No one knows.

The assembly ends at lunch. Disappointed, I return to my room. Festus comes in to tell me that he has evidence of Communist activity: someone has been going in and out of the duplex basement late at night. Excited, he leaves to arrest whomever.

Next, Londa enters. Her hair is disheveled, her clothes obviously slept in. Her mascara is smeared; puffy bags accent hollow eyes. Her lips and hands tremble. She sits down. "Mr. G. . . ." Her eyes brim.

I kneel beside her. "Tell me. What is it?"

At first she shakes her head, but then she puts her head in her hands and, crying, says between sobs, "I tried . . . I tried to kill myself. Pills. They . . . pumped my stomach. At the clinic."

Then she blurts, "I'm terrible at Problem Solving! I can't keep up with the boys!"

Fear makes me flush. "You took pills because of Problem Solving?"

She grabs the Kleenex box from my desk, blows, wipes, reaches for more tissue. "Because of my boyfriend. The way he treats me. You don't understand. No one does."

Then she says, "I have to make it to the finals! I have to! But no matter how hard I study, during tests I freeze up. Merle carried me on the prison problem. It was all Merle! If I freeze up on the qualifying problem we won't make state. It'll be my fault!"

"We can play a three-person team." My eyes search hers out. "You don't need to do Problem Solving if it's not good for you."

"Don't you understand anything? Don't you know why I'm in Problem Solving?" She is crying again. "I want to go to Anchorage to see my mom, Mr. G." She puts her head in her hands, her whole body shaking. "I want to see my mom."

"We'll get you there," I promise her, a hand on her shoulder. "You can go as an alternate."

In the end, we agree to what proves a masterful strategy. In exchange for the free trip, she will study even harder than before. Since Merle, Marshall, and Boone hate to be outdone in anything, they too will work harder.

Two weeks later, the teams play the Greenhouse Effect problem. The answers are good but not great, as everyone expected. This one, I remind the kids, really is just for practice.

In a high school faculty meeting that afternoon, without thinking through the possible consequences I announce that the teams have sent in their second problem for the year. Gerald and Lars start in again. The kids have an unfair advantage, Gerald insists. "He's a professional science fiction writer," he says. "It is *Future* Problem Solving, after all," Lars adds.

Mr. Dan changes the subject. Later, when I tell Mary what happened, she says to forget about the program's detractors. But I can't seem to let it go.

That night I am so exhausted I cannot sleep. When I wake up I have trouble lifting my arms. Mary wants me to fly to Nome to see a doctor, but I am sure that the feeling of utter inertia will pass, though I am more tired than I remember being any time the year before. I choose to walk to school, rather than ride the snowmachine, hoping that some exercise will *exorcise* whatever has its hold on me.

As I near the school, I make a decision that nearly derails the kids' efforts. It seems logical at the time. Only years later will I realize how much a product of utter physical and emotional exhaustion it really was.

"I'm not going to coach you on the state qualifying problem," I tell the junior high and high school teams.

They stare at me, dumbfounded, thinking I'm joking.

"Oh, maaaan!" Marshall says, after a moment.

"Is Bruce going to be our coach this time?" Kasha asks hopefully.

"I will coach the elementary team. The rest of you won't have a coach."

"The other teams have coaches," Marshall says.

"We'll never make state," Londa says.

"It's not fair," Marshall says.

"What's unfair," I say, handing out more readings, which they accept without so much as a glance at the papers, "is if you make state and people say it was all the coach's doing. If you win state, some will say that anyway. But at least you will know you got there without my help."

"Lawrence coaches us in wrestling," Boone says.

"Keenan and Wymena coach us in basketball," Romie says.

"I'll keep giving you resources, but making the finals is up to you. If you make state, I don't want you ever to doubt that it was your brains and hard work that got you there."

"How will anyone know that you didn't coach us?" Merle asks.

"You'll know," I tell them.

"But what if we *want* you to coach?" Romie asks.

"Then make the finals."

Meredith crosses her arms, her body stiffening. "This is all Gerald's fault."

I ignore them and check my watch. "You have a teleconference with George Harper in eight minutes. Do you all have questions identified that you want to ask him?"

Grumbling, the kids get out their questions from their notebooks. Marshall's papers as usual are in such disarray that they look pulled from a trashcan. I remind them to go over their questions with their team members, so they change places until each team is gathered around a table, talking low and occasionally glancing at me in disbelief.

Despite my announcement, they know that a speaker-phone session with George Harper is not to be missed, so soon each team gets down to the task of prioritizing what questions they wish to ask. This is the second time they have interviewed him via phone—the first time was on the prison problem—and their respect for this man they have never met is obvious. A science writer living in Tacoma, Washington, he has no college degree, yet he has lectured in universities on subjects ranging from physics to philosophy. But what most fascinates the kids is that he was a WWII commando and once killed a headhunter in a knife fight while attempting to canoe up the Orinoco River and portage to descend the Amazon.

I hook up the convener and place it on a middle table, dial his number and, after some initial static, his voice comes through. "Hi kids!" he says.

"Hi George!" they reply almost in unison.

I head to the office. What information they derive from his wonderful intellect must be their decision, now that they are on their own. Allana, the gifted typing student I had taught the year before, has this year assumed a lot of the school's secretarial duties. She looks up from her typewriter as I watch a plane that, because of the winds, is trying to take off across the tiny runway instead of down it.

I stifle an urge to rush back into the classroom and countermand my announcement about not coaching. Maybe the kids *do* have an unfair advantage, I decide, given my background as a writer and science magazine editor. But don't most high schools look for coaches with excellent sports backgrounds? Are athletics and academics really so different?

Still, I can't seem to bring myself to go back in there and rescind my decision.

"There's got to be something more to life than typing," Allana says, watching the plane with yearning, as if she wishes she were on it.

"Aren't you planning on being the school secretary after you graduate?"

She sighs and turns back to her work. I go into the gym to shoot some hoops. On the hour, I return to the class and ask how the interview went. Those who answer at all do so in grunts and monosyllables. I give each group a famine problem to scrimmage and leave the room.

When I return twenty minutes later, the junior high team has produced eight answers, the high school team ten; usually they would have five times that. I know I should be angry at myself, not them, but instead I storm from the room. Two or three minutes later I slam back through the door and stack three six-packs of pop on a table, go back to the janitor's closet for two more, which I also deliver to the classroom, then rummage through my desk for another practice scenario to be scrimmaged, and hand out a copy to each team. "You have twenty minutes! If the bell rings, keep working! If you have less than thirty problem ideas when I come back, then your team goes thirsty. Got it? Thirty . . . or thirsty."

I return to the gym and, after the end-of-the-day bell rings, I watch kids shoot baskets. I glance at my watch. When twenty minutes are up, I enter the classroom.

The junior high team has eighty-seven answers, the high school team has eighty-nine.

As I pass out pop—two cans to each high school student, one can to each member of the junior high team—Allana comes in and looks around shyly.

"Can I join?" she asks.

The kids look at one another. Merle, Marshall, and Boone glance up at me, questions in their eyes. I know what they are thinking: if Allana joins, whose place will she take on the high school team?

Londa looks up at me with eyes that beg me to replace her on the team.

"It takes months to learn the process," I tell Allana. "If you really intend to join, you won't be an alternate. To earn a trip to Anchorage, you'll have to be ready to play the state-qualifying problem in less than a month. Mess up, and no one goes."

She reflects for a moment, and sits down, determination in her eyes.

Merle slides her a can of pop. "Have a drink. You'll need it."

Barbie and books, Gretchen tells herself over and over, willing her resolve to surface, as the other third and fourth graders file from her classroom. *Barbie and books, Barbie and books.*

Each day after school she must choose between helping in her mom's classroom or running home amid taunts. It's bad enough that Mom selected *Gretchen the Witch* as the class's supplemental reading the year before. Or that Mr. Dan suggested that she skip second grade, so she is now the youngest and smallest student in the third/fourth grade classroom. Or that the Yupik instructor mocks her because, unlike Meredith, she cannot speak the language.

Worst of all, this year her class is dismissed out the back door. With its long hallway and its abrupt turn down a short flight of stairs, it forms a tunnel secluded from the rest of the school. There, most days, a gauntlet of kids awaits.

"Gretchen the witch! Gretchen the bitch!"

"White trash! White trash!"

"Get her!"

Even on the best days, when the other kids aren't there, she flings herself down the stairs, hoping someone is not holding the door shut, blocking her exit as they sometimes do, and runs past the playground, which often empties in pursuit. She stumbles over snow mounds and lurches into her house.

She huddles in the corner beside her bed, Barbie next to her, books surrounding her. After her heart slows, and on days when kids do not beat on the walls, she reads to Barbie. Sometimes she sticks her head out the door, checks the area, and runs to the next house, where nice Mr. Russell, who carves ivory, lets her play with Bosco, his huge black lab.

Her three Bs, as she calls them: *books, Barbie, Bosco.* They comfort her.

Meredith has warned her against telling Mom and Dad about what goes on at school, what really goes on, lest the two girls be sent to live with their aunt, or Mom and Dad quit and lose their licenses. The kids have stopped picking on Meredith, who has begun punching them back or telling them off in Yupik.

Now their anger is directed at the smaller sister.

Sometimes, Gretchen thinks, Meredith does not understand anything at all.

30

The weeks fly by, during which the junior high and senior high teams struggle with articles and videos on famine. I continue to help the three sixth graders, but it's getting harder and harder to teach, due to my continual exhaustion. I just need to get through the school year, I tell myself. Wasn't that supposed to be the best part of teaching—having summers off?

In a late February faculty meeting, Mr. Dan announces that for the next two weeks we will spend each afternoon preparing the kids for the CAT, the once-a-year achievement tests.

"You mean teach to the tests," Gerald says, sitting back smugly.

Mr. Dan's gaze snaps around. "I don't mean that at all."

To the rest of us he says, "Starting Wednesday, we'll cancel the regular classes and have the kids do a round robin, moving among science, math, reading, and English. You've all been teaching the scope and sequence, so this will be," he looks at Gerald, "a review."

"Right." The special ed teacher makes a little circle with an uplifted index finger.

"Keenan, you and Lawrence split up the math and science curriculum," Mr. Dan goes on. "There's no way that Bruce can handle all the language arts, so he will take the reading and also review English skills with the top kids. And George, you'll review writing and grammar with the low kids. Lars, you'll do refreshments. We're going to give the kids lots of wholesome snacks. Gerald, you'll take spelling."

"Spelling?"

"You do know how to teach spelling, don't you?"

"Of course I know how to teach spelling!"

"Then spelling it is."

Scowling, Gerald breaks a pencil between his fingers and shoots each half at the trashcan.

"We're under the gun in terms of time," Mr. Dan says. "As you know, at the end of next week, the wrestlers and cheerleaders leave for the tournament in Unalakleet. They return that Sunday, and the CAT starts the next day."

"The following Thursday, the Problem Solvers play the qualifying problem," I say.

"As if we cared," Gerald says.

"What if both teams make the finals?" Meredith asks that night, as I lie on the ratty couch we have scrounged for the year. "Will the district pay Londa's way to Anchorage?"

"Not with Allana on the team. They only pay for four."

"Londa can go in my place, Dad."

"Don't be ridiculous."

She plops down beside me. "Didn't you say that the district would probably send a short-story winner to the awards banquet? What if I won?"

"Your mom and I have decided to pay Londa's way, if the team makes it."

"But if I won the story competition, could a fifth person go from my team?"

"I think that's right."

"Okay, Dad! I'll write a story!"

She disappears into the girls' bedroom.

"That's all we need in this house," Mary says, frowning. "Another writer."

But she need not have worried. Meredith's story, about a basketball-playing Eskimo boy who helps bring about world peace, is terrible. When I try to help her, our mutual frustration causes her to run into her bedroom and burst into tears. I end up standing before her curtain, angry at her and even angrier at myself.

Two days later, kids troop into my classroom for grammar cramming.

Having taught grammar for several years before coming to Gambell, I am comfortable enough with the subject that I avoid the rules and especially all the insipid nomenclature—object, objective case, subjunctive—and show Lobert and the others simple tricks to take them through the test. "For example, most people don't know when to use 'who' and 'whom.' Just remember M&Ms," I say, passing out candy. "'Whom' ends in 'm,' and so does 'him.' If you can say the sentence and use 'him,' the answer will be 'whom.' If you can use 'he,' the answer will be 'who.' If either fits, the answer usually is 'who.'

"For example, if the test asks, 'Who or Whom is getting married?' we could say, 'He is getting married.' The answer therefore is 'Who.' Or if the test says, 'Who or Whom is the package for?' we could say, 'The package is for him.' Therefore, the answer is 'Whom.' Him: Whom. M and M. Finally, if the test says, 'Pass the ball to whoever or whomever is the best shot,' then the answer is 'whoever,' because 'he' and 'him' both fit: 'Pass the ball to him' and 'He is the best shot.'"

We practice several examples, with mixed success, and move on to the next concept, that of grammar courtesy. "If there are two people, and you're one of them, always put yourself last," I tell them, and hold up little red and blue Nerf balls to indicate people. "You don't say, 'The book belongs to me and Bob,' because your friend is always more important, so the *I* or *me* always goes last."

I look at the kids, and everything seems blurry. I suddenly feel so weak that to keep from falling down, I have to hold onto the little teacher's podium that sits atop a table at the front of the room. I continue talking but feel so disembodied that the words seem to come from outside myself.

"Next, pretend that Bob leaves," I manage to say, putting the ball marked "Bob" behind my back. "You're by yourself. You wouldn't say, 'The book belongs to I,' so the answer is, 'The book belongs to Bob and me.'"

"You have a friend named Bob?" Chip asks me, clearly confused.

Darrel blows his nose in a dollar bill and tries to pass it to the next table.

I lean on the podium, feeling too tired to speak. I have Festus hand out photocopied grammar problems to be worked.

Moments later Dale raises his hand. "I can't work this one," he says. "I can't work number five. It has a tree in it. I've never seen a tree."

"Have too," Chip says.

"Only on TV," Dale says, pouting.

"This one has a car in it," Lobert points at another example. "You can't grammar a car."

When Festus looks at him as if for guidance, Lobert tells him in a tone of authority, "You can't grammar a car."

31

During lunch I climb into the school attic and lie down on the plywood floor of the storeroom. There, on a lower bookshelf, I find *Foxfire* books.

The real books of that famous series are compilations of essays on local crafts, written by kids from Appalachia. These are a couple dozen portfolios bound in construction paper and held together by ribbons. Perusing them, I see that every English teacher here until Bruce has tried the same thing—among villagers who fear calling attention to their culture, lest the world denounce them for hunting whales and walruses.

As Greenpeace has done. And as Cousteau did, when the islanders permitted him to film a walrus hunt so they could show its economic and spiritual value. He "rescued" a walrus pup and, in the film, called the Eskimos murderers.

Each year's Saint Lawrence Island *Foxfire* effort sits here gathering dust. Not that my teaching of English last year had been much better. Despite my disdain for the practice, I had used the "proven" method of having kids free-write for twenty minutes at a session, on whatever subject came to mind. And if nothing came to mind? Our composition textbook told them to write "I can't think of anything" until an idea took hold.

Each time, Chip and Dale wrote "I can't think of anything" the entire session. The rest wrote vacuous prose about basketball or boating. Or wrote nothing.

It was not just because of the exhaustion that I have taught only social studies and Problem Solving this year.

I climb down the ladder and get ready for the next session. Then Lobert walks into my class carrying one of the tiny, exquisite ivory swans his father carves—a man who has no fingers, only thumbs—and I remember what Mr. Dan had told me about the elder who insisted that education is like a barbell.

I rush to the sports closet in the gym and return lugging a weight set.

After I let the kids practice curls for several minutes, I ask them, "How would you like to do anything better?"

"Like what?" Lobert asks, eyeing his biceps as he works the weight.

"Anything."

"Whaling?" Chip asks eagerly. For reasons I have never understood, he is not allowed out in the boats.

"Or carving," I say.

"You know about those?" Dale asks.

"I know about everything," I tell them.

"Cool," Chip says.

Lobert looks at me appreciatively as he puts down the weight.

Fine-tuning "what because why" in Problem Solving has taught me that subjects consist of relationships. In workable subjects, as in clearly defined real-life relationships, there are two variables. *Like the ends of a barbell,* it has today occurred to me.

With a little manipulating, I get Lobert to admit what I already know—that he wants to be an ivory carver.

"I want to be a carver," he repeats as I write it on the board.

"Why?" I ask him.

"Because . . . because I like it?"

I write that as well. Then I show the class that *like* in the second half of the sentence is already implied by *want.* "And that's repeating yourself," I tell them, "which you don't want to do. What Lobert has ended up saying is, 'I like being a carver because I like it.' The *'why'* statement," I underline the second half on the board, "can't repeat the *'what'* statement, the first part."

Taking the funnel from my desk drawer, I quickly teach them about funneling, all the while wondering why I have never used Problem Solving techniques in *all* my classes. Was it elitist not to have thought of applying the techniques to goal-setting?

Together we focus each element in the sentence.

"You see?" I ask.

"Lobert Ayaatana wants to be a famous ivory swan carver because his father is," the board now says.

I divide the board into three columns, label them "Lobert," "swan carver," and "father," and then we list information under each. "Just like a grocery list your moms probably give you," I tell them.

Under "Lobert" we list what carving tools and training Lobert already has and how much money he will need to support himself and a family. For "swan-carver" we brainstorm where and how he can sell ivory swans, and under "father" we discuss how he can use his father's influence to create markets. Then, with numbers, we prioritize the information in each column, and the kids get to work writing up the result. Even Festus burrows in, his tongue sticking from the side of his mouth as he concentrates.

When they finish, I have the kids give me sentences from the essays they have created, and together we write up a master essay on the board. Afterward, they look at the result in awe. Never before have they composed something so long or so meaningful to their lives outside the classroom.

"Do me next!" Dale says, waving. "Goal me too!"

"A carving isn't done until it's inked," I remind them, for the moment too exultant to feel ill. "So before we do your own goals, we'll make this essay pretty. We'll work on whatever grammar we need to help readers understand it."

To my surprise, no one groans.

The next day, I sit through a faculty meeting Mr. Dan has abruptly called after his return from an emergency meeting in Unalakleet.

"The Unalakleet water system has frozen," he tells us, "and maintenance says that there's no thawing it soon. I therefore offered Gambell as the tournament site. Wrestling and cheerleading teams from sixteen villages will be coming here. We have twenty-four hours to prepare. Lawrence and Linda will be busy getting the wrestlers and cheerleaders ready, so it's up to the rest of us."

Everyone asks questions, for the CAT tests are to begin on Monday, and the kids need to be focused, not exhausted from a sports festival. I do not voice my concern. I anticipated losing

Garnet and Meredith, who are cheerleaders, and Boone, a talented wrestler, for the weekend.

Now, just before the state qualifying problem, I will lose them all.

For generations, Siberian men in bulky sealskin pants and anoraks of walrus gut would beach their skin boats and steal onto the island, seeking larders of seal and walrus, greens refrigerated in permafrost caches, and, above all, women and children to enslave. They would be met by single-minded men armored in baleen and in sealskin so hardened by fire that an arrow could not pierce it—men who knew that they dare not lose.

Finally, perhaps worn out by centuries of killing, the Siberians and islanders agreed to meet for shows of physical strength instead of warring prowess. The islanders trained at every extra moment for the annual event, running up and down the mountain all day and carrying huge rocks great distances. They would compete in long-distance running; the one-foot and two-foot high kick; the ear pull, a loop of sinew stretched between the two straining men; and the seal hop, seeing how far a man can travel with only knuckles and toes touching the ground. Losing was not an option, for the Siberians might not think the islanders formidable foes, and the raiding might again begin.

Of all competitions, it was at wrestling that the islanders truly excelled. Determination, diet, and rowing gave them almost superhuman upper-body strength. They wrestled year-round. Grainy film footage by early anthropologists shows them stripped to the waist, practicing moves at twenty-below.

Such is the heritage that the island students bring to wrestling tournaments, so when word of the tournament passes through the village, all interest in the CAT stops. The school becomes a frenzy that seems to move around me in a sweaty fog. I stumble through the day in a fugue.

When I oversee the move of the wrestling mat down through the emergency door that connects the attic to the gym's upper reaches, a wrestler struggling with the huge thing accuses me of costing the school money for a second mat. His father has told him the funds went to the two Problem Solving trips last year. I don't feel up to explaining that academic and athletic funding come from different pots. He would not believe me anyway.

For the weekend I am assigned to making and selling popcorn in the home ec room. By the first match, Festus and I have popped corn for a hundred bags. They are gone in half an hour, some kids arriving with rolls of bills as big as my fist, others doling out pennies and dimes. "Depends on whether a village has access to ivory," Mr. Dan says.

A couple hours later, my efficient apprentice abandons me. Realizing that some wrestlers are from Little Diomede Island, three miles from Soviet territory, Festus puts down his apron and heads home to find his badge and handcuffs, readying to arrest Communists.

After each match, people surge in for popcorn. Then the door slams shut, and I am left alone with oily smoke and the constant popping, the corn spilling out like laughter from beneath the lid of the machine's little bucket.

On the other side of the wall, people yell and cheer. When they start stomping their feet in unison so hard that the walls reverberate, I know that Boone is tearing up an opponent twenty or thirty pounds above his weight. I feel a strange, searing pain, and I look down to see my forearms have formed charley horse knots the size and color of purple eggs. My skin is slicked with oil and sweat. And in the mirror above the sink, I notice that my face is covered with red rash. I stand in my stupid apron, wondering what it must be like to be Lawrence out there . . . what being a *real* coach must be like.

part 4

◄ Saint Lawrence Island Yupik child in parka. *Photo by John Wensley.*

32

"We can kiss good-bye any hope of good CAT scores," Lawrence tells me.

I had taken the Sunday evening flight to Nome to see a doctor, but weather delays kept the planes grounded until Tuesday morning. The doctor has given me pills to help me sleep, plus prednisone for the flu and Xanax for muscle spasms, so I am feeling better. But the students aren't.

Someone in the tournament brought in a flu bug, and now I am wondering if it was me. It was a bunch of very sick kids, Lawrence says, who tried to take the CAT. Knowing how much the tests mean to funding and to school pride, they showed up at school flu and all.

"Bless their hearts, they answered as many questions as possible and put their heads down," he says, his huge body showing his deeply felt emotion.

As ineffective as the Tuesday night's practice turns out, those Problem Solvers who are not sick might as well be. When I finally coax them into talking, they grouse about my only coaching the elementary team. Alvin, though, summarizes what really bothers them.

"Finding problems isn't hard for famine," he says. "Even figuring out unique ones isn't that bad. Thinking up original *solutions* without your help, that's what's tough."

The others second him.

"But you *have* unique ideas!" I pull down the world map. "Here's Ethiopia. In all probability that's where the test question will be set. Now, what's one problem that may result from the famine there?"

"Loss of culture," Kasha says, without her usual enthusiasm.

"Give me a solution to loss of culture from famine," I say.

She looks at me, unsure of herself.

"Give me a solution to loss of culture *anywhere,*" I tell her.

"Dance." She loves to Eskimo dance. "Have a dance."

"What besides people can dance?"

"Animals," Alvin says. "Some of them, anyway."

"Plants dance," Merle says. "When the wind blows."

"Thoughts dance around in our minds," Romie says.

"Dust!" Kasha says.

"Sunbeams!"

"Clouds!"

I gaze out the window, up into the darkness. "What else dances in the sky?"

"Um . . . birds?" Romie asks.

"Helicopters!" Kasha says. Everyone looks at her. She pouts toward them and shrugs as if to slough off their unvoiced criticism.

"Starlight!" Merle says, waving his hands as if to pull everyone back on track.

"The aurora!" Kasha says.

All look toward the window as if expecting the Northern Lights, rare in this part of Alaska, to be bathing the village in green-gold.

"What if the famine happened here?" I ask. "You all know that there were famines here in the old days. Let's say you survived the famine and wanted the aurora to Eskimo-dance to celebrate your culture. How could you do that?"

They mull the possibility, and I wonder if I've lost them.

Then Alvin says, with his usual lack of enthusiasm as if the rest of us are too short-sighted to see the obvious, "Shoot argon lasers at the aurora. From satellites. Tuned to the aurora's frequency."

"But the problem involves a famine in Africa!" Marshall says. "Stupid, man."

I go to my desk and flip him the smelly sock package. Wrapped in a Ziploc, the sock stays for a night with whoever criticizes someone else's ideas. He catches the package with an embarrassed look and sticks it under his table.

"Beam down a transmission," Alvin says. "Show Africans how Eskimos do it."

"MTV!" Kasha says, clapping her hands. "We could do it on MTV!"

Following Alvin's lead, I draw the aurora and the Earth on the board and show satellites and the transmission as best I can. From my desk I take out our funnel. "Funnel down ideas," I remind them. "Make the ideas specific. That gives you the imaginative ones. Original thinking is precise thinking."

Setting down the funnel, I add, "You have an advantage over other teams. You have your culture. Apply ideas from your background. No other team can do that—not Eskimo background, anyway. You'll be the only Eskimos at state."

"You think we'll make it?" Romie asks.

"If you don't keep getting down on yourselves."

The kids hunker down, thinking about my words, looking at each other.

"How long is practice going to be?" Marshall asks at last, picking up his basketball. But he appears to be speaking more to break the silence than from any desire to leave the room.

"That's up to you." I gaze around the room. "All of you."

"Two hours," Kasha says.

"Three," Boone says. He looks with confidence toward Merle.

"Three hours," Merle says.

Marshall nods.

As I exit, Kasha pushes past me, hurrying toward the bathroom.

Halfway down the hall she turns my way. "I joined Problem Solving because I wanted a trophy. Next, I played for the trip to Anchorage. Now, I play for the ideas."

She enters the bathroom. I know that, unlike Puffin, she soon will be out again.

The next afternoon, Boone sets down his Dremel tool on the shop workbench. Trying to control a rising self-anger, he stares at the lump of ivory in his hand. Lump. That's how he thinks of what he has been trying to carve. It is supposed to be an owl, but it looks more like some weird petrified marshmallow.

The other students work diligently, some already producing carvings that are certain to sell, often for excellent prices, in the Anchorage gift shops. Even the girls in the class are better carvers than he is. He cannot seem to focus—to see the animal in the ivory, as he has been taught to do, his task but to free the carving from its unworked medium.

What is frustrating is that he does so well at Problem Solving, but when it comes to translating that mental ability into craftsmanship, he cannot seem to make his hands do his mind's bidding. He tosses the ivory onto the table. It rolls with a clatter up beside the Dremel tool.

Conrad, the carving instructor and assistant shop teacher, walks over and puts a hand on Boone's shoulder. He picks up the ivory and quietly puts it down again. Boone is afraid to look up at him, lest he see any hint of disappointment in Conrad's eyes.

Conrad is one of the most respected elders in the village, a man of great knowledge and almost infinite patience and caring. Boone knows that the elder will never voice disapproval, but on the other hand he will not give undeserved praise. Ivory carving is by far the village's most important income source, so it is imperative that the next generation of carvers be able to compete with the best in the state.

"I'm not worried about you, Boone," Conrad says softly. "You're going to college and eventually will become a high school history and P.E. teacher. We all know that. All of our friends here need to learn to carve"—he habitually refers to all young villagers as *our friends*—"but for you there's another destiny. Isn't that what really matters—that you travel your own road?"

That afternoon as he trudges home through the snow, Boone reflects on Conrad's words. *Hands, head,* he thinks. When he was in Anchorage, without losing a single player he had broken the record for the most points ever scored on the Chuck E. Cheese's video game console. He had attributed it to dexterity, but all the while he had known it was mental dexterity, and not a manual one, that had garnered him the position at the top of the Pac-Man machine's champions.

He walks over to Kasha's house. They have been friends all their lives, but only lately has he truly begun noticing her growing beauty and obvious intelligence. He finds Romie and Kasha chatting about Problem Solving as Kasha cooks dinner—as usual, not just best friends but also study partners.

He samples the stew. Kasha's eyes go downcast, her face glowing with delight, when he says how good it tastes. Romie glances from Kasha to Boone, and beams, then quickly sobers when she realizes that Boone has seen her happiness at his interest in Kasha. Romie also looks down.

After a moment Kasha returns to stirring the stew. "Romie and I have been talking about who should play on the team and who should be alternate," she says.

"If we make state," Romie says.

"You will," Boone says. "I know you will."

"Yes," Kasha says. "We will."

This time, when their eyes meet she does not look away. Kasha's eyes are clear and moist and calm, and for the first time in Boone's life, looking at her, he feels his heart skip a beat.

"Meredith and Alvin," Kasha says, in a voice that seems somehow separated from Boone's focus. "They definitely should play. And Bess, too, I think. If it's between Romie and me for the other spot, then I'll play in the individual competition instead of on the team."

"My brother wants me to play on the team rather than in the individual competition," Romie adds.

Her brother, Boone knows, has taken intense interest in Romie's progress in Problem Solving. It's one of the things he talks to her about when he writes or calls from prison. In a way, she is playing as much for him as for herself.

"I guess who plays will finally be up to George," Boone says.

But he isn't thinking about George. Nor about Problem Solving or about ivory carving. He cannot take his eyes off Kasha.

The door opens, and Kasha's mother, Lydia, enters. She smiles at Boone and indicates for the girls to come help with the walruses that the boats have brought in. There is meat to cut up and hides to clean. Soon the girls will be seated as Lydia makes expert cuts on the animal with the *ulaaq*. Kasha and Romie will watch silently, not even, as the rules of subsistence dictate, allowed to ask questions.

Boone exits, filled with a strange, profound happiness as he leaves the women to their work.

Word comes from the Problem Solving national office that the two-hour test has been deemed too stressful for elementary school kids. All elementary division teams will play the state-qualifying problem in one-hour blocks on successive days rather than in the usual two-hour block.

I have insisted that the junior high and high school teams work on Problem Solving by themselves, but, because of their age, I am continuing to coach the elementary kids. As soon as Garnet and Groper have recovered from the flu, we have our first practice.

"Name ten transportation problems regarding famine relief in Ethiopia," I tell them.

After the girls huddle for a couple of minutes, Summer rattles off, "Problems with trucks, busses, trains, planes, ships, boats, canoes, airplanes, helicopters, cars."

Canoe in Ethiopia? I don't comment on the possible irrelevance. "Now, *funnel.* Take a general idea and make it specific. Give me, for example, ten problems with trucks. If you can't think of a word for what you want to describe, then just write something close to what you want to say, and underline it."

After another huddle, Summer says, "Problems with maintenance, driving, maps, long hills, loading, unloading, boxes shifting, theft, overheating, getting stuck in the sand, flat tires, overinflated tires, Bedouins taking hostages, sabotage by the rebels in Eritrea, payment for drivers, animals in the road, kids in the road, broken headlights, broken taillights . . ."

Two years in Problem Solving *has* paid off. Nineteen ideas in under three minutes. "Now let's funnel one of the problems you just identified," I tell them. "Give me ten problems with truck maintenance. You have five minutes."

In two minutes they have a dozen ideas, including repeated ones. "Flat tires, overinflated tires, broken headlights, broken taillights, engines going dead on the climb from the sea to the plateau, can't see the driver behind you, some mechanics maybe only have metric tools and it's an American truck, sand in the <u>back thing,</u> radiator bursts, hose breaks, belt breaks, brake breaks."

After some discussion we clarify "engines going dead" to "Vapor locks MBAP on the climb from sea level to Ethiopia's 6,000-foot plateau" (we had earlier pored over a topographical map of Ethiopia). "Sand in the <u>back thing</u>" becomes "Sand in differentials MBAP for truck convoys involved in famine relief in Ethiopia."

But I am stumped by "can't see the driver behind you."

"Why is that a mechanical problem?" I ask.

The girls giggle. "Some trucks have steering wheels on the wrong side!" Groper says.

American trucks and British Commonwealth trucks, in the same convoy.

So obvious and yet to me, as an adult, so opaque.

Kids thinking and talking—and poised to play.

33

On the day of the junior high and high school test, and the elementary team's second day of testing, Bess is too sick to participate. Alvin, who hasn't prepared, fills in for her. Meredith plays despite a fever, as does Allana, my talented typist turned Problem Solver.

As if on cue, the power goes out.

The elementary team plays in Mr. Dan's apartment, where there is an emergency generator. The other two teams huddle in the gym, with only two small emergency lights high overhead.

When I call time after two hours, no one sticks around to shoot hoops. The kids are worn out from eyestrain.

I snowmachine to Mr. Dan's to pick up the elementary team's booklet, the first half of which they completed the day before. If these solutions are anywhere near as good as the previous day's problems, I figure the kids will easily have earned themselves a trip to the finals.

Mr. Dan shakes his head as he hands me this day's booklet.

Within is only: "Tools that are metric on one end and American on the other MBAS."

"When I came in here, they were seated in three different parts of the room, backs to each other, fuming," he tells me. "They said they got into an argument over the first solution. They must have sat here and sulked the whole time."

Angry and helpless, I lean my head against the wall. Another year wasted.

At least last year's coloring had been creative.

The snowmachine knows I am down in the dumps.

For four months, since the day of its dash to the sea, it has huddled outside my house, waiting for the right time to make another flight toward freedom.

Sensing that the throttle is sticking, perhaps frozen, I clip the safety coil to my sleeve before pulling the starter cord. On my first two yanks nothing happens. The engine does not turn over.

On the third pull, the machine roars into life and roars away, the coil ripping from my sleeve instead of detaching from the machine and stopping the engine.

It screams up the snowbank toward Mr. Dan's living room windows, then turns and roars along the snowbank, heading between the Old Village shacks, while I run behind it like a crazy person.

Again it turns, this time toward the skin boat racks.

It careens along the side of a berm, misses the racks, hits a piling sticking a couple feet above the snow, flies into the air, and smashes into a shack, each ski buried up to the cowling on a side of a stud, the back end of the machine digging itself into the drift, down and down until gravel mixes with the rooster tail of snow spewing out behind.

Merle, wearing a T-shirt, sweatpants, and tennis shoes, emerges from within the shack as I race to the machine.

He pushes the emergency stop. The machine shudders, coughs, and halts, the rooster tail dying. "You could have just knocked," he says with a grin.

"I had the emergency coil clipped to my sleeve," I tell him, feeling foolish. "In case the throttle was frozen open."

He tries pulling on the emergency cord. It does not free itself from the machine. Rusted.

He beckons me inside, the entrance a little door cut small to keep out polar bears. Within is a double bed made from an old mattress and a couple of sleeping bags, a black-and-white TV, a desk created from varnished plywood placed across Chevron gas-can crates, a chair with the ubiquitous *Gambell Schools* stenciled on it, and several pictures of Alaskan scenes cut from magazines and framed with wood trim. On the desk: a stack of lined paper, three sharpened pencils, a clock. All neatly arranged.

"My home away from Nome," he says. "I made this place so I can study, when I need time away from my brothers. The building belongs to the store, but no one minds if I use it."

He shows me the shack's other, considerably larger room, separated from his study by a plank door. Within stand a couple dozen tanks of propane gas looking like huge bowling pins, the snowmachine skis sticking on each side of one of them.

If the stud had broken, the snowmachine would have smashed into the tanks. The explosion could have killed Merle and me—who knows how many others.

Bunnie enters, looking fearfully at Merle. "You okay? Oh, hi George." She shyly smiles.

"George and his snowmachine were just remodeling the side of the house," Merle says.

"Well, that's good," she says, obviously confused as she peers back outside toward the machine.

Turning his attention back to me, Merle indicates a trashcan half-filled with wadded up notebook paper. "I've been trying to write a short story. For that new competition in Problem Solving this year. But nothing. No talent, I guess. Are writers just born?"

"All writers are born," I tell him.

"You know what I mean."

"Try to relax. Let the words flow."

"I've tried that. I've tried to psyche myself up. I've tried drawing pictures." From one of the crates he pulls a picture depicting a prison space station. The detail is startling. Like most of the villagers, he is an excellent artist. Not the talent that Alvin is, but certainly adept. "I try to write but I keep thinking, 'This isn't right, and that isn't right.' So I try rewriting. Then it doesn't seem right at all."

We exit the house and pull the snowmachine from the trough it dug. The cowling is crumpled. I feel more disgusted than angry. At my request Merle retrieves paper, duct tape, and a black marker, and I tape a FOR SALE sign on the thing.

"People here love to buy teachers' machines," Merle says. "Teachers take good care of them." He laughs. "Usually."

That evening, I climb the pressure ridge and watch the sunset turn the ice and sea pinkish orange. I think about Merle and Meredith, both unsuccessfully attempting stories for the competition, and I think about my own early efforts as a writer.

We graduate students brought in stories, all horribly flawed, to be workshopped by the rest in the class: the ignorant sharing ignorance. There was no instruction on how to write. Have I so easily forgotten my frustration? The year I taught high school in Washington, I used the workshop method I had learned. In the waning light I can see the face of the boy who had tried to hide his tears as my class critiqued his work. His distress had so wrung my heart that I swore never to teach fiction writing again.

His problem had been the same as mine when I began. He had no stories to tell. Lacking worldly experience, he had no world to give the audience.

Here, a wealth of background exists. Four thousand years of ancestral tales amid the rocks—the tundra and sea alive with the islanders' stories. Though I am directly descended from William Brewster, head of the *Mayflower,* the longevity of my American ancestry is but a footprint on a beach by comparison.

It begins to snow. Flakes, undulant in the breeze, drift down across the sun. I think about Meredith's tears as she struggled to compose her entry, and I think about the wadded-up papers in Merle's wastebasket: tears there too, different in kind if not in degree. Why, I ask myself, must fiction and frustration go hand-in-glove?

An idea comes to me. In an epiphany amid the flurries, I imagine another way stories might be created. I doubt that it will eradicate all the pain involved in trying to produce an art with words for brushstrokes, but it just might contain it.

34

When I announce a special evening workshop for anyone wishing to enter the Problem Solving short-story competition that is a corollary to the team competition, Meredith, Merle, and—to my delight—Bunnie show up.

"Storytelling and writing fiction are different mediums," I tell them. "The origins of storytelling are just that, storytelling—whereas the origins of fiction writing are in theater. A couple of nights ago I started thinking what life must have been like here not many years ago, when people would sit around the seal-oil lamps in the *nenglut*"—the sod houses. "I'll bet there were some gifted storytellers.

"It occurred to me that the two mediums could be combined, that stories could be developed orally—not like told stories, but incorporating the sensory details that make good fiction—and *then* written down. People think writing fiction is a solitary activity, but it's not. It's a social one. Professional writers don't write alone. They usually have friends look over their manuscripts, and they have agents and editors and copyeditors who offer ideas.

"You have ten days until the deadline. Instead of trying to find someplace quiet and writing the stories and then rewriting and rewriting, what if you tell the stories to each other, or tell them to me. Then we'll ask you questions about the different parts, like what's going on in a scene, what kind of furniture or trees there are, what the people are saying to each other, things like that. Tell the story and reshape it orally, and *after* you are satisfied with it, write it down. I'm not sure it will work, but it should reduce the frustration of so much rewriting."

They look at each other, and Bunnie nods, as if she has been chosen spokesperson.

I explain that, since everyone in the competition must write on one of three situations—the Ethiopian famine, a world peace conference, or the prison space station—then it would be a good idea to have a scientific or sociological gimmick to give the story punch and to set it apart from other entries. "Instead of trying to brainstorm an idea, why not use ideas that already exist?" I ask them. "But ideas that aren't well-known."

I bring out a stack of *Omni* and *Discover* magazines that were in the school storeroom, plus copies of *National Geographic* and a couple issues of *Western Wildlands,* the science magazine I edited for two years.

After perusing magazines and talking over possible ideas, Meredith settles on an *Omni* news report about an attempt to develop aneutronic energy through cold fusion, and Bunnie decides to build a story around a *Western Wildlands* article that describes how huge flocks of passerine birds are one cause of the African famine.

Wanting to set his story in the space-station prison, Merle has considered and discarded a dozen possibilities. "I'm going to use the article on galvanic skin-resistance tests," he says. "It got me originality points on the prison problem. I'll stay with a winner."

Each time we meet, Meredith and Bunnie have progressed with their stories, without writing anything down except for scribbled notes about what might be added or deleted. We role-play dialogue and discuss how to keep a story's setting and characters unified.

After reading a *National Geographic* article on the rebels of Eritrea, a country that borders Ethiopia, Bunnie composes a tale of a rebel who fights the Ethiopian army and the passerine birds that carry off what few crops he has left. Meredith transforms her story about the basketball player into one about a shy teenage Eskimo genius who uses dream transference to share his breakthrough regarding aneutronic energy.

Merle, strangely reserved, produces nothing.

The day of the deadline, Meredith and Bunnie's stories are ready for mailing. When I ask Merle if he intends to send in a manuscript, he says, "I'm thinking about it." I don't press him, figuring he does not want to tell me that he will not be submitting an entry.

At 3:45 he knocks on my door, lets himself in, and announces, "I'm ready to write."

"The post office closes as five. You'll never make the deadline."

He grins. "Herbie's my uncle. He said he'll stay open until six. But not a minute later."

"Can you have it typed up by then?"

The grin does not waver. "Don't you remember? I don't know how to type."

Teenagers. "Give me the pages," I tell him, resigned to my fate. "I'll type it."

"I don't have any pages."

"Are they in your study shack?"

He touches his temple. "They're in here."

Teenagers can drive you crazy, but Eskimo teenagers can make you chain yourself to the bed frame rather than ever leave the loony bin. For the next two hours he dictates as I type, and at 5:57 he runs out the door, jumps onto his snowmachine, and races toward the post office.

For two weeks we wait for word of how the teams fared on their state-qualifying test. The evaluators have agreed to phone us rather than rely on the mail, but no call comes. All of us become increasingly depressed.

Merle, Boone, and Marshall have a chance for two weeks of vocational education training in Unalakleet. When it becomes clear that we did not make the finals, they swallow their pride and board the plane.

The next week, Romie, Kasha, and Bess prepare to depart for the Future Homemakers Competition in Anchorage. Unlike Future Problem Solving, the FHA competition is open to anyone who can raise the money for the trip. The girls in home ec have been holding bake sales to pay their way.

The day before departure, Romie tells me, "I don't want to go to FHA."

"Me neither," Kasha says.

Bess, quiet as ever, nods to indicate that she too does not want to travel.

"I want to stay here and study Problem Solving," Romie says.

"There's nothing to study," I tell her. "Not this year, anyway. We would have heard by now if Gambell had made it."

"Maybe their phones are down," Kasha says. "Maybe our line isn't working."

"The phones are fine," I tell her. "Go have fun at the Future Homemaker Competition. Come back with a bunch of blue ribbons."

In the hope of making the finals, I had photocopied articles on nuclear waste disposal, the state topic. As they file out, the girls pick up several. "Just in case," Kasha says.

The Saturday after the girls leave, I borrow the school's snowmachine to haul water. It's an Alpine, a one-ski affair so enormous that I can place two thirty-gallon trashcans in the luggage rack.

As usual, the ice from the hose dripping outside the village laundry is a couple of feet thick and blued with veins, like geological striations. I fill the cans, use bungee cords to secure their lids, zip up my thick snowsuit, and mount the machine.

Partway home, I round a berm—like riding the crest of a wave— and the machine, its poor balance worsened by the water's weight, begins to tip. I leap off.

Not far enough.

The machine lands on top of me, only the handlebars keeping me from receiving its full weight. I'm not hurt, but I'm pinned. Night is coming on, and no one is around. After struggling unsuccessfully to free myself, I lie back, wondering whether machines know how much I hate them and whether the feeling is mutual.

Only one solution. Lighten the load. I zip up the snowsuit as tightly as I can, reach up and pull off the bungee cords, and let sixty gallons of water pour on top of me. At last I can crawl out from underneath.

The machine is too far over on its side for me to pick it up.

Now to walk the half mile home.

Thanks to the Refrigerwear snowsuit, I am dry and proud of myself. I had spotted the outfit, popular on North Slope oil rigs, on sale at the Anchorage Nordstrom's during the state finals the previous year. My size was not available, but the salesman assured me that the store would honor the sales price the next fall.

Traveling through Anchorage upon my return to Alaska that August, I headed to the store, only to be told I would have to pay the full—hefty—price, despite the promise. I said pleasantly, "Well, I'll just call Jim and ask him." The salesman, nonplussed, asked, "Jim who?" I smiled. "Jim Nordstrom. I grew up with him."

Five minutes later I was out the door, a sale-priced Refrigerwear snowsuit in hand.

My self-congratulation—we don't get many chances like that—does not last long.

Though the snowsuit keeps me dry, the water on the outside of the outfit begins to freeze and my progress slows, like a scene created in time-lapse. One moment I am headed home, smiling. The next I begin to crinkle.

By the time I reach the house, I am lumbering like Frankenstein, arms frozen away from my sides, the Refrigerwear's green vinyl icy-white. Unable to move my hands well, I kick the arctic entry door. Mary answers, Gretchen beside her.

"The Abdominal Snowman!" Gretchen cries out, eyes wide.

"*Abominable* Snowman," I correct.

"That's what I said. Abdominal!"

It takes pliers and considerable pulling on Mary's part to unzip me, but as I step from the prison she says, "The Iceman Cometh . . . and so does the mailman."

She hands me a Future Problem Solving Program envelope that Mr. Dan had brought over while I was getting water.

Seven junior high teams have made the finals. Gambell, sixth.

And the high school team, fourth out of four.

35

The next day I scurry around photocopying more of the reading material I had been collecting on nuclear waste disposal, the subject of the finals. As I pass out selections to the remaining Problem Solvers I swear them to secrecy about making state. I do not want word getting to the kids who are off-site, for I know the high school boys will not pay attention to their vocational education training, and the ninth-grade girls will not want to participate in FHA.

But word leaks out.

No sooner has Lars returned from the FHA competition the next week than he bursts into my room.

"What do you mean, trying to ruin those girls' Anchorage trip!"

Having no idea what he is talking about, I just look at him.

"After the FHA competition, I took the girls to a movie. I wanted to make things special for them, especially after having been cooped up in the university's dorms for two days. But I practically had to browbeat Bess to get her out of the car, and Romie and Kasha refused to come into the theater. They said they would rather sit in the car and study goddamn Problem Solving."

As he exits my room, he adds, "You're a joke, and so is your program."

Knowing there is no way he will believe that I had not tried to hurt FHA, I vow to venture from my classroom as little as possible for the remainder of the year. It's a recluse who works with the Problem Solvers throughout the weeks that follow.

When Boone, Merle, and Marshall return the next week, we hold our first real practice, a night session. "We have nine days until state," I tell the kids. "The other teams have been studying for five weeks."

I lecture on nuclear waste and radionuclides, the particles that can flow through the food chain. Trying to make the information as relevant as possible, I mention the nuclear reactors in Siberia, homeland to most Saint Lawrence Island migrating wildfowl.

Marshall slams a fist down against his desk, face blazing with anger.

"You mean our ducks eat that crap?"

"Calm down, man," Merle says.

"No, let him speak," I say. "I think he's onto something. Use that anger." I pull down a U.S. map and point to Florida. "Boone, what Indian tribe lives here?" I ask, testing his recall from material we had in U.S. history class.

"Seminoles."

"Can you memorize every tribe in the U.S. in a couple of days?"

"No problem. Just find me a list."

"For the state-qualifying problem, you focused on culture," I tell everyone, sitting down and thinking aloud. "Let's ratchet up that approach. The test situation at state will probably be set somewhere in the U.S., so Boone will memorize every Native American culture we can come up with. Romie, you do the same for the junior high team. No matter what problem they give us, try to apply as many problems to things that might affect indigenous peoples. Legal matters? Make them Native. Environmental problems? Show how the local Natives will be negatively affected. What other issues are heavily Native-oriented?"

"Hunting, man," Marshall says. "There's always hunting."

"Weather," Merle says. "We think about weather differently than white people do." When the others look at him quizzically, he adds with a grin, "They think about weather. We think about whether or not. Like, whether or not we're going hunting."

"What about business, Dad?" Meredith asks. "Wouldn't Native businesses be hurt by nuclear-waste leakage?"

"White people always seem to feel guilty about everything," Kasha says. "Isn't that a problem?"

"People getting angry," Marshall says. "Natives, I mean."

"Lawsuits," Bess says. "There would be lawsuits."

We look at The Silent One, stunned by her participation.

"I can file *two* lawsuits," Boone says. "I'm half Indian and half Eskimo. I get to be twice as angry."

Everyone laughs.

"Before, white people took our whales," Marshall says, after the laughter subsides. "Now they want to keep us from whaling."

"It seems like it's always them against us," Merle says. "The powerful against those of us struggling to keep subsistence alive."

"Like David and Goliath," Londa says. "Them against us."

The kids stare off into space, contemplating the discussion.

In a mix of awe and fear, Kasha shouts and points at the window. "Look!"

Outside, the heavens have come alive. Green and gold ribbons of light dance above the village. The aurora undulates and shimmers, the houses caught in iridescence.

The kids sprint outside, me following, where they dance and run about, arms raised, whistling shrilly. "If you whistle at the aurora, the spirits will come down and cut off your head," Kasha explains to me, laughing.

We all run back inside.

The kids' faces glow with delight, as if the aurora has imbued them with power. "Our ancestors," Marshall says proudly. "They're talking to us. To *us,* man."

Londa looks at me. "That's because . . . because we're the Kids from Nowhere."

I expect smirks, but instead there are smiles.

"The Kids from Nowhere," Merle says, and extends a fist.

Soon all the kids, except Boone, who has gone to use the phone, touch fists.

"The Kids from Nowhere!"

Boone reenters the room and says something in Yupik.

Marshall and Merle are up out of their seats and headed toward the door so fast that it seems instinctive. "Sea's opening up," Boone tells me. "We have to be ready to hunt first thing in the morning."

"You have to hunt *tomorrow?*"

As if only now realizing how close the finals are, the boys halt. *Something mystical comes over them,* the former principal said.

"We'll study nuclear waste while we're boating," Marshall says.

"We'll strap notes to our legs," Merle says.

Then they're gone.

That weekend, Bruce and I schedule cram sessions, but this latest walrus hunt goes well, so some of the girls are soon pulled away by subsistence duties. The girls attend the sessions as much as they can, as do Merle, Boone, and Marshall, the boys bone-weary from the long, merciless hours at sea.

On Sunday evening, one of the few times that everyone is present, Bruce and I suggest a desperate strategy. "We can't out-research the other teams this time," I tell the kids. "There aren't enough days left."

"We think you guys should choose a scenario you think might likely be asked," Bruce says, "and concentrate all your energies and research on that. Then hope you get asked what you studied."

"You think it will work?" Allana asks.

"Worth a try," Bruce says.

We leave the kids alone to brainstorm. As coaches, we will help them fine-tune their game plan, but the decision is so important, and the odds against success so great, that we feel we need to let the kids make the call.

The high school team decides to examine how to improve the quality of life for nuclear waste repository workers who might be exposed to radiation. "The exposure could be devastating," Merle says. "And not just physically."

"Psychologically, financially," Boone adds, ticking the ideas off on his fingers. "Effects on the family, the community, on friends, on coworkers . . ."

"On management, and on . . ." Allana joins in, then says something to the boys in Yupik. ". . . on other people in the same church," she says.

Marshall's eyes light up. "Even when people are buried!" As everyone looks at him, he explains, "Man, who would want to visit a cemetery if you knew a body there might be leaking radiation?"

"People might even stage protests over it," Merle says, defending Marshall's idea.

The kids laugh and decide to use the idea if they can. Weeks later we will learn from the national news that Brazilian street children exposed to radioactive material sadly had been denied burial for precisely the reason that Marshall postulated that Sunday evening.

The junior high team decides on a scientific tack. Having been skimming books and articles on nuclear waste disposal since the day we received the invitation, Meredith has discovered that radionuclides do not emanate randomly but rather travel along specific biochemical lines, including the food chain, aquifers, and wind currents. "If we could identify those lines before a leak happened at a repository," Kasha says, "couldn't we set up detection stations?"

"Or even stop the leak if it does happen?" Romie asks.

I have reservations about a subject of such complexity, but Bruce reminds me that the game plan *is* the kids' call, so we give the students the go-ahead. Soon all the junior high team members except Alvin are plowing through books and articles that Bruce and I had mailed to us by the college libraries in Anchorage and Fairbanks.

Meredith and Bess have their heads together as they pore over the materials. Romie reads with one finger on the page of text and her other hand rapidly going through the dictionary, her head bobbing back and forth. Kasha seems to find every opportunity she can to ask Boone for help. Alvin continues to draw, apparently oblivious to everything except art.

36

On Monday, fog rolls in. Hunting is out of the question. For a skin boat to be caught in the soup of Bering Sea fog might mean a crew never comes home.

The Problem Solvers are comatose during classes and spend every minute of free time studying nuclear waste disposal. I feel sorry for the other teachers, having to deal with such sleepy kids, so I stay in my classroom rather than endure the criticism or hard looks.

To prepare for the finals in nine days is a gargantuan undertaking. To prepare in nine days the way the Gambell kids do approaches the impossible. Each idea they cull from their reading and brainstorming must be graded for probability of originality, prioritized according to the possibility of fitting various scenarios we think might be asked, written up, and memorized.

During sixth period and again in the evening, Bruce and I scrimmage the junior high team against the high school team, to fine-tune their performance and to see if the kids can fit the latest ideas to the increasingly difficult scenarios we devise.

"Discuss the test situation for exactly five minutes before you write a word. Not a minute less!" I remind them, stopwatch in hand as Meredith and Merle, the team captains, open the envelope of whatever scenario Bruce and I have dreamed up. "If you think an idea might fit the situation but you're not quite sure how, ask the other team members. Work together! You're all in the same boat. Succeed or sink!"

Once the room is abuzz with the teams discussing the scenario, the junior high team talking in Yupik and English and the high school team only in Yupik, each student familiar with everyone else's ideas, everyone checking with everyone else to make sure that the ideas fit the situation and counting the number of ideas that fit and inventing new ones on the spot, I leave the room lest they eye me whenever they are unsure of something.

Two hours later Bruce and I check the kids' work, and we all discuss which ideas fit the situation, how much time each part of the process took, and how everyone might work better next time. Then they go home to read for new ideas and to rehearse old ones.

Meredith, who memorizes best when she's on her feet, walks around and around in the tiny house, mumbling problems and solutions. Alvin draws imaginary pictures in the air as he stands on the blue ice beside the laundromat and fills the water jugs that he will cart home to his grandparents. Romie and Kasha drill each other as they cook and babysit. Marshall, Merle, and Boone brainstorm as they ready their hunting equipment, should the weather break.

Then comes the Night of the Blond Screamer.

It is Tuesday, nearly midnight. We leave for Anchorage Friday morning. The junior high kids have gone home, and the high school kids, though exhausted, have stayed for more practice. They are trying to brainstorm solutions for radiation burns, when a shrill scream erupts in the gym. Thinking someone is hurt, we rush from the classroom, only to find Gretchen and Mary playing badminton, Gretchen jumping around and shrieking when she misses, which is always.

"We got tired of watching Meredith pace, mumbling to herself," Mary says.

We return to the classroom, and soon Gretchen joins us, unsuccessfully trying to shoulder her way into the huddled team members. "Watcha working on?" she asks.

"Radiation burns," Boone says. "You wouldn't understand."

"Graft on worm tissue," Gretchen says.

"That's dumb," Boone says.

"Boston University Medical Center," she replies, "is putting worm tissue stuff on people with bad burns. It's called lecture-troll-assist."

"Electrolysis," I correct her. And to the team members, who are staring at her, I say: "Her mother reads to her. A lot."

That night Boone gets the smelly sock, and he gives Gretchen a new name: the Blond Screamer, Mascot of the Kids from Nowhere.

The next day the fog lifts, and most of the high school boys are back out at sea. I find Lobert, who lately only shows up for lunch, rummaging through the janitor's closet. He grins what I recognize as his warning grin: up to no good.

Sure enough, stashed behind the bleachers are several six-packs of pop. Regardless of the administration's edict that we need to keep kids in school at any cost, I sit him down and tell him either to come to school all day or not to show up at all. During the last parent-teacher conference, his dad had told me that Lobert has been using school as an excuse to avoid being taught more about carving.

"If I stay home, can I still come to open gym at night?"

"If the pop gets put back where it belongs."

Lobert grins, gathers up the six-packs, and hustles toward the janitor's closet.

The next day he does not show up for school.

The sea is calm. Sunlight sparkles off the icebergs that dwarf the skin boat, its sail snapping in the breeze. Boone's father, Langdon, leans his weight against the tiller, Boone beside him, the other men of the extended family sitting hunched, some smoking, everyone contemplating weather and water. Carefully laid out between the men is the harpoon with its grenade-like bomb attached, the primers ready. Attached at the end of the coils of rope is the sealskin poke that will identify the bowhead's location should Boone, who is now the boat's striker, harpoon it. Knives are stuck in the gunwales, in case someone gets caught in the rapidly uncoiling rope. And beside everyone is a rifle, in case walrus are sighted or in case the fog rolls in again and the crew is trapped at sea, with only wits and weapons to sustain them.

Boone leans close, Langdon wondering if his son wants assurance or has a particular question about the seascape and the world of the whale.

"Dad," Boone asks, pushing his parka ruff forward so the wind will not blow his words away, "if there were a nuclear waste disposal site in, say, a salt mine in Kansas, could the salt corrode the canisters even if they were made out of titanium?"

Langdon looks in bewilderment from his son to Baylor, Langdon's younger brother, whose lips tighten in his effort not to laugh.

"I really don't know," Langdon tells Boone.

Boone returns to contemplating the sea and Problem Solving. Everything has changed so much this year, now that he is a striker and now that Problem Solving has become so serious. Merle's insistence that they are playing not for themselves or even for Gambell, but for Natives everywhere, has made him read, thoroughly read, material that a year ago he would have left in his locker or skimmed only after he had wearied of playing Pac-Man. Or maybe because he alone among the team members bears the blood of two peoples, Tlingit and Siberian Yupik—maybe that is why he has pushed himself so hard to win at everything. Some villagers have never approved of his father's marriage.

Feeling a lump in his pocket, he pulls out the smelly sock in its Ziploc bag and shows it to Baylor. "George made me carry this for teasing his daughter," Boone says. He knows that Baylor and George, who are the same age, greatly respect each other and often end up as opponents on the basketball court, both small, slow guards.

"You teased Meredith?" Baylor asks. "She's a firecracker, I've heard."

"It was Gretchen. I just said one of her ideas was stupid. You can't do that in Problem Solving—ridicule other people's ideas, I mean. George says one coach makes his players carry toilet seats, if they do that."

"Make a good life preserver," Baylor says. "The air-filled kind, anyway."

Boone grins and, replacing the sock in his pocket, finds his folded-up notes—what he originally was searching for when he found the sock. He and Merle decided that the ink on notes strapped to the leg would probably run. So a pocket was a wise substitute.

The CB crackles. It's Merle, several miles away. *"Uukna qerngughtaqaa, aniingughnaqnaquuqut"* . . . The ice is packing in, we're going to try to maneuver through it.

The lead to open water must have closed, Boone figures. The Apassingok family crew may end up having to decide whether to push their boat over an isthmus to more open water. Killing a whale is one matter, bringing it back another. There must be open water the entire return trip for the harvest to be successful.

Langdon shifts the tiller, the sail snapping as the boat responds. He moves toward another lead but is careful to stay in contact with the Apassingok boat. Boone reads through a paragraph he wrote the night before, intent on memorizing and thoroughly understanding the ideas behind the words of his second language, and puts the paper away.

He looks at the harpoon and, out of mental preparation rather than vanity, sees himself as the striker his age and athleticism have earned him, ready to throw down at the rising bowhead and hoping that the whale does not capsize the boat and send everyone into the frigid sea. For the moment, he puts Problem Solving—the kind he is taught at school—from his mind.

It is midnight by the time the boats return and the high school boys drag themselves to school for practice. The teams are not ready. Boone, Merle, and Marshall are exhausted, their eyes glazed. Disappointment shows in their faces, for the village has not even seen a whale much less harvested one.

Romie is also tired, and is still struggling with the science concepts, her weak vocabulary a hindrance. Kasha is in bed with the flu, so Bess will take her place. Bess is smart but so shy that she almost never offers up ideas and information. And Alvin—how much does he know? How much reading has he done? With Alvin there's no telling.

Marshall can barely stay awake. "Ecoterrorists," he says in a voice that seems to hang wearily in air. He adds, "Kamikaze ecoterrorists. Like suicide bombers or something like that."

I can tell that Meredith admires his mental quickness. He lacks Merle's and Boone's depth of understanding and drive to read about a subject but makes up for it in intellectual audacity.

Picking up Marshall's lead, she waves her hand to get my attention. "People willing to blow up a nuclear waste repository just to prove how dangerous it is."

"Give it a try," I say. "Just get going. You all have a week's worth of material to plow through even to have a fighting chance." I indicate the new pile of photocopies on the table near the blackboard.

"If we studied eight hours a day for a week, would we be in the ballgame?" Merle asks, a look of bemusement entering his tired eyes.

"You don't have a week," I say. "You leave Friday morning. Friday evening in Anchorage there's the introductory get-together. You play the first thing Saturday."

Merle is doing multiplication on a piece of paper. "Eight hours for seven days, that's fifty-six hours," he says. "We have two days—forty-eight hours—until we leave. Plus another, what—eight hours Friday, including travel time." He looks up at me and opens his hands as if to say *no problem*. "Fifty-six hours."

"That's two days if you don't sleep," I tell him.

"Mr. Dan said we could cut our other classes these two days, right?" Merle looks around at the other team members. "During the spring hunts no one sleeps. Not just the hunters—no one. There's too much to do. For the next two days, we treat this like a hunt." He looks intently at Boone and Marshall. "Right?"

The two look at him with determined confidence—and then nod.

37

I should not be depressed on the flight to Anchorage, but I am. The short-story winners have not been announced, but Mr. Dan went over the heads of the Unalakleet bottom-feeder administrators and approached the superintendent directly, thereby getting approval for the alternate team members to make the trip as well.

But I'm worried about Bess.

During the jet flight from Nome, Meredith leans close to me and, knowing the reason for my funk, whispers, "It's okay, Dad. She's been talking to me for a long time."

I look at Meredith incredulously. "You mean Bess?"

She grins, sticks her tongue out at me, and crosses her eyes. "She just doesn't talk when adults are around. Didn't you know that?"

We check into the hotel and board the elevator—all except Bess, who balks. No verbal persuasion can make her enter. Finally one of the boys grabs her arm and pulls her within.

"She's never been in an elevator before," Kasha says.

"She's never been in a hotel before," Romie says.

"Have you?" Kasha says.

Romie shakes her head. Everyone is looking up, watching the numbers.

"I've been in a hotel," Marshall says. "I was here last year."

When we reach our floor and pile out, Bess remains in the elevator. The door closes. I look around fearfully.

"Don't worry," Kasha says, pulling her suitcase toward her room. "She wants to ride."

I wait by the elevator as the kids find their rooms. Up to the top floor the elevator goes, and back down to our floor. When I ask Bess if she is getting off, she looks downcast and shakes her head. Down the elevator goes and all the way up again. I don't interrupt her. Down and then up and down again. Then at last the door opens.

"You ready?" I ask.

She smiles shyly. "Ready," she says, and walks off toward her room, her bag cradled in her arms.

I am still smiling to myself as I find the room I am sharing with Bruce. Bess at least thinks she's ready, so there's only Kasha to worry about. Her flu cleared up in time for her to make the trip, but too late to have her prepare for the team competition. She will compete in the individual competition, where she will face opponents the likes of Dillingham's Jennifer Hill, whose Problem Solving abilities regarding science subjects are said to be of national caliber. Kasha has only had a day to cram.

"What do you think?" I ask Bruce as we settle into our room.

"I think we should order out. Burgers and shakes, and a double order of fries."

After the opening ceremonies that evening, I tell everyone to get a good night's rest. The kids dutifully head for their rooms. An hour later Merle stops by to discuss one of the concepts. "Tell everyone lights out at midnight," I remind him. "That's fifteen minutes from now. Some of you haven't been in bed for two days."

"We're going to study right up to the test tomorrow." He grins.

"I don't want a bunch of zombies taking the test."

But I'm talking to his back. He's already headed to his room, papers in hand. "You worry too much," he says over his shoulder.

The next morning, after another sleepless night—the pills the doctor in Nome gave me do not seem to help anymore—I am so worried that I only stare at the breakfast we buy at McDonald's. Then everyone piles into a bus for the trip to a nearby church, where the test will occur. A few kids who were at the competition the year before say hi to Boone, Marshall, and Meredith. For many of them the state finals is *terra cognita;* some of the students have been participating in Future Problem Solving for five years.

Sharon Green, the state director, reads the final instructions to the sixty kids who have made it to the finals, after which the Gambell kids and I huddle in a corner of the church's all-purpose room.

"When you receive the test, read everything through carefully, together," I remind them. "Discuss the situation to make sure everyone understands it. Meredith and Merle? Don't just assume that everyone understands. Insist that everyone gives feedback immediately. Play smart. Play to win."

We do our usual hands-together *Win!* Then the kids file into their respective rooms. Londa and Kasha join those kids who will serve as monitors. Their own tests—for Londa also has decided to play in the individual competition—will take place after lunch.

On the way to the coaches' meeting, Bruce and I contemplate our chances. "Everything rides on the question," I tell him. "Everything. If it's a repository in a salt mine in Kansas, we have a good chance. Anything else, we're dead in the water."

"It's up to the kids now," he says.

Each year, while the kids play, the coaches and evaluators meet to discuss strategies for fine-tuning the scoring of booklets the following year. Some of the coaches are among the best educators in the state. I consciously set my shyness aside and summon the resolve to ask about what has weighed on my mind for months.

"For a long time I have wrestled with a dilemma," I tell everyone. "One that," I glance at Bruce, who gives me a knowing look, "has severe ramifications not only with how we teach Problem Solving in Gambell but also with relations among faculty and between the district administration and me.

"The rulebook tells coaches how to teach the process, but it doesn't say how much input we can have regarding the information the kids need. On the first practice problem I helped them with the readings and helped them analyze the ideas they brainstormed. I didn't help them on the qualifying problem, but went back to being proactive, though less so than on the first practice problem, for these finals.

"I apologize for being so long-winded, but this is extremely important to us on the island. At the risk of having our teams disqualified in case I've done something I shouldn't have—just what exactly is the coach's role?"

The response delights me and defuses my worry. "We spend long afternoons kicking around ideas," says the Dillingham coach, the recent recipient of the Alaskan Educator of the Year award. "I have my input and they have theirs, and sometimes we fight over who's right."

"I have fourteen junior high teams," the Kenai coach says. "I can't offer extra support to one team without offending the rest. But if I had only one team per division? I'd empty my brain trying to fill up those kids' minds. Aren't we in education to *teach,* not just to stand by and hope the kids learn on their own? I give my teams as many ideas as I can find, and hope they're bright enough to work with the ideas without duplicating each other."

An evaluator is the next to speak. "We want the coach to have tremendous input into the process," she says. "Otherwise, wouldn't we be advocating classrooms without teachers?"

"There was concern in the past," Dr. Green interjects, "about teams just memorizing information they did not truly understand, and coming here and writing it down. If the situation were broad enough, that would be possible. But this year, as you know, *every* answer the students give must address the test situation exactly or else the answer isn't counted. And to guard even further against mere memorization, for state and national competitions the national office now is listing possible problems that simply will not be counted—as you will see." She passes out sealed envelopes marked TEST.

I feel better from what she and the other coaches have said. Yet my hands shake as I open the envelope and read the exam—and my heart sinks.

"It's an undersea nuclear-waste repository!" Merle says as he, Boone, Marshall, and Allana press together around their tiny table, reading the scenario. He switches into Yupik. "A thousand miles off the coast of Hawaii."

"Oh man." Marshall's voice is almost a wail. "How could there be nuclear waste exposure *there?*"

"And look at this list at the bottom of the situation," Allana says, holding up the second page. "The following are not problems:

'Transportation of nuclear waste canisters to and from the site, earth movement from volcanic eruptions or from shifts in tectonic plates, the presence of commercial shipping or pleasure boats.'" As she reads, she switches back and forth between Yupik and English. "It's a pretty long list."

"A lot of what we have won't work," Boone says, affirming Allana's summary.

"I have some other stuff," Marshall says. "Brand-new stuff. I put a list in my shoe."

Boone leans across the table until his nose nearly touches Marshall's. "You take that shoe off, and I'll break your leg."

"You take the shoe off and George probably will break your other leg," Merle adds.

Allana thrusts out her lower lip and blows her hair from her eyes. "What to do now?" she says in a quiet voice.

Merle settles back and for a moment is lost in thought. "A lot of our ideas won't work. But I'll bet that a lot of other teams' ideas won't either. I doubt if anyone thought of this scenario."

"We're going to win by default?" Boone asks.

"The repository is isolated. We understand isolation, don't we?" Merle looks around. "Well, don't we?" The others nod. "I have an idea." He gestures for everyone to gather close. "Listen . . ."

38

Voice tight with desperation, Meredith reads the scenario aloud to her teammates.

"How are we going to monitor pathways the radionuclides might take," Romie asks when Meredith finishes, "if the repository is in the middle of the ocean!"

"All of our ideas involve monitoring on the land," Meredith says.

"Think of something, Alvin!" Romie says.

Head against the chair back, he stares at the ceiling, as if resigned to failure.

"Alvin!" Meredith says.

"ALVIN!" Bess blurts, in a "Chipmunk Song" voice.

The girls giggle, and someone shouts from the other side of the industrial accordion curtain that separates the room from the next team's, "Knock if off in there! We're trying to think."

"Alvin," Meredith says in a low voice, "we all know you're a genius. You have to think of something. You just have to!"

Alvin briefly closes his eyes and when he opens them he says, "Island," without taking his head from the chair back. "We monitor from an island."

Romie shoves the paper toward him. "There *is* no island! Can't you read?"

"We build an island."

"Sure. We build an island."

"Smelly sock to you," Alvin says. "We build a floating island and monitor the biochemical pathways from there."

"It would float away," Bess says.

Alvin tips forward in his chair and, grabbing up scratch paper, draws furiously. "We attach the island to the ocean floor with bungee cords. Like this."

"Look here," Romie says, pointing to part of the scenario's text.

"It says that there are no animals in the area *except for a few worms and microscopic organisms.*" She looks at her teammates, and grins. "Biochemical pathways—and the food chain, right?"

"We can't use most of our ideas, but some of them will fit," Meredith says with growing excitement. "Let's write those down and brainstorm after that. That'll work, won't it?" She looks at Romie and Bess. "Well, won't it?"

After a moment Bess lifts a hand to give her a high-five. "All right, Mere!"

"*Please* shut up!" comes from the other side of the curtain.

After lunch, while Londa and Kasha compete in the individual competition, the other kids engage in the required skit competition, during which teams act out their best solution. Most junior high and high school teams find the skit competition silly, given the depth and breadth of the research they did for the main competition. But the skits do provide mental relief.

Alvin ends up running through the audience dressed as a radio-nuclide particle wearing only his underwear and a garbage bag stuffed with newspaper, and Boone shows the audience that he is a victim of radiation exposure due to bad genes: he rips his *jeans* apart, the seams of which we have taken apart and put back together with Velcro. The boys set the crowd laughing.

That evening, Londa shows up at my room with her mom, both of them smiling. As Londa's mom and Bruce talk, Londa tells me privately, "I don't think I did very well on the test. But I didn't freeze up, Mr. G! I wrote for the whole two hours."

She is the happiest that I have ever seen her. She and her mom walk hand-in-hand, arms swinging, as they head to the elevator.

Sunday arrives. After a day's shopping we are as ready as we ever will be for the banquet. I am hoping for two second places. The junior high kids have told me about their man-made island. The high schoolers argued that repository inspectors or maintenance workers might be exposed to radiation leaks and might have to endure long periods of shipboard isolation. The ideas are good, but probably not good enough for a first place, I decide, after the Gambell kids keep running back to me with word of other teams' ideas.

We'll lose Merle and Allana to graduation, I tell myself as we find our table, *but this is their first finals and we shouldn't expect a win their first time out. Everyone else should be back next year.*

We pick through our food, all of us except Bruce too nervous to eat. We endure the scientist giving his guest lecture, as he drones on about the need for problem solving in an increasingly complicated world. The state evaluators comment about the excellence of this year's booklets, and at last Dr. Green stands to give out the awards.

Soon my head is swimming:

"Short-story competition, senior high division. First place, Merle Apassingok, for the story of a young Eskimo," she pauses as squeals from the Gambell table erupt, "who fights his claustrophobia, while in prison, by projecting a hologram of himself back to the tundra wilderness that he loves."

Merle goes up to receive his award, and is halfway back when Dr. Green says, "Second place, high school division, Bunnie Boolowon, Gambell," more squeals from our table, "for a heartbreaking tale of an Eritrea rebel who must watch his meager crops being eaten by passerine birds while he himself is pinned down by Ethiopian troops."

Merle glances at me and I send him up again to receive Bunnie's trophy.

No sooner has he sat down and is looking from his plaque to Bunnie's, such pride in his eyes that I think his heart will break, than Dr. Green announces:

"First place, short-story competition, junior high division, Meredith Guthridge, Gambell," more squeals and laughter and applause, "for a story of a youthful genius who learns that true giving comes not from the head, through his science, but from his heart, from his Eskimo culture."

Those three trophies mark the beginning of an evening that is truly, deeply *ours:*

"Individual competition, junior high division, first place, Jennifer Hill, Dillingham. Second place, Kasha Kapaaka, *Gambell*."

"Skit competition, junior high division, first place, Anchorage. Second place, *Gambell.*"

"Skit competition, high school division, first place, *Gambell*."

"Team competition, junior high division, first place, *Gambell.*"

"Team competition, high school division, first place, *Gambell.*"

As coaches, Bruce and I go up to the podium with the kids for the team awards, and when we return the second time, Bruce offers me a hand and gives me the finest congratulations I have ever received.

"All that emphasis on research. I really didn't think it would work. But you were right. You were right all along."

On our table is a forest of trophies, earned by kids whose school could have been closed.

After the banquet, the Cordova coach, whose team won the elementary division, and I meet with the evaluators and Dr. Green, to begin preparing for the national finals.

The head judge pulls me aside. "It was a pleasure reading your kids' booklets," she says. "The ideas combined science and culture. Arguing that indigenous Hawaiians would demand local hire, which in turn could cause lawsuits by other potential repository workers . . . pure genius.

"But one thing puzzles me. What happened to your elementary team? The first half of their qualifying test was *way* beyond any other team's efforts." She flutters her hands for emphasis. "But we opened the second half of their booklet, and nothing. I mean, *nothing.*"

I have to laugh, sadly.

Dr. Green, smiling though looking harried from the weekend of running the competition, is next to speak. "As you both know," she says to the Cordova coach and me, "the subject for nationals is not announced until after the state finals. That's so no team can get a head start. Also, no research help of any kind is sent out to the teams. In a nutshell, you have forty-four days to prepare your kids to compete against the best and brightest America has to offer, and you're on your own. Given where we live, Alaskan teams are hugely handicapped, that's especially true for your kids, George.

"Another thing you both need to know," she continues. "Each year, approximately 80 percent of the teams at nationals are from schools or programs for the gifted. For those, winning a national academic competition of this caliber is a *big* feather in some administrator's cap. Many of those schools have top libraries at their disposal, they have computers, and they bring in experts to prep the kids—whatever it takes to walk away with a trophy."

She hands us each a packet containing rules, dates, and other procedural matters.

"The subject matter for nationals this year," she says, "is genetic engineering."

Looking through the packet, I realize that, while my goal all year was to have at least one team win the state championship, I have never really thought beyond this level. That they now will compete for the *national* championship frightens me.

As I walk back to my room, I decide what my goal with the kids will be. A goal I dare not tell them for fear that they will throw in the towel.

My goal for them will not be to place at nationals, but to go the distance. Given where we live and the teams we are up against, there is no way that we can win a national championship. But what if the kids from Gambell could hold their own against the best in America? Wouldn't that be trophy enough?

I find that the kids have piled up the beds of one of their rooms against the wall, and are dancing, swilling down pop, and stuffing banquet cake into their mouths. They shut off their boom box and sit on the floor for the announcement they are awaiting: the subject at nationals.

"Genetic engineering," I say.

Except for Meredith, who has been raised around science fiction, their faces go blank.

"What's *that!*" Marshall asks, his tone suddenly fearful.

"It's when scientists manipulate genetic structure."

"Oh, you mean like in a cell," he says. He looks around at the other high school team members, and they relax a little. They have either had, or are taking, sophomore biology.

"What's a cell?" Alvin asks.

Romie's and Bess's eyes duplicate his confusion.

"Like in prison?" Kasha asks.

"You don't know what a *biological cell* is?" I ask the ninth graders.

In unison they shake their heads, a baffled quartet of wide-eyed innocence.

We have forty-four days.

39

Students mob us when we land in Gambell on Monday. Mr. Dan is there to greet us, Keenan pumps my hand, and Lawrence pounds me on the back. From the moment I stumble, ecstatic, into the school, I can hear the phone ringing from the kids' parents and from the elementary teachers.

"We're having a faculty meeting for the middle school and the high school teachers," Mr. Dan tells me at lunch. "It will be in your room instead of in home ec." I start to ask why we're using my room, but then I smile inwardly at his strategy.

Because that's where the trophies are.

I imagine an ice cream social, a faculty—finally—of friends. Wymena had received heartfelt adulation from the rest of us when she coached the girls' basketball team to second place, Keenan when his boys made state in basketball, Lawrence for having coached winning squads during the wrestling tournament, and Linda when her cheerleaders won a number of awards. Hadn't Bruce and I led kids to the first academic state championships ever won by a team of Native students? Hadn't Gambell become the first school in Alaska to win two age divisions in Future Problem Solving in the same year? *It was our turn, now.*

The teachers are strangely quiet as they enter my room. Mr. Dan strides to my podium instead of sitting down, as he usually does, and stands there looking down at Gerald and Lars—waiting, I am sure, for them to be the first to officially congratulate Bruce and me and, in so doing, unofficially apologize for the obvious animosity they had held toward the program.

Lars is the first to speak. "In light of what George has done," he says, "three of us are petitioning to have Future Problem Solving here in Gambell dropped. Effective immediately." He hands Mr. Dan a piece of paper.

"The kids are studying too hard," Gerald adds. "It's bad for their health and for their emotional well-being. They should be learning for learning's sake, not for trips and trophies."

"George has been ruining our classes by piling on homework," Lars says, sitting back and folding his arms in a look of resolve, his gaze straight ahead as though he fears to look my way. "Furthermore, he *purposely* set out to try and destroy the trip for my Future Homemakers Program. He told those girls they should be studying while they were with me in Anchorage. The problems *that* caused!" He snuffles loudly.

"I still haven't seen any transferability of the skills they're supposedly learning," Wymena says.

"Just rote learning, is all," Gerald says.

Mr. Dan glances toward me, his gaze a mix of anger and sorrow. I feel numb. All I can think is, *I am going to resign.*

Mr. Dan's gaze moves to Bruce, seated apart from the others, by the window.

"I have to admit," Bruce says, looking down at his clasped hands on the table, "that at first I didn't believe in these methods either. All this insistence on research and on practicality in what is a competition involving futuristic ideas. But what has happened here," he continues in an even voice, turning his bulk to face the three petitioners, "changed the history of Future Problem Solving. The kids here *won* using those methods, and the program will never be the same, certainly not in Alaska, probably not anywhere. Bright kids no longer are going to walk into the finals and win with brilliant, flash-in-the-pan thinking, as was often the case in the past. To beat kids like *ours*," with a forefinger he thumps the table for emphasis, "kids who are willing to put in the time reading and digging for ideas, kids who will *sacrifice* to take home the hardware, they will have to hit the books like never before."

He looks at Lars, at Gerald, at Wymena.

"Say what you will," he adds, "but what has been accomplished by the methods that were developed here is amazing."

Gerald lifts his head as if to object, but Mr. Dan gives him the hawkish look he effects for errant kids. "This is *not* going to be another attack-George session. I've put up with it all year, and I'm sick of it. It's going to end *now.*"

"What about our petition?" Lars says.

Mr. Dan holds up the folded paper, eyeing it as if debating whether to tear it up, and sticks it in his front pocket. "I'll forward it to the superintendent. I'm sure he will be interested to know that we have some teachers here who believe that studying hard is detrimental to learning."

That evening we are supposed to have our first practice in preparation for nationals, but when Alvin arrives to say that the other boys have gone boating, I am thankful to cancel practice.

"Let's wait until we have everyone present," I say.

But it's a lie. In truth, my heart isn't in the program.

I don't want to coach Problem Solving anymore.

I don't want to teach Eskimos anymore.

I don't want to teach—period.

I turn off the light, trudge home through what is left of the snow, and end up canceling Problem Solving for the week. There are too many subsistence and end-of-year activities to distract the kids, I tell myself, but it's just an excuse.

Still, I know I must finish walking the path where Problem Solving is taking me. Though I am almost too angry to read, I dutifully plow through the books on genetic engineering that Bruce and I grabbed from the Anchorage library before flying back. And I submit a funding request to take the kids to study in Seattle for ten days on the way to the finals.

Our only hope for a respectable showing at nationals, Bruce and I have concluded, is to get the kids out of the village as early as possible before the competition, find a hotel near a major library, and somehow give them an understanding of genetics, away from the distractions at home. But the more I read about the subject, the more morose I become. Even if I can teach them such material, how can they come up with information that other teams won't have? The library books we got from Anchorage are horribly outdated.

On Thursday the head of special ed for the district phones to say that the superintendent has approved our travel request. "Just be glad the district is flush with cash," she adds. "And good luck."

No sooner do I hang up than Bruce bursts into the secretary's area, *Newsweek* in hand. Its cover depicts "Mighty Mice"—bigger, stronger, and smarter mice that a scientist has created through bioengineering. "I'll bet *he* has some unique information and ideas," Bruce says. "And he's at the University of Washington."

He grins slyly. "We'll be in Seattle anyway. You can't get a dance unless you ask."

Fifteen minutes later, after wending via phone through the halls of academe, we are talking to Dr. Palmiter, hoping to be granted a brief interview while we are in Seattle.

"You say that these are Eskimo kids preparing for a national championship in academics?" he asks. "And they'd like to interview me? I'll go you one better. How about I take a few hours off and give them a crash course?"

Bruce and I are so excited that when we hang up we jump around like children.

Then, returning to earth, I wonder: *How can we possibly raise the kids' knowledge of genetic engineering so they can comprehend what he will tell them? Will they understand what they learn? Will they be able to apply it?*

40

During sixth period, Merle comes in to tell me that he needs to talk to me privately. "Tonight," he says. We agree to meet up on the mountain. After dinner I take a thermos of cocoa and climb among the boulders, where I use binoculars to look for polar bears. I have never seen one except in a zoo, though their tracks are often outside my door. Spotting one of the huge animals that enter and exit the village so stealthily has become a dream of mine.

"The secret of seeing a polar bear is knowing where to look," Merle says as he joins me.

"Where should I look?" I hand him the binoculars.

He scans the frozen sea and gives them back. "You have to look where the bears are."

After pouring himself a cupful of cocoa, he sits down to watch the water. Great chunks of ice, some looking like spired crowns, others so flat they seem like stepping stones, float past on their way south. Around them the sea is milky gray, the water further out cobalt blue. It occurs to me that I never tire of the Bering Sea's changing moods.

I lower the binoculars. "I don't think I'll ever see a bear."

"Sometimes people get their hopes too high. They see what they want to see." He gazes out across the ocean. "They see what isn't there."

Then he says, "I can't go to nationals, George."

It takes a moment for me to internalize his words and their impact. Without the motivation that Merle gives, there are no teams.

"It's a problem with—with Bunnie."

He takes a bag of sunflower seeds from his pocket and sticks a handful in his mouth. He appears dazed.

"She's pregnant," I say. It's a guess, but the answer is apparent. "We're only going for a month," I remind him. "You'll be back to her by the second week of June. She certainly isn't the first high school girl here to have a baby."

Teenage pregnancy is common in village Alaska. There is no stigma. In fact, for some it is a proof of fertility that raises rather than lowers a girl's prospects for marriage.

Merle spits a shell. "I haven't entered bride service yet. I don't even know when I will. It's up to our parents. Besides, my dad wants me to go to college. We're too young. Just babes in the woods." He laughs a small, bitter-sounding laugh and sags back against the boulder. "As if we had any woods."

I have never seen him so abject. "The baby will go to Bunnie's parents," he continues. "That's how it is in our culture. They're wonderful people, but we don't want to give up the baby. Bunnie's really shook. She needs me *here*." He hangs his head and blinks away tears. "Sometimes I don't understand my culture at all. It's so complicated! You white people have it easy. You see your relatives when you feel like it, you support whichever ones you wish. You usually only have to worry about your own family. Just yourselves and your kids. What do sociologists call that group, the father, mother, and their kids?"

"You mean 'nuclear family'?"

Again the bitter laugh. "Sounds like a bomb classification."

He rises with what seems great effort and wanders down the slope. I do not follow or try to advise him. Had he wanted my advice he would have asked. I will not burden him with more troubles by reminding him that there is no sense in our going to Cedar Rapids without him.

I expect Merle to phone during the weekend, saying that he has changed his mind and will go to nationals, but he does not call. On Monday, during my first-period prep, instead of showering (having no running water, we shower at school), I sit staring at the trophies, wondering what to do. Take the rest of the kids, leaderless, to a slaughter?

Not wanting to face the ninth graders with news about Merle, I dismiss my geography class to play basketball. The school is almost empty anyway. Most boys are out boating. The afternoon rolls around, and I have just given an assignment to the three kids who remain in

American history when I hear shouting and people running. Kasha sticks her head into my classroom and yells, "Boone got a whale! Boone got a whale!"

The hall fills with kids laughing and giving each other high-fives, then grabbing coats and running out to zoom off on three-wheelers and snowmachines as if the boaters will bring the behemoth onto the beach at any moment, when in fact getting a whale to the village, much less over the shelf ice, is a lengthy and arduous undertaking.

After the whale is harpooned and the grenade explodes, *if* it explodes, the hunters must wait for the animal to rise. Sometimes it comes up under pack ice, and the harvest is lost. If the whale surfaces in open water—the hunters spying the seal poke that balloons up to the surface long before the whale does—each boat ties its rope to the main rope that is attached to the whale.

Then the sails come down, and all boats motor home in a line, forming a string across the golden sunset as they pull the prize. Other men bring the village's two bulldozers and long, thick ropes and block and tackle down to the beach. As the boats near, people pour from their houses; others arrive by snowmachine, some from as far away as Savoonga, all coming to help and to take away large hunks of *mangtak* (whale skin, which tastes like almond-flavored chewing gum) which they love to eat fresh.

This whale is small, about thirty feet. At the usual ratio for bowheads, that means about thirty tons. But even if it were smaller, or were a small species, such as a minke whale or even a Dahl porpoise, the villagers still would bring down the bulldozers and the big ropes, lest its spirit be offended by its being underappreciated.

Observers from Fish and Game and two from Greenpeace have flown in from Nome. Shrugging off professional dispassion and, for the Greenpeacers, official dismay over the practice of whaling, they grab hold of the rope that now leads from the ropes around the tail. Workers hook up the other ropes to the bulldozers, and everyone heaves, for hauling a bowhead up over the shelf ice is difficult.

By what I doubt is coincidence, Merle ends up behind me on the long line of people manning the ropes. Like everyone else, he seems in high spirits.

"Heyyyy-up!" someone with a megaphone calls.

"Thirty-one tons, and what'd you know," Merle sings in a Tennessee Ernie Ford voice as everyone pulls mightily at the ropes. I look back, and he grins. "Another day older and deeper in snow. . . ."

"Heyyyy-up!"

"Saint Peter don't you call me, 'cause I can't go . . ."

"Heyyyy-up!"

"I'm much too busy being Es-ki-mo."

But the whale will not budge. The ice shelf is too ragged, the current flowing beneath it too fierce, and the men fear that the ropes from the bulldozer, strained to the point of snapping, could break, sending the huge hooks flying among the crowd. The only solution is to reduce the whale's weight while it is still in the water. Despite the cold, and despite the Bering Sea's freezing waters, getting the whale onto the shore and cut up as quickly as possible is imperative. A bowhead gives off such tremendous body heat that, in death, it can quickly cook itself and spoil the meat.

And it is the meat, not the blubber, that the Eskimos seek. The idea of Eskimos subsisting on blubber is another of the many misconceptions that most Americans have about life in the north. Only in times of starvation, or else to supply themselves with essential fats, was blubber ever a significant food for Eskimos. It mainly was used for heat and to feed the dogs.

Men climb onto the whale and, using crescent-shaped cutters attached to poles the length of broomsticks, begin slicing through the skin, which is then attached to sharp hooks and dragged ashore by one or two dozen villagers at the ropes. The strips of whale skin, perhaps fifteen feet long, are extremely heavy. Only when they are ashore and are sliced up can they be lifted. They are diced until they fit in bread sacks and Ziploc bags, but little of the cutting is random. Everything is doled out according to the size of shares owed to various relatives.

The work goes on until after 11 P.M., when darkness makes the work too dangerous. All head home for a few hours' rest.

Mr. Dan phones the next morning to tell us that school will be held "on the beach." I pull on my coat, boots, and gloves and head outside, only to find Merle coming down from the drift that still separates my house from the rest of the world.

"An apple for the teacher," he says, handing me a bread sack.

Within is whale meat.

Mary and I have dined almost exclusively on Native meats since coming to the island. Seal, walrus, polar bear, duck, goose, cormorant, seagull—we have come to love them all, and have relied on canned goods only for fruits and vegetables.

But bowhead is our favorite, its black meat reminiscent of sweet beef and so fat-free that we must add oil to cook it. I'm savoring the meal we are going to make when I tell Merle, "It'll make a great roast."

"You're going to need it. Got to keep your strength up." He grins. "What did you tell us about Vince Lombardi?"

I rattle off the great coach's oft-misquoted maxim. "'Winning isn't everything. It's the endeavor to win that's everything.'"

He nods, starts up the snow mound but looks back. "I thought about a lot of things when I was out boating, and decided that some things aren't personal. They're bigger than that. It's time we started endeavoring again, George."

41

I work all day helping with the whale and becoming increasingly depressed, despite Merle's change of mind. I spend the evening perusing ideas I have lightly underlined in the library books on genetic engineering. No way will the Problem Solvers understand such complexity!

Unless . . .

An idea of how to teach the subject forms in my mind. I dig under my bed and, pulling out my box of *Scientific American* and *Omni,* thumb through various issues, marking articles and passages. Then, excited, I phone my cousin. Besides being an astrophysicist, he is one of this country's leading authorities on Superlearning, a memorization method that, originally developed in Bulgaria, is so powerful that the Soviets classified it as a military secret. As I speak to him at length, I mentally outline how I can tweak and torque the method to suit our needs.

Next, I call my genius friend, George Harper.

When I mention what I have in mind, he chuckles.

"Long-term learning," I tell the Problem Solvers, "is made up of four Rs: rhythm, rhyme—mnemonic devices—repetition, and relaxation. You need to learn to study *smart,* not *hard.*"

I dim the classroom lights, quietly play soft music, and have the kids stand and stretch to reduce their stress as much as possible. Then I tell them to sit down again, relax, and shut their eyes. "We want to reduce distractions," I tell them.

Next I softly say, "Repeat after me: 'The helix's nucleotides have paramagnetic properties.'"

Their faces tighten with confusion but they keep their eyes closed and mumble the sentence. My cousin informed me that the brain seems to work best if it receives information in four-second intervals, so I wait four seconds before having the students repeat the sentence, which they do until everyone says it perfectly, despite having little idea what it means.

"Scrabies are cells that, like viruses, lack nuclei," I next tell them.

After twenty similarly short sentences—the concepts condensed to seven or eight words, to fit into the four-second interval—I have them open their eyes. Then I tell them to fill out a simple worksheet, without talking. It consists of the sentences we have just repeated, with key words left out. I warn them against guessing. I do not want them to implant a wrong answer when they are so receptive to learning.

Next, I have them stand and verbally exchange any answers they lack. When all worksheets are filled in, they sit down again. Though everyone still looks confused, the confusion appears lessened. A few are smiling.

I turn on the overhead projector and show cartoon transparencies that Mary has drawn. We see a chromosome jailed in a cell. "Being in the cell really has our Mr. Chromosome upset," I explain, placing the next transparency onto the machine. "His insides are twisted like hell. Like a hellix . . . a *helix.*"

Several transparencies later, I unveil my *pièce de résistance,* which has been sitting, covered with a cloth, on my desk. Before them is a rickety model I made with a dowel, toothpicks, and little marshmallows. "What is this?" I ask.

"A hellix," Marshall says. "Helix."

"And these are?" I ask, pointing.

"Marshmallows?" Bess asks.

Everyone laughs.

"Nucleotides!" she says, proud of herself.

"What kind of properties do they have?" I ask. "What kind of qualities?"

Blank faces for a moment, but then Meredith asks in a tentative voice, "Paramagnetic?"

"That's right! Paramagnetic. What's that mean?"

"They have two magnetisms?" Romie asks.

I hadn't anticipated such an answer. A lot of teaching in ESL classrooms consists of anticipating and correcting vocabulary confusion before wrong definitions become learned. I write "pair of" and "para" on the board, and explain that the latter refers to "weak" or "similar to."

Understanding dawns on Meredith's face. She, Kasha, and Romie put their heads together, Meredith mumbling in English and Kasha telling Romie something in Yupik. Romie lifts her head. "Those *things,*" she points to the nucleotides, "have something like magnetism."

"But not really," Meredith adds.

Yes.

I pull up the map, behind which on the board I have drawn a helix broken into two parts. "From what I understand, genetic engineering consists of scientists separating a helix and introducing another gene into that spot." I jam a marshmallow onto a pencil and pretend to insert it into the dowel-and-marshmallow helix. "Now, if the new gene is introduced into the wrong spot," I pretend to insert the pencil elsewhere, "what do you think could happen?"

"Bad genes!" Boone blurts and pats his Levi's. Marshall gives him a high-five.

"What's one way, from what we have learned," I ask, "that we can help assure that the gene to be introduced goes to the right place on the helix?"

"Magnetism, man," Marshall says. "Er, *paramagnetism.*"

I grin, bring out pop, and soon the kids are rattling off connections between the Superlearned concepts and the model of the helix. Then I pair up the kids and give them photocopied articles from *Scientific American* to read, and stand back to watch—in awe.

In half an hour, the kids have gone from almost no understanding of genetic engineering to concepts George Harper gave me—"ones that in some cases aren't even in the professional journals yet," he said.

The kids have been able to tackle such advanced concepts because we have reversed the usual sequence of teaching.

Most teachers work from the simple to the complex: they introduce basic ideas and try to have students master them before moving to difficult ones. What if, I had wondered after Merle brought me the roast, we reversed that? What if we started with the complex, *but did not tell the kids the ideas were complex?* How fast could they make sense of the advanced concepts?

Watching Merle wrestle with his dilemma regarding the pregnancy, it had occurred to me that kids do not imprint cultural traditions by necessarily starting with simple concepts. Each day, the Eskimo children are exposed to village practices without realizing the degree of conceptual difficulty some of those involve. What they do not understand they just accept, for, unlike in most Caucasian communities, Eskimos frown on questioning cultural authority.

The following afternoon, Mr. Dan dismisses school early. Everyone is readying for the annual Yupik Days celebration, which this year is especially poignant, given the whale.

I give the Problem Solvers the afternoon off. We are leaving in thirty-six hours and everyone needs to pack. The district is allowing Bruce, Mary, and me to end the school year a week early so we can accompany the kids. I'm grateful for the reprieve, for my flu is back.

At 4:30 Mr. Dan pokes his head into my classroom. "Better come into the office. There's a phone call you need to hear."

The call is from an administrator at the district office. I figure he has called to give us the district's final blessings before the trip.

"I'll get straight to the point," he says. "We at the D.O."—like many district office administrators he loves acronyms—"have been examining the itinerary you submitted for taking the kids Outside. We have decided not to let the Gambell teams attend the national competition. The trip isn't academic enough to warrant the expense."

I nearly choke on his last sentence. "Not academic enough?"

"That's right," he says confidently.

"Not academic enough?!"

Mr. Dan desperately signals for me to lower my voice, but I wave him off.

"There's no reason for you to be upset, George," Mr. Administrator continues. "And there's certainly no reason for you to use that tone of voice."

"They're going to compete in what is probably the nation's most difficult academic competition," I ask in a voice bordering on hysteria, "against kids from schools for the gifted, and that's not academic enough?"

"It's not the competition we dispute. It's the time you're spending in Seattle."

"In Seattle they're being given a class by one of the top scientists in the world. They're also going to interview George Harper, a science writer, and visit a high school science class and a genetics lab. On top of that Bruce and I will lecture four hours a day, and the kids will study on their own at least another four. That's not academic?"

"You also have them scheduled to see a Mariners' baseball game, for heaven's sake. And a ride on a ferry—just what is that?"

"They'll be in class or studying from morning until evening. You don't want them to take any breaks? Would you study nonstop for ten days? Did you do that in college? Did you?"

"There's no need to make this personal. We're not talking about me, and we're not talking about college. We're talking about what you purport is an academic trip. It just isn't academic, George. I'm sorry, but it isn't."

"The hell it's not!"

"You'll just have to tell them they can't go. That's the end of it."

"Look, you little pencil-pusher!" Mr. Dan half rises to stop me, but I so scowl at him that he sits back down. "If these were Unalakleet teams, or if these were white kids, you'd be out here holding the door open for them. The students are home packing right now. You waited until the last minute, didn't you! If you want to tell them they can't go to nationals, after all they've been through, then fly out here and tell them yourself!" I slam down the phone.

"I'm glad you said that," Mr. Dan says. "I wish I had."

The energy seems to have gone out of his face, and he gazes out the window, toward the runway. "Every time I turn around, there seems to be another deputy superintendent trying to stop us," he says. "And I can't go over his head, this time. The superintendent's in Anchorage, fighting his court case. He won't be back for a week. Even if I could find out where he's staying, I doubt if he's in any mood to be bothered by more problems."

I walk back to my classroom in a daze, so angry that I want to break something. Instead I sit down backward in a chair, chin on the chair back, and stare at the awards, wondering if anyone except the kids and Dan and me cares about academics. Romie's confidence and reading ability have skyrocketed, Kasha is writing excellent essays in Yupik and translating them. At his own insistence, Boone is reading excerpts of Plato and Aristotle to give him ideas that *no one,* as he says, will think of applying to genetic engineering.

Thinking about the kids, I begin to reassess the situation.

What would *they* do in my situation! I ask myself.

What would *they* do if this were a scenario on a test?

How would the Problem Solvers answer Mr. Administrator?

Use the techniques you teach the kids, I decide.

I formulate the issue by using the syntax I have had the kids memorize for expressing the central problem a team has decided to examine: How might we + verb + qualifier(s).

"Do your thinking on paper," I am forever reminding the kids.

I grab a piece of paper and jot down a tentative problem statement:

How might we overcome the administrator's objections about being allowed to go to the Problem Solving nationals via a ten-day study stint in Seattle?

I start brainstorming ideas, scribbling them as if for a last-minute grocery list, writing feverishly, not worrying about logic or feasibility.

Shoot him is number one.

I am half a dozen ideas into the list when understanding dawns.

I return to my problem statement, cross out "overcome," and insert "circumvent."

42

Two phone calls later, I dial Unalakleet. "If this trip isn't academic," I ask Mr. Administrator as soon as he answers, "then why are half my kids enrolled in a college course I'm teaching in Seattle? All of the high school team are taking English 197, Science Writing, offered through Northwest College."

There is silence at the other end of the line, and I hold my breath for fear he will let the high school team go but not the junior high team. I had called up the little college in Nome and asked if they would like a science-writing class taught. Yes, the five students who will comprise the class are at least sixteen years old—a small lie, for Boone will not turn sixteen until the trip is nearly over—and yes, I used to be a tenured English professor in Iowa. No, there is no need to pay me for my services. The class, I explain, will be taught in Seattle, while the students are on an academic road trip.

Unlike some teachers and administrators I have encountered, those at the college in Nome loved the idea of challenging Native kids. Nor was having the class taught in Seattle any problem. Because of its rural setting, the college is accustomed to being flexible about where an actual classroom is.

I now have Mr. Administrator backed into a corner, and he knows it. If he is does not recognize my vulnerability regarding the junior high team, then he has no choice but to back down. My next move, as I am sure he is aware, is to take the matter to the school board— and to the media. He might keep the kids from going on the trip, but I will have his head on a platter. Besides, what can he possibly gain by fighting us?

"I just needed ammunition to demonstrate the trip's academic value," he says in an almost saccharine voice. "Just so there will never have been any question. Now I can give the trip a much more careful look."

"The trip's already been approved," I remind him. "I don't have the time or the emotional wherewithal for anyone to vacillate on the decision. I need to know *now.* Are we going or not?"

"As I said before," his voice still syrupy, "I'll give the trip a closer look. But I think it's safe to say that everything will be approved."

I say good-bye without thanking him, and hang up.

I stay in my room the next morning as the Yupik Days celebration progresses in the gym, to finish paperwork and get my semester grades in, and to avoid being thrown high in the air during the Eskimo blanket toss. I hated trampoline practice when I was in middle school, and, given how nauseated I feel, I better avoid it.

I am eternally grateful when Chip and Dale drop in, laughing, to tell me that Lawrence broke the sealskin blanket.

Later I hear Eskimo drumming. The people are dancing in celebration of the whale and of spring. I don't have time to watch. When the pounding stops, the drummers apparently between songs, Lawrence enters my classroom.

"Dan wants you in the gym," he says. "Remember the CAT disaster? Maybe it was some phase of the moon, because despite being sick, our kids had the highest increase in English in the district. You and Bruce are getting awards. Since you and the Problem Solvers won't be here for the final awards assembly, Dan wants to make the presentation *now."* He emphasizes the last word by poking a thumb over his shoulder.

Lawrence's mischievous grin tells me he will enjoy my unease at being singled out. "You coming quietly," he steps toward my desk, "or will I have to throw a fireman's carry and haul you out?"

"The only thing you can throw is bull," I say, reluctantly rising.

Friends for two years, we enjoy teasing each other. The summer before, he won the cow-pie pitching contest at the Iowa State Fair— in high school he had been the state discus champion—and I have never let him forget it.

I enter the gym, waiting for Bruce and Dan to come forward.

Lawrence gives me a gentle shove and blocks any possible retreat.

Pandemonium erupts.

"Hey George!" someone yells, and many people start chanting, "George! George! George! George!" Kids stamp their feet on the bleachers.

A low-level terror seizes me as I wait for Mr. Dan to emerge from the crowd so we can get the district's silly award business over with. But instead, the crowd quiets as Mary and Londa, wearing *qiipaghaat,* rise from the bleachers and come toward me, Mary holding a shopping bag with a red bow on the handle, and Londa grinning.

"An early birthday present." Mary hands me the bag. I untie the ribbon. Inside are sealskin dance boots, with their sinew straps, and a white, hooded dance shirt. When I lift up the boots, the crowd *ooohs* and applauds.

"My auntie made them," Londa says. "Mary traced a pattern from your shoes."

I shake hands with Londa and give Mary a hug, everyone clapping. At Londa's urging I sit down on the nearest bleacher and pull on the boots. It's a snug fit. The soles, made of walrus hide, are so slick that I slip slightly when I stand.

"After a few weeks the soles will be soft as worn leather," Londa says. She lifts out the dance shirt and urges me to put it on.

"Now, you dance," she says when I'm finished dressing.

In the new boots, my feet nearly go out from under me. In a daze, I step away from the bleachers. "No way," I whisper to her.

She gestures toward the crowd, and several other girls come forward.

The ancient woman whom Gretchen and Meredith met their first day in Gambell totters through the crowd, everyone stepping back to give her plenty of room. She stops at the crowd's edge, not stepping out onto what is now the dance floor. *She's come to watch,* I realize.

I have not danced since the previous year, under Bietha's tutelage, but when the drummers start playing the song she always had me dance to, I realize just how much this event has been choreographed. I watch the girls dance, and I enter at a point with which I am familiar, my hands telling the story of a woman kneading bread and of her husband harpooning a walrus. I am hesitant at first, worried about slipping, but then the drumming takes hold of me.

I forget about slipping or making mistakes.
I dance.

Afterward, as I am taking my jacket from my locker and Gerald is getting his things from his, he says with a sneer, "Quite a show you put on for the villagers."

"It was just dancing."

"Right." He pulls on the jacket and adjusts the collar. "Something I thought you should know. In case the district doesn't give me the village I want next year, I've been applying elsewhere. My girlfriend won't move up here with me, so I might go back home to Seattle no matter what. I'm not like you. I haven't had the luxury of having a family up here. You don't know what it's like to live in Alaska alone."

I wait, wondering where this is going.

"Anyway," he says, "I thought you should know that I put on my résumé that I was in charge of the state champion Future Problem Solvers. Technically, I was, since it's a gifted-and-talented program. But if you have a problem with that . . ."

"Do whatever you want," I say, and walk out the door.

It is nearly midnight by the time I finish packing. I return to my classroom, having forgotten Mr. Dan's memo about making sure the chairs are up on the tables so Jones can give the floor its annual waxing and buffing. As I finish, I see Lobert at the window, grinning at me. He indicates for me to let him into the school, so I do.

"You going to take Merle and them to that thing huh," he says.

"To the competition. Yes, we're going."

His grin broadens, and I start to worry.

"I'm going away too," he says.

"To fish camp?" I ask, trying to be polite. "You going camping for the summer?"

"Nope." Even his eyes seem to grin. "Going Oregon. Job Corps," which he pronounces as *corpse*. "So I bring you this."

From inside his jacket he draws out a small dark-brown teddy bear, across whose tan stomach is penned GEOG G. "And this, too."

He pulls out what is obviously a gift, wrapped in toilet paper. I remove the paper to find myself holding a tiny swan that, much smaller and though more roughly worked than his father's, is in some ways more exquisite. This, unlike his father's, has no feet—the swan is meant to be floating on water—but the arch of the neck is wonderfully carved, and the India inking of the beak and eyes is almost Japanese in its delicacy.

"I don't know what to say, Lobert. Except thanks."

When we shake hands, he isn't grinning. He's beaming.

The next morning, as the plane lands to pick up everyone, the kids, extremely excited, are hugging parents and racing off on three-wheelers to grab some forgotten item. Bruce and I run around making sure the kids have all of their materials on genetic engineering.

We are just about to board when Lars roars up on a three-wheeler and frantically motions me over as he unstraps a white baker's box from the machine. "Cinnamon rolls," he says. "I made them for you and your teams."

I gratefully accept them.

"I haven't had a chance to tell you," he mentions as we walk back toward the plane, me holding the fragrant box, "but two days ago I got the results back from the problem-solving part of the FHA competition in Anchorage. It's a written test, so it's not judged right away. I don't know if you've heard, but Romie, Kasha, and Bess all won blue ribbons."

We shake hands without breaking stride, the pilot gesturing for me to board. "I guess I was wrong about a lot of things," Lars says. He puts a hand on my back as I start up the steps. "Good luck in Iowa. Give 'em hell."

43

"Wow!"

"Cool!"

All the Problem Solvers except Meredith and Boone, who have been to Seattle before, crowd toward the windows as the jet approaches Sea-Tac Airport. The flight attendant has to remind half of them to buckle up as we start to land.

Alaska Air has been kind enough to discount the airfare tremendously, and Best Western has given us a great rate on two suites—one for my family, and one to serve as Bruce's room and a classroom—plus three regular rooms. Perhaps because they are Eskimo or just because they are kids, the teams do not mind that the outdoor pool is freezing. The pool is unheated, and the weather is chilly, fairly typical for mid-May in Seattle.

After allowing them all afternoon to turn blue, Bruce and I deliver two-hour lectures followed by brainstorming sessions. The students resolutely take notes, but their ideas lack the hard-edged, almost driven thinking that won state.

"Something's wrong," I tell Bruce.

"Probably just jet lag."

I am not just talking about the kids, though. I feel exhausted, but like any good male with too much testosterone and too little sense, I put off Mary's suggestion that I phone a doctor.

The next morning there is no change among the kids. They are polite but mentally lackadaisical. I grow increasingly worried and irritated but try not to let it show. "What's going on with everyone?" I ask Meredith after the session. She shrugs.

Back in their rooms, the teams are supposed to read the photocopied materials Bruce and I have given them, then apply the usual process of grading, prioritizing, and writing up the ideas they have culled from the pages, lectures, and brainstorming sessions. The rooms seem abnormally quiet, even for such an academic undertaking. After knocking, I use the passkey I insisted the management give me.

The rooms are empty.

The pool is not.

"We'll learn it!"

"Just a few more minutes!"

"C'mon, George."

"No way, man, that this stuff is going to be a problem for us."

The clock in my head is ticking. It's as if I'm listening to a time bomb. Seventeen days.

The morning is overcast. After the cold, dry spring of Saint Lawrence Island, Seattle has chilled me to the bone. I walk away without speaking, lest I say something I will regret.

The kids' ideas in the pre-lunch session prove worse than in the morning. Only Meredith seems intent on wanting to work as a team. Kasha scowls at her, and Meredith flashes me an angry look. Alvin draws animals. When I tell everyone to read, Romie stares at her book.

That afternoon we drive to Tacoma to visit George Harper, who seems overjoyed to see the kids. They sit in awe of him as he questions them about Alaska, having spent a winter camped on the tundra after WWII, testing army equipment. He asks about genetic engineering, but breaks off the discussion when they appear reluctant to answer.

"Smart man," Boone says as we drive away.

"Nice man," Kasha says. In the rearview mirror I see her slip her hand into Boone's.

We are at a stoplight, signaling for a left, when by happenstance Gerald—who also left school a week early, though for personal reasons—pulls up behind us. The kids in my vehicle climb over each other in their efforts to make it to the rear seat of our Suburban. They wave and pound on the back window. From my rearview mirror I can tell that he sees them. He turns off his blinker and drives straight as the light goes green and we turn.

"How come he didn't wave?" Kasha asks in a voice filled with hurt.

"Maybe he didn't see us," I say.

The silence tells me they know I'm lying.

The next morning the kids are in the swimming pool even before I've had breakfast.

"Any way we can drain it?" I ask the manager. "Only my kids are using it."

He commiserates but refuses my request.

I usher the kids from the pool. They go grumbling. "Tell me what's wrong," I say after they have changed clothes and are in the study room. "Tell me before we close up shop and climb back on the plane, for Gambell."

"That's where we should be," Marshall says. "Everyone's hunting, man."

"I'm homesick," Allana says.

"Me too," Bess says.

Most of the others nod.

I go to the window, not speaking, to collect my thoughts. How to deal with mutiny, especially one that is so understandable?

"You will never again have an opportunity like this," I say, my back to them. *"Never.* You didn't come here to turn blue and shrivel up like peapods in a hotel pool. You didn't come to act like children, wanting to run home to Mommie the moment you landed. You came to win a *national* championship. You came because you are the Alaskan champions, but more than that you came because your loved ones were willing to sacrifice. We all know that you're needed at home for the spring hunts. Others are doing your job out in the boats and in cutting up the meat. They're doing that so you can have the chance—and frankly it's not a very big chance—to walk away with a trophy that a lot of people in the world, including some in your own village and even in your own school, think you are too slow and stupid even to compete for."

I open the door and turn toward them. "Part of your problem is that you have no idea whom you're competing against. You're not going to beat them because you're nice kids. You're not going to beat them because you're Eskimo. And you're damn well not going to beat them by spending half your time in the pool and the other half staring at the ceiling or pretending to read. There are kids right now plowing through books and listening to experts, hanging onto their every word, because they want to win. Sixteen days from now the teams with the trophies aren't going to care if people like you are white or black or brown or polka dot. The only color they will care about is gold—the color of trophies. They will have it, and you'll wish you did."

I walk to the front of the room and face them. "If you want to keep acting the way you've been these past two days, I'll understand. But I won't be going to Cedar Rapids with you. I won't take a team that will get laughed at. Bruce can, but I won't. I'll never, ever, coach that kind of team. You want me to help you, you'll have to earn that help. You want my help preparing for nationals, then this is what I require."

I write "150" on the portable blackboard, and underline it twice.

"You have sixteen days to put in—what? Maybe a hundred and fifty hours of homework. That's what it will take to get me to accompany you to Cedar Rapids. You can't play for the national championship like you did at state. In Anchorage you prepared this much," I draw a small circle on the board, "hoping you would be tested on the tiny part of the topic that you studied. You weren't asked that, and you proved that you have the smarts to adjust to a difficult situation. You proved to yourselves that you're a lot smarter than anyone thought you were.

"But now you're in a bigger game. You can't rely on that basic intelligence, no more than an Olympic athlete can rely on athletic ability. You can't hope that you'll be given a difficult scenario on the test and other teams won't be able to adjust. You aren't playing against four or five other teams this time—there are thirty-three teams per division. Thirty-three teams that are coming to Cedar Rapids prepared.

"If you want me to coach you, you'll have to prepare like Eskimos. Because that's what you are. Even Meredith there," she seems to shrink, her gaze riveted on the floor, "because she's not Caucasian any longer. Your culture changed her. And I think that she's the better for it.

"You aren't some city kids who might go out on the ice and get into trouble—*They don't think ahead.* When you hunt, you prepare for every emergency. If you don't, you come back empty-handed, or maybe not come back at all.

"*This* is the way you need to play at nationals, and *this* is the way I'm going to coach you." I slam the *150* with my fist, then lower my voice and let my gaze drill into them. "If you're *my* teams, you're going to be prepared for *every* area you might be tested on!" I write "Genetic Engineering" on the board. "*This* is what you should be thinking about. Home will always be there. Home is familiar. It's safe. But *this*"—I thump the board—"is where your focus must be. You're out on the ice, and if you don't have your complete attention on *this*," again hitting the board, "you'll fall through and drown." As soon as the words spill from my mouth I regret them because of Marshall's mom, but his gaze is riveted on the board—eyes filled not with anger or sorrow, but with resolve.

"Bruce and I have identified five areas that genetic engineering encompasses," I continue, drawing five circles and labeling them as I talk. "*Plants . . . animals . . . medicine . . .* and *humans.* And, finally, *the business of genetic engineering.*

"We don't think you will be asked about genetically engineering humans—cloning people and things like that. It's too controversial. Bruce and I could be wrong, but we don't think that the national office will risk upsetting parents, especially with elementary school kids playing." I make an X over that circle. "And the business applications— that's probably too dry. So if I coach you, *if* I coach you, you're going to prepare for all five areas but concentrate on these three." With the chalk I thump *plants, animals, medicine.*

"Some kids, because they slide through school on a prayer, will prepare only one area. They'll roll the dice, and if they roll right, they're fine. But if they roll wrong, and the chances are four out of five that they will, they're toast.

"The very best teams, those with the drive and the desire of champions, they'll prepare for every contingency. Every scenario the test might ask. Just as you will, if I coach you. Because if I coach you, you won't be swimming any longer in some hotel pool in water so cold that only a bunch of dumb village Eskimos would ever venture into. You're going to be swimming in information. You're going to know these areas," anger wells up in me, and I smash the board so hard that the easel collapses, "you're going to know them upside down—"

"Inside-out, forward and backward," most of the kids say, almost in unison, in voices barely above a whisper.

"Or else get yourself a new coach!"

I throw the chalk against the wall and walk out the door, shutting it behind myself with a quiet click.

Fifteen minutes later there's a knock on my door.

I open it to see ten kids crowded at the door, looking in at me.

"We want to win," Merle says.

Nods from the others tell me that he speaks for all of them.

"We'll skip the baseball game," Boone says. "And the ferry ride. And," there is a wistful sadness in his eyes, "going up the Space Needle."

"And swimming?" I ask.

"No more swimming," Marshall says.

"The pool doesn't exist," Merle says.

"Let's get to work," I tell them.

We return to the makeshift classroom, read for half an hour, discuss concepts, and have the kids brainstorm and then each write a paragraph, flipping through books and photocopied material for information. Some sit at a table, some flop onto the floor. Alvin turns a lounge chair onto its back and sits on it upside down, back on the carpet and the paper in the air.

When Bruce and I review what are supposed to be rough drafts, I am stunned at how much the kids understand about genetic engineering and how well they can follow the "what MBAP because why" paragraph pattern. The depth of their learning is almost comical, were it not so impressive. Because Bruce and I have made no distinction between the simple and the complex, the kids don't either. They accept as second nature concepts that other kids might groan over.

From Meredith, with her usual love of parentheses: "Risk capital in genetic engineering MBAP, because it promotes the starting up of companies based on capital rather than on research. (Genentech, a genetics lab, for example, had a $691,000 deficit and only earned $81,000 in the first half of 1980. Despite the high risks, investors purchased $35 million worth of stock in the first four hours of stock sales!) With so much money available, genetic-engineering entrepreneurs may be overanxious to start companies (but not all companies can possibly have Genentech's success). Loss of money for the investor, human frustration, and unsafe working conditions (in an attempt to 'save' a company in trouble) may occur."

From Romie: "Unfair educational advantages MBAP because of genetic engineering. For example, if two groups were going to the same school, and one group was rich, they might buy the brain peptides MSH/ACTH. Which can help people learn more better. The book *Life for Sale* says that brain peptides have been isolated. And will be available soon. Therefore, the rich would get smarter and richer, while the poor could be dumber."

From Merle, with his usual emphasis on moral issues and his liking for lists: "What philosophy-of-science author June Goodfield calls 'humankind's technological imperative' MBAP if genetic engineering becomes widespread. Technological imperative is the feeling of 'We are powerless to stop technology!' This results from: (1) human drive, the urge to understand and be productive; (2) technology's self-perpetuating momentum—society tending to think in technological terms; (3) existentialistic views. Genetic engineering increases technological imperative, because scientists are manipulating life instead of just manipulating the environment. Thus, there may be a growing sense of loss of individuality, less self-assertion, loss of self-confidence, social frustration, and more nihilism."

And from Marshall, the last to finish writing down his idea, bent over his work, scribbling and crossing out, discussing his idea with Merle and Boone, reworking the paragraph, now handing me his paper and looking at me with an intensity that could melt an iceberg: "Lysenkoistic overreaction MBAP in genetic engineering. Lysenkoism is the belief that somatic (of the body) and environmental influences are the primary cause of heredity. Instead of gene and gene interaction. People may argue that environmental change is the solution. Instead of genetic engineering. Public and legal battles may result."

This from a kid who eighteen months ago wrote, "Seeing UFOs might be a problem because our telescopes might be bum and so we might not be able to see them."

I finish reading, so proud of him that I could hug him. I raise my fist and utter the only thing I can think of: *"Yes!"*

"You want me to go study it?"

"Upside down . . ." I say, drawing a couple of arrows in the paragraph to eliminate the sentence fragments.

"Inside out, forward and backward." Grinning, he grabs the paper and leaves the room.

I am left to look at an open door and a hotel classroom littered with pop cans and empty potato chip sacks and a couple dozen wadded-up papers on the floor. For the first time that I can remember, the kids were too intent on reading, writing, and discussing even to shoot baskets at the trashcan.

Late that night, when we meet for a summation of what we have learned about genetic engineering that day, Merle lifts up a calculator for me to see. "A hundred and fifty hours. We have sixteen days left. That's only ten point four hours of studying a day." He glances around at everyone else, and back at me. "We can do that."

I look at my watch. "It's 1 A.M. It's been a good session. You've each written and memorized good ideas. Off to bed."

Eyes bright with confidence, the kids file from the room, talking not about sports or travel or hunting or swimming pools, but about science.

"Good stuff," Bruce says after everyone is gone.

"Somehow we have to ratchet up the research," I say, picking up the litter before the maid has to deal with it. "Except for the ideas that George Harper gave us, what they have, they garnered from books. We've got to get hold of material that no one else has. No one."

As I put the chairs along the wall so the maid can vacuum more easily, I wonder when it was that I stopped thinking about just having the kids not embarrass themselves and started thinking about a trophy.

"Three weeks ago I was just hoping to prepare kids to go the distance," I tell Bruce. "I'm not willing to settle for that anymore."

He slugs down a root beer. "This isn't *Rocky.*"

"The hell it's not," I say softly.

44

The next morning, I awaken so exhausted that I have difficulty raising my arms. Mary has to help me into my shirt. "You better see a doctor," she says. "Bruce can take them today."

I do not answer her, because she already knows the answer. *And miss Dr. Palmiter?*

We arrive at the University of Washington to meet with him. As we near a pond amid the manicured lawns, the boys chase a duck. I run after them as well as I can, given how I feel. "You can't kill a duck on a university campus!"

"Why not?" Marshall asks, stopping and coming back.

"Because you can't!"

"We can't because we can't? That's circular reasoning."

"It has a broken wing," Merle says.

"We were going to take it to Denny's and see if they'd cook it," Boone says.

"Broken wing or no broken wing, the duck is on university property," I say.

"Ducks don't attend college," Merle says as we file toward the science building. "So it can't belong to the university."

"We were going to put it out of its misery," Boone says.

All my education and experience, yet I haven't a clue how to refute their logic.

"Inside. All of you." I open the science building door.

We locate Dr. Palmiter's offices, only to find that he cannot see us. "He has an unexpected meeting," the receptionist says. The kids' faces darken with disappointment but brighten when she adds, "Two colleagues of his, a microbiologist and a botanist, have agreed to work with you today, since Dr. Palmiter can't be here."

We are led into a lecture room, Marshall whispering to me, "But its wing was broken. Couldn't you see that?" Before us are semicircular rows of seats looking down upon a laboratory table upon which sits the biggest microscope I have ever seen. The receptionist leaves. Marshall appears to be in a dark mood as he and the other boys wander to the other side of the room, away from me, to sit down.

A short, slim woman from India strides in. She is snappily dressed—hair in a bun, frilly blouse, light gray suit, dark nylons, short black heels. After giving the kids a warm smile, she places a hand on the microscope with the deference accorded something sacred. "This," she says in a British accent, her gaze moving among the kids as if she is giving each student an equal measure of her attention, "is . . . a . . . microscope." She speaks each word slowly, perfectly artic-ulated, as if the kids do not understand English. After pulling down a picture of a paramecium from the charts above the whiteboard, she says, "This . . . is . . . a . . . cell. An animal. A one-celled . . . animal." Again the smile and sweeping gaze. "But let's begin with the . . . micro . . . scope."

As she goes through its parts—ocular, tube, slide clips—the kids' eyes glaze with disinterest, and her body language shows her growing unease. Her speech speeds up.

I see Marshall lean over and whisper to Alvin, who stops doodling and raises his hand. Suddenly I *know* what Alvin, at Marshall's urging, will ask.

He will ask about the damn duck. He will ask a professor of microbiology who is willing to take time away from what I am sure is a hectic schedule, why it is wrong to chase a disabled duck on a university campus.

"Question?" she asks.

My heart stands still. I chide myself for prepping the kids to ask questions. I sit wondering if there is some way I can tell her that Alvin is not allowed to ask questions, that his hand goes up habitually, an automatic response for which he is not accountable. I slink down in my chair.

"If there is a mismatch between a gene to be expressed and . . . and the helix receiving the new genetic material," Alvin says, "can extra chromosomal material in the host cell, um," he seems to struggle for a word, ". . . create parity?"

The professor's mouth goes agape, her head tilts down as if on a hinge and, recovering herself after a moment, she says, "You mean parity of function?"

"Yeah," he says. "Parity of function."

She blinks as if awakening from a fugue, looks at me and again at Alvin, perhaps to assure herself he is not being a smart aleck. His face is calm, neither eager nor arrogant. "You study parity of function out in *Gambell?*" she asks.

"Of course," he says, frowning in confusion.

"In Gambell, Alaska?" she asks. "In an Eskimo village?"

She looks over at me, and I nod.

Her whole face brightens, and she pushes the huge microscope to the side. "Let's talk *genetics!*" she says.

Word that on campus are Eskimo kids anxious for information about advanced genetics apparently races through the halls of academe. After the session with the microbiologist, we have lunch at the Commons, troop back into the science building, and walk into the surreal.

Professors poke their heads from their offices, thrusting textbooks and academic journals into our hands, some walking alongside us, pointing out important passages, scribbling notes in the margins, everyone offering ideas and congratulations and good luck, the kids moving in a daze, foreigners in a world of well-wishers.

We crowd into the botanist's tiny office, he the quintessential professor: a nice man with a horseshoe of white hair, leather patches on the elbows of his tweed jacket. Leaning back in his chair, he gives an overview of how genetic engineering is changing the essence of botany, right down to its roots, he says, frowning when the kids miss the pun. He sucks his unlit pipe, tamps tobacco, and continues talking.

When he mentions that cells that undergo genetic manipulation experience temporary energy loss, Meredith, seated cross-legged at his feet, eyes downcast in what I know is deference but what might be misconstrued as disinterest, sits up straight. "You mean like someone who, you know, has had surgery?" she interrupts.

He nods toward her, and chuckles. "I suppose you could think of it that way. I guess it *is* the same for plants." He cocks his head, as if mulling the idea. "Plants . . . patients. *Nice.*" He leans over his desk for a better look at the skinny middle schooler. "You've a real understanding. Going into science?"

She glances at me and shakes her head.

"Too bad," he says. "Some of my graduate students couldn't have made that analogy. I'm always telling them that we botanists can't see the forest for the trees," again chuckling at his own joke. After he asks her name again and, in answering she explains that I'm her father, he says to both of us, "There's a real need in science for people who can explain complex processes in terms that laypeople can comprehend." To Meredith: "Don't lose that gift, young lady."

On the way to the hotel, she and the ninth graders huddle in the back of the Suburban, all of them whispering, her hands going ninety miles per hour.

That evening, Bruce and I lecture for a couple hours, the kids study until 2 A.M., then everyone is up early for breakfast and for the trip to a Tacoma high school. I double the dose of prednisone and it seems to help my exhaustion. I don't want to miss this latest excursion any more than the kids do. It will be, we all are certain, the trip's academic highlight. They are eager to meet kids in a big school, and I am eager to witness their pleasure.

We arrive to find out that the administration had no idea we were coming, despite previous assurances that everything was a go. The science teacher seems angry when the principal, upset with the information breakdown, takes us to the biology lab. Instead of brainstorming about genetics with the Tacoma kids, as we had hoped, we waste the first class we attend watching them take a final on frog dissection. That the kids in the class are unprepared after what they tell us has been a two-week unit is obvious. Most miss even the simplest questions.

Merle asks the teacher if he can take the test. Though he has never seen a frog, he glances at the anatomy chart for thirty seconds, and does not miss a question.

"Frog's insides aren't much different than those of a seal," he tells me.

His enthusiasm is short-lived. The students in the next class we attend do not want to help the Gambell kids brainstorm about genetic engineering, so Bruce and I end up putting on an impromptu slide show regarding life on the island. "Gross," one of the Tacoma girls mutters, when they see our Eskimo students out on the ice, hunting and butchering walrus. Some of the kids lean away from our students as if our kids are lepers. One girl openly slides her desk away.

"After school they'll eat at McDonald's, and tonight they'll go home and eat what someone else slaughtered and tell their parents that we're murderers," Merle angrily tells me after the class.

"They don't understand about people who harvest their own food," I say.

"They don't want to understand," he says.

Even the one promise that our kids have looked forward to—a breakdancing exhibition by several Tacoma black kids—ends in disaster. When the Tacoma teachers urge our kids to Eskimo dance, the Tacoma teens snicker and sneer.

Ten very subdued team members travel to our next destination, a genetics lab.

The woman who shows us through the lab is outgoing and professional, but when her questions are met with silence and downcast eyes, she signals me aside and asks if anything is wrong. "Just tired, is all," I tell her.

Tired of ignorance.

45

The next morning—the only day we are in Seattle that drizzly clouds do not hang over our heads—I take Mary's advice and phone a doctor, only to find that the earliest appointment I can get is a week away. I have just hung up from the sixth or seventh call when Dr. Palmiter's secretary phones. He's available this morning.

I down more pills and go look for the kids at Denny's. There, Alvin is breakdancing before the windows, using them as mirrors. The customers applaud when he moonwalks. Realizing that he has an audience, he bows. *That boy,* I think, unaware that this new interest of his will later prove of great importance to us.

Next, Dr. Palmiter gives us a fascinating four hours, including a tour of his lab and a long question-and-answer period. We learn about genotyping when he shows a batch of genetic material being mixed. He mentions that the mixing is random.

"Random?" Merle asks, suddenly excited, peering at light-purple material in the tubes. "You don't just maneuver a single gene to a single point on the helix?"

"That obviously would be best, but the science isn't that sophisticated yet."

Merle thoughtfully holds up the tube. "Isn't there a danger of turning on pseudogenes?" From their reading, they have learned that genetic manipulation can turn on weak genes—called pseudogenes—that contain poorly inscribed genetic coding. The result can mean plants lacking resistance to disease; in animals, the result can be deformities and mental defects.

"And introns?" Boone asks, eager not to let Merle upstage him.

Dr. Palmiter smiles. "You mean, ancestral genes that aren't expressed anymore? What genes turn on in the helix—that's a primary concern of ours as well. The media loves the big mice we're producing, but our main research involves oncogenes—cancer-carrying genes. We're trying to find out what causes those to turn on."

Merle looks at Boone and Marshall, and it is as though nonverbal communication passes between them, because suddenly all three are out of their chairs, peering at the test tube.

Allana and Londa come forward, the whole team huddling around the test tube as if it's a magic elixir, and I sit there in a sick daze, thinking, *Please God, don't let them drop it, don't let them shake it, and above all don't let them drink it.*

My racing pulse slows when Merle hands the tube back to Dr. Palmiter.

"This random mixing method," Merle asks the professor. "Does it always work?"

"If it did, it wouldn't be random." Dr. Palmiter chuckles. "We test to see which parts of each batch *take*—that is, which cellular material accepts the gene we are introducing—and we discard the rest."

I am forever telling the kids to look for some simple but novel idea around which to build a great argument. So when I see Merle eye the others on the team, I sense what he is thinking.

What about this for a central idea? Will it fit almost any problem we could be asked?

"Cool," Marshall comments, and for the rest of the four hours the high school kids follow Dr. Palmiter around like puppies.

When we get back to the hotel, I try to nap while the kids review Palmiter's material, and then Bruce and I lecture into the evening, going over the material again plus new material that Bruce and I have gleaned from what is now a small mountain of books on the central table, while the kids scribble in their notebooks and discuss genetic engineering with renewed enthusiasm.

All except Romie, who lately looks withdrawn.

When I call on her late that night, asking about these latest ideas, her eyes go downcast. I ask about the previous day's material. Her head tilts down, and she shrugs. The material of the day before *that.* Another shrug, and now she's pouting. When I ask about the ideas from three days before, her head seems to retreat into her shoulders like a turtle's.

I explode.

"You mean you haven't understood anything these past four days?"
She shrugs.

"I don't speak Eskimo shrug!" I yell. "I'm not a mind reader! You don't understand something, you're to ask me." I thrust up an arm, showing her how easy it is to raise a hand. "That's what we agreed to, remember? That's what we agreed!"

Her lower lip starts trembling.

"What *do* you understand! Tell me!"

Tears well in her eyes.

"What is this!" I demand. "And this! And this!" With each question, I slam the chalk against the blackboard drawings of a genetic problem we were discussing.

The chalk breaks in my hand, and I pitch the pieces against the wall.

"You don't understand something, you ask! We're not on a picnic!"
I stomp from the room.

Back in my room, I try to slow my pulse. That I let real anger surface during Problem Solving leaves me shaking. Part of me knows that we may have reached a level of genetic engineering that has surpassed Romie's understanding no matter how hard she tries. Another part knows that exhaustion has so gripped me that I cannot control my emotions.

When I return to the study rooms an hour later, the kids are hard at work. No one talks to me. I pull Romie aside and apologize to her, then to everyone else, for losing my temper. Romie promises to ask if she doesn't understand something. In minutes, things return to normal, but as I look at the kids studying, Meredith and Merle helping Romie review the concepts, I stand there feeling embarrassed and deeply ashamed.

The next day, I phone Lawrence in Iowa. We'll be staying for three days at his farm. When he informs me that there's a good country doctor there, I again double my dosage of pills and decide I can tough out the illness while in Seattle. Things are frenzied with the kids. Having their coach gone or having them worry about me, I convince myself, might stop their momentum.

Each team has put together several dozen possible problem ideas they might be able to use, depending on what the test asks, and they are bugging me to work on possible solutions. My insistence that the teams spend 90 percent of their time identifying and analyzing problems, in contrast to other teams' preference for solutions, wears on the kids' patience, no matter how consistent it is with a subsistence lifestyle.

When at last the kids seem able to brainstorm problems with ease and precision, I announce that we're ready to start on possible solutions. The kids cheer.

"You'll start tomorrow morning," I tell them, "and tomorrow night I am going to unveil our newest secret weapon. But now you're going for some much-needed R&R."

Perhaps because of my tongue-lashing of a few days before, Romie protests that the teams need more time to study, but I remind everyone that today is my birthday, and they run for the cars. As I climb into the Suburban, I look back at the faces watching me with anticipation. They have been studying so hard and have had such little sleep that their cheeks are hollowed, their eyes sunken. The faces frighten me. Maybe Gerald was right. Maybe I do expect too much from kids. Maybe I do push too hard.

Right now I can only provide a few hours' respite, for all of us.

We take them up the Space Needle and to a Mexican dinner. I do not feel like eating, but the kids surprise me with a briefcase for my birthday present, so I exit the restaurant feeling as if I am flying. Next we're off to the baseball game that so upset Mr. Administrator. And at midnight they become what I am sure is the only class of Bering Sea Eskimos ever to attend the *Rocky Horror Picture Show*. Seeing college kids open umbrellas and dance in front of the screen as the movie plays leaves my kids open-mouthed. "Something's wrong with these people!" Marshall whispers to me as other members of the audience throw toilet paper toward the stage.

The next night, after the kids spend eight hours brainstorming solutions to test scenario after test scenario that Bruce and I dream up, our secret weapon arrives: eight Seattle science fiction writers and fans come for pizza, root beer, and brainstorming. They show the kids advanced methods of extrapolating known science to unknown situations, and we team up the kids with the science fiction people and run through a mock competition.

As the guests leave, one tells me, "They really know their stuff." Another says, "I wish my own kids had such dedication."

I go to bed happy, only to be roused an hour later from my insomnia by a pounding on the door. "Come!" Allana says.

I run barefooted down the cold, wet concrete of the outdoor hallway to one of the girls' rooms. There, Kasha, Romie, and Bess stand atop a bed, screaming, arms around each other.

"I turned on the light," Kasha points toward the floor, "and there they were!"

In the corner is a half-eaten Big Mac . . . feasted on by a dozen large ants.

"Bugs!" she blurts.

"Yeech!" Romie says.

Bess does not say anything, perhaps because she's trembling so much.

I close up the hamburger box and am taking it outside when Alvin runs up.

"Come quick, George! It's Boone!"

More ants?

We find Boone curled up on the floor of the boys' room, groaning and clutching his stomach, his face chalk-white. "Too much pizza?" I ask, hoping for the best.

"I don't . . . know," he gasps.

Bruce rushes him to the hospital while I keep an eye on the rest of the kids. An hour later Bruce phones. "Ulcer," he says.

"Do we have to send him home?"

"That's what they're determining. It doesn't look good."

What to do if we lose him? I ask myself.

Then Londa will have to play.

46

Too worried to wait for Bruce and Boone to come back, I drive the Suburban to the hospital, pulling into the parking lot just as they emerge. Boone gives me a sheepish smile and heads toward Bruce's car. "Definitely an ulcer," Bruce says. "Trying to impress Kasha last night with how much Tabasco sauce he could put on a pizza didn't help."

"Are we sending him home?"

"The doctor says Boone is so competitive that sending him home will do more harm than good. He didn't just approve Boone to go to Iowa—he insists that he play."

Feeling woozy, I sit down on a retaining wall.

"You look white as a sheet," Bruce says.

I am too drained to reply.

"Maybe it's a good thing you came too," Bruce says, and at his urging I enter the ER.

Four hours and several tests later, the doctor tells me that I have mononucleosis. When I argue that the doctors in California had ruled that out last summer, he explains that I have an uncommon form, one that is stress-related rather than viral. He is Chinese, young and confident, and is, I suspect, proud of his diagnosis despite his professionally neutral demeanor.

"Sometimes people overlook the obvious," I say. "They see what they want to see."

"I hear that." His thick glasses, behind which his eyes shine like dark, polished stones, reflect the light as he peruses my chart. He explains that I apparently produce too much adrenaline, which is consistent with my insomnia and which also suppresses my immune system. "That accounts for the rashes and extreme muscular pain. In a nutshell," he adds, "the last thing in the world you should be doing is coaching. Especially at the level your young protégé told me about." Then he says, with a bemused shake of his head, "He really reads Plato?"

"You keep this up and we won't be putting you to bed," Mary angrily tells me as she helps me into bed. "We'll be putting you in a box. Let Bruce take the kids to Iowa."

"I'm going."

"You told me that the doctor said you should be in the hospital *now.*"

"There are doctors in Iowa. Besides, it's only five more days."

"You're goddamn suicidal."

"You're probably right."

In fifteen years of marriage I have never before heard her swear.

When I look up from the bed I see Meredith in the corner, in her pajamas, looking apprehensively from her mother to me. "Stay here, Dad," she says. "We'll be all right."

"I . . . am . . . *going.*" I cannot keep the anger out of my voice. "That's the end of it. And you are not going to tell the others. It's going to be our secret."

Her concern becomes a glower, and she runs through the door that separates our room from the other part of the suite, where she and Gretchen sleep. "I hate secrets!" she says, and slams the door behind her.

I start to rise, angered further by her outburst, but Mary gently pushes me back down. "It's just the competition," she says. "Everyone's on edge. I wish it would all just end."

She climbs into bed, but neither or us can sleep or talk. I feel distanced from her. I want to tell her what else went on in that doctor's office, but cannot bring myself to do it. I want to tell her how, when the doctor started talking about the pressures of coaching, I came apart. I started trembling uncontrollably, my head swimming. The next thing I knew I was crying and he was standing beside me, a consoling hand on my shoulder, more priest than physician, and between sobs I was telling him everything. About how I never wanted to be a teacher in the first place. About Lars and Gerald. About the district office.

"You have mononucleosis," he said as I fought for self-composure, "coupled, I suspect, with a panic disorder. Swallowing these like candy certainly hasn't helped," indicating the vial of Xanax I had revealed. "You're verging on drug addiction. And on a nervous breakdown."

Then he told me that the hospital had a special wing.

"You mean 'ward,'" I said, guessing his intent. "A mental ward."

"Not the one for the psychos. One for professionals."

I smiled inwardly at his dichotomy but could not commit to mental *or* physical help. Perhaps I was deluding myself, but I felt I was not insisting on finishing the trip out of masochism or martyrdom. For nearly two years everyone had been telling us "no."

To me, the illness was another Gerald.

Just as new pills that the doctor gave me start to kick in, there is a screaming. *It's Meredith.*

We are used to her talking in her sleep, often loudly, but this time she's shrieking. We rush into the kids' part of the suite and awaken her, Gretchen looking up at us groggily and, used to her sister, instantly falling asleep again. Meredith collapses into Mary's arms, shaking all over. "It's just a bad dream, honey," Mary keeps saying.

"No," Meredith says, her breaths coming in little gasps. "More than that."

Blurting the story in bits and pieces as she sobs, she tells us about the many times other kids in her class would slap her face with chalk-covered erasers, reveling in her whiteness, and about the night they almost killed her. By the time she is finished, Mary also is crying and I am sitting there on the sofa bed wondering if my decision to come to Alaska, made on impulse, was not the most foolish thing I have ever done in my life.

But then Mary looks at me with absolutely no accusation in her eyes. When she reaches out and takes my hand, there is warmth there, not only in her touch but in her body language, a sense of family, of decisions jointly made, and I understand what every man probably wants from the woman in his life—absolution if not from our sins then from our stupidity.

I still am occasionally trembling, my mind in tumult and my body begging for a few hours' sleep, when the next morning we all say good-bye to Gretchen and Mary, who are staying in Seattle, and fly to Cedar Rapids. It's a humid afternoon when we arrive in Iowa, the fields around the airport stubbled with new corn, the air reeking from a nearby hog farm.

"Stinks worse than a dead walrus!" Londa announces as we pile into a passenger van. Instead of going directly to Coe College, where the national competition will be held, we head west, past Des Moines, to Lawrence's farm for our final two days of studying. He greets us wearing a John Deere hat, and Merle grins—he has his on too. "Mine cost fifty thousand," Lawrence says. "The combine that came with it was free."

No sooner have the kids piled out of the van than I know that my decision to bring them here was unwise, as least before the competition. I had not figured on how seductive a farm can be to kids from a Bering Sea island. Within an hour they are riding tractors, feeding chickens and pigs, and helping make strawberry pies. Alvin climbs the highest tree he can find, and soon is sitting on the grass, tablet across his knees, using charcoal to draw a boy in a tree.

"Shouldn't you be studying?" I ask him. "You've hardly cracked a book."

"Already know everything."

"What's the relationship of, say, introns to pseudogenes?"

He does not look up from his work. "Ask me about parity of function."

"I'm asking about introns and pseudogenes."

He does not answer.

"Nice picture." I mean it, despite my anger. I go back into the house, letting the screen door slam behind me. He keeps drawing.

Another day passes. The new pills have helped considerably, so I forgo Lawrence's offer to take me to the doctor, for fear someone— Lawrence and his family, most likely—will insist that I check myself into a hospital. The two study sessions go so poorly that afterward I sit on the porch, watch the clouds corkscrew above the rolling hills of plowed earth, and wonder what possessed me to take the kids out of Seattle before they are due in Cedar Rapids.

The screen door creaks open. "Let's go for a drive," Lawrence tells me. When I protest that the kids need me, he says, "I've coached too, remember? I know when kids aren't focused. Maybe your absence—rather than your presence—is what they need."

He drives Bruce and me through a county of red barns, rail fences, cottonwood and poplar windbreaks, farmhouses with widow's walks and wraparound porches sporting rocking chairs and swings. The town, a county seat, looks sprouted from its surrounding fields of dark soil.

Prosperity here seems a dream gone sour: businesses with grimy windows, signs with missing letters. The town square's sidewalks lead to a bandstand in need of paint. Later in the summer, Lawrence informs me, the local band will play old songs and patriotic songs, and people will sing without embarrassment. Despite the foreclosures and fields in need of rain, or too much rain, there will be cotton candy and balloons, hamburgers and horseshoes; for this is the heartland of America. This is the Midwest I once called home.

"I think we should go back," I tell Lawrence and Bruce.

"To the farm?" Lawrence asks. "It's only five miles, by the back way."

"Back to Gambell," I say. "I won't have the kids embarrassed at nationals. I won't have them laughed it. That Tacoma high school was bad enough."

"You don't think the kids have a chance?" Lawrence asks.

"No."

I look at Bruce, in the backseat.

"They're not ready," Bruce says. "They're too erratic. I thought they were getting there in Seattle, but now…?" He shakes his head sadly and sucks his lower lip in contemplation. "Back to the island without competing?" he asks me. "It's your call. Whatever you decide."

"You'll be fired if you take them back without competing," Lawrence says.

"I don't care anymore," I say.

47

We arrive back to find some kids on the tire swing. Merle and Boone are helping Lawrence's brother milk cows. Alvin is drawing. Only Kasha and Romie are studying.

Meredith climbs off the swing and comes running. She looks troubled. "We need to go somewhere quiet, Dad. Where there aren't so many distractions."

Lawrence's father is the principal of the local elementary, so we are soon on our way to the school's library. "Are you going to tell them what we were talking about?" Bruce whispers to me when we arrive.

"They have to make up their own minds. I'm through threatening them."

We leave the teams at the school. Bruce helps Lawrence and his wife prepare the turkey feast that is to be the kids' last dinner before heading to Cedar Rapids in the morning. I lie on a couch, feeling sick but unable to nap despite the pills.

They all agreed to study at the school, I tell myself, trying to assure myself that *this* decision was not the exhaustion talking. *If they've been fooling around at the library, that's it. We'll stay at the farm a few more days, and fly home to Alaska.*

When we arrive back at the library, Meredith is watching Marshall race around swatting flies with a rolled-up magazine. Merle and Boone are arm wrestling. Allana and Londa are talking in a corner. Only Romie and Kasha are bent over their books.

"You're supposed to be studying," I tell everyone.

"We did," Marshall says.

"Doesn't look that way to me."

"You see?" He hands me up a paper. I unfold it. On it are written *Fly's eyes genes.*

"This is it?" I try to contain my disappointment and anger. "This is *it?*"

287

"He doesn't understand," Marshall says to Boone and Merle, an impish gleam in his eyes. "I told you he wouldn't."

"Fly's eyes," Boone says. "The gene to be expressed needs fly's eyes genes."

"We graft them on," Marshall says proudly. "Onto the gene to be expressed."

"We didn't feel right about all the technological stuff," Boone says. "A fly has four hundred eyes. The gene to be expressed can *see* its way to the proper locus on the helix."

He and Boone give each other high-fives.

Then everyone is talking at once, and slowly I come to understand: they have translated many of the ideas they have garnered during the trip into solutions that are not so technological.

Londa and Allana have redesigned monoclonal antibodies to become "homing genes" that will guide the gene to be expressed into the helix. Thanks to Alvin, the designer drugs that the biotech lab technicians had told us about are now like Lego toys that can be manipulated for gene splicing. Meredith, Romie, and Kasha decided that a Kirlian camera, which photographs energy, can help a shaman identify genetically engineered cells whose energy levels have declined.

"Kid talk, Dad," Meredith says. "We just needed to play."

"With ideas, instead of in a swimming pool," Boone adds as everyone else heads out the door. He hands me a paper.

"The breaking down of barriers between prokaryotic and eukaryotic organisms MBAP in genetic engineering," he has written. "Prokaryotic organisms, such as bacteria and viruses, have no nucleus; eukaryotes do. For example, if a flu virus develops a nucleus or other advanced cell structures due to recombinant techniques, the virus would become stronger and harder to get rid of. Epidemics may result."

"We can win," he says with quiet confidence. "We're Eskimos."

After dinner we have a timed practice. I give the teams a moderately difficult test problem and put them to work. They handle the situation well, but are a half hour overtime.

I show them my watch. "You've got to analyze the situation, come to grips immediately with how to approach it, and write at lightning speed. Fail to finish, and you'll lose so many points that you won't have a chance."

"I can't write any faster," Romie says. "My hand almost fell off."

"If we try to shorten our time analyzing the scenario," Merle adds, "we're likely to misinterpret what the problem says. And we shouldn't reduce our brainstorming time."

"Sleep on it," I tell them. "And I mean sleep. No late-night talking, no pillow fights. Maybe someone will have an answer in the morning."

That night, before I drop off, I consider our situation. The kids have good material, and they *know* that material, but how can they cut their time so they can finish within the two hours?

Since we want to be in Cedar Rapids by mid-morning, we get the kids up at dawn for a practice before breakfast. The test situation we give them is difficult, and though their answers are excellent, neither team finishes within the two-hour limit. The high school team takes twenty minutes too long, the junior high, twenty-five.

"Load up in the van," I tell them, and we head down the road, everyone quiet, concerned about the timing.

We're nearing Cedar Rapids when Meredith lurches halfway into the front seat.

"Abbreviate!" she says. You know how many times we have to write 'genetic engineering'? How about 'g.e.' instead?"

"Could we leave out the research?" Allana asks.

"The judges wouldn't believe a lot of your answers," I tell her. "You want those research points. *Every* point will be crucial."

"Trying to get in all that research is hard," Kasha says.

"What if there were some simpler way to put it in?" Bruce asks.

"Such as?" I ask.

"Don't know. Except for Meredith, they *are* writing in their second language."

I feel like laughing angrily. Merle's comment about overlooking the obvious has again come true. I have taught the kids to write little essays, but I had forgotten that melding in their research while writing in a second language takes time, too much time.

As we near Cedar Rapids, I have an idea.

"Abstracts!" I tell Bruce. "The kids need to work research into their answers, but then they don't have enough time to finish."

When he nods in agreement, I add, "You know how scholarly articles have little summaries that precede the article? What if, instead of an abstract, the kids list their data at the beginning of each little essay? Then they could concentrate on addressing the test situation instead of worrying about how to put in their research that supports their idea."

He mulls the thought for a moment and then says, "Okay."

I use the rearview mirror to look back at the kids. "What if you use a separate sheet of paper for each problem or solution, write 'Data' at the top, and list your research information before you begin each answer?" I ask them.

The kids put their heads together, murmuring, and Merle says, "Might work. But we're going to have a lot of pages to turn in."

"Baffle 'em with B.S.," I say.

He and Boone laugh. The others look confused, not knowing what B.S. stands for.

As we enter the city, a huge electronic sign blinks, CEDAR RAPIDS WELCOMES FUTURE PROBLEM SOLVERS.

"How did the sign people know we would be passing by right this minute?" Kasha asks.

I give her an Eskimo shrug.

48

We arrive at Coe College and unload the van. The manicured lawns and brick dorms remind me of Loras College, ninety miles to the northeast, where my teaching career began and that of Om, my best friend, ended in suicide.

"I wish we were back in Gambell," Allana says. "I'm tired of being good."

We attend the opening ceremonies, the Gambell Problem Solvers awed by the presence of four hundred kids in the auditorium. Afterward, I remind them that they must attend the gift swap.

"We have to?" Marshall whines.

"Bruce said that the other teams will have state pins and buttons and school pens to give away," Boone says. "No one's going to want our stuff."

"Over ten families donated whiskers," I remind them. "And Romie's dad . . ."

From their expressions, I see that they are sorry they spoke. Walrus whiskers are useful as ornamentation in ivory carvings, so parting with them is not insignificant. Romie's dad also donated a sack of walrus teeth, each of which could have been carved and sold.

They take the whiskers and teeth and trudge off toward the gym, then return an hour later, grinning. "We were mobbed!" Boone says.

"Everyone wanted our stuff!" Marshall adds. "I thought they were going to fight over the whiskers!"

"When we ran out of stuff, they wanted to know all about Gambell!" Romie says. "They wanted to know about us!"

Soon, everywhere we go on campus, kids stop to watch us or to trot up and say hello. "You really hunt whales?" they ask. "You eat walrus? Cool! Speak some of your language for us! How could you study in the middle of nowhere?"

"Some guys from Montana were laughing about the girl on their team," Alvin tells me, "because on the state problem she said that ecosuicide bombers might try to blow up nuclear waste repositories. They wouldn't let her write down her idea."

Everyone looks at Marshall, whose identical idea had earned the team five points for original thinking, and we burst out laughing.

"Smelly sock!" Marshall says.

After dinner Bruce and I give them the hardest genetic engineering situation we can imagine. The answers are excellent, and both teams finish in just under two hours. We use the dorm lounge to review, and then I send the junior high team to bed so I can have a second review with the older kids, whose opponents are certain to be more intellectually sophisticated.

Merle looks troubled. "We have some good ideas," he says, "but nothing great. If we get the chance to use a lot of our material, then we need," he makes a fist, "something *dynamite* that might work for a best solution."

"Not something technological," Boone says. "The city kids will have that."

"Something *Yupik*," Marshall says, and Allana nods.

We kick around ideas for ten or fifteen minutes, but nothing feels right.

Then I remember Bietha, and suddenly I see a connection to something I read.

I ask Marshall if I can talk about his mom, and when he agrees, I tell them Bietha's teleporting story. The kids appear to accept her having flown on her grandfather's shoulders.

"Maybe it's just my science fiction background talking," I tell them, "but there's some evidence to suggest that the way people look at the world—I mean, the way white people look at the world—may be shutting out whole realms of possibilities. Stephen Hawking"— the Problem Solvers are familiar with the world-famous physicist—"says mathematics indicates that other dimensions must exist. Maybe, by insisting on a rational, ordered universe, the white man's world has shut itself off from a greater physics than we're aware of. Maybe people really can teleport, but because white people assume it's impossible, then it is, for them."

"Cool," Marshall says when I finish.

"But even if people can teleport," Boone says, "it's not going to fit genetic engineering."

"Maybe Lobert has the answer," I tell them.

They look at one another, start laughing, and then look back at me incredulously, realizing that I am serious.

"I remember seeing something in here." I dig though my new briefcase, which is bulging with books and articles. I find an interview I had torn from a *Playboy* I confiscated from my young reader of *Moby's Dick*. The interviewee is Francis Crick, the geneticist who together with James Watson originally identified the helix and began the revolution regarding DNA.

"I'm pretty sure that somewhere in here Crick mentions that thought itself might be electromagnetic, like a chemical pattern," I say.

Merle's eyes meet mine. "Like a math formula," he says excitedly.

"And therefore decipherable," I say.

Heads together, we go through the article, me running a finger down the paragraphs, all the team members except Merle obviously confused.

"If thought is biochemical and can be decoded, then maybe . . . " Merle says.

"Maybe it can be transferred," Boone says, now keying on his cousin's thoughts. Then, his face tightening in confusion, "Not 'transferred.' What's that word?"

"Projected?" I ask.

"A shaman could do that," Marshall says. "In the old days."

"Modern explanations, ancient technologies," I say.

The kids sit back, satisfied with their reasoning, happy with themselves. Then Merle grabs a piece of paper and hunches forward. "What if thought really isn't projected?"

He skillfully draws an Eskimo and then what at first appears to be a parka. "Pretend this is the aura," he says, referring to the electromagnetic force that surrounds all living things. "What if the mind doesn't occur only in the brain, but in," he looks up at me for affirmation, "in the entire being, even in the aura? Instead of projecting thought, couldn't two brain patterns," he draws a second figure and intersects the two auras, ". . . like, meet?"

"I still don't see the connection to genetic engineering," I say.

"What if the mind," Merle says, leaning back against a couch, "isn't in just the brain and the aura," he closes his eyes in what seems intense concentration, "but in the cells themselves? In every cell, not just in brain cells?"

"Plato says that all truth is within us," Boone adds. "But didn't he also believe in those Form things? That there's a greater truth? Truth is everything. . . ." His voice breaks off.

He glances at Merle, and that unseen, unknowable communication passes between them. The next thing I know, Merle is drawing a tree. He puts an aura around that as well, points to it, and Boone nods. ". . . and everything is Truth," Boone finishes. "Every living thing."

"Every living thing can communicate," Merle says. "On the cellular level, in the overall body, in the aura. Change one part through genetic engineering, then everything changes."

"Genetic engineering," Boone says, pointing to the tree's aura, ". . . is communication."

"Communication is precision," Marshall says, parroting what we had drilled on so many times. "And so is genetic engineering."

It is a very mature young basketball player who looks at me.

There is silence among us.

At last I say, "Time for bed, now."

"What if," Marshall says as he rises, "the aurora is the world's aura? What if it shows what the earth is thinking?"

"Next you'll be genetically engineering the Northern Lights," I tell him.

"They got us here," he says.

49

As Marshall enters his room I see Alvin, his roommate, at his desk, hunched over a book. Finally.

"The girls' ideas are good," I tell Alvin, pulling up a chair. I wait until Marshall heads down the hall, towel in hand, and then quietly tell Alvin, "Your ideas are sketchy, and I don't mean like in drawing. I mean information-sketchy. I know you're some kind of genius. It's time to prove it. Either be ready by morning, or I'm replacing you with Bess. She's ready, Alvin. You're not."

He does not say a word, but he is back poring over the book as I exit.

I go to my room and climb into bed, only to awaken in a sweat, a nervous knot that feels the size of a grapefruit in my chest—and not from mono, this time. I can *feel* that something is wrong.

My watch says 2:30. Bruce is snoring. The glow from a street lamp slants through the blinds, ribbing the wall with light.

What's the problem? I ask myself. *The timing? The high school kids' concern about too much science?* No, we are good to go on those.

I think about Palmiter's lab, and realize what's worrying me.

"Get up!" I tell Bruce. "We have a problem! I mean a big one!"

He grumbles and rolls over. "Go to sleep. I don't care what it is."

"You've got to listen to me! You've just got to!"

Bruce moans and sits up, supporting himself with an elbow as he rubs his eyes. "What!"

"Everything we've worked on, everything we've taught the kids, involves problems in genetic engineering as it's taking place. That's only natural, because the information came from books on genetic engineering and from genetics labs."

"So what's your point?" His voice has not lost any of its irritation.

"This is *future* problem solving. We overlooked the obvious! The test isn't going to ask about problems during genetic engineering.

The kids will be given some invention or process, something created from genetic engineering. None of their material will fit!"

"Let it go, George." He lies down again.

"We're dead in the water. I'm telling you, the kids are going to drown."

And it's my fault, I don't need to add. *I didn't see what was right in front of me.*

"Nothing you can do about it now. They're as prepped as they're going to be."

I lie looking at the ceiling, waves of anxiety rushing through me. *Just let it go. Nothing we can do now.* Developing a whole new game plan, with all its days and days of reading and writing and memorizing, and all before eight in the morning? Now that, truly, is impossible.

Just lie here, I tell myself.

But I can't. Because before each skit, the team reads their best solution to the problem the test gives.

If that solution does not deal with the test question, people will laugh but not aloud. The kids here are too socially astute for that. But they will know. They will decide that the Eskimo kids are not in their league.

I climb from bed and pound on doors. Everyone except Alvin is asleep.

"Meet in Meredith and Romie's room!" I tell everyone, not wanting to use the lounge and risk awakening kids from other teams. "Hurry!"

In pajamas and shorts, the kids bustle in bleary-eyed, crowding onto the beds, chairs, floor. Heart thudding with anxiety, I explain the situation as well as I can. Only Romie does not seem to understand the dilemma.

"Five hours to learn a whole new game plan?" Marshall says, moaning. "No way, man!"

"Is it possible?" I ask.

Meredith shakes her head. "Even if we could develop new stuff, we'd lose. The ideas wouldn't be good enough. If we don't score some originals, we don't have a chance."

But at least you wouldn't be laughed at. At least you would be addressing the test question.

"So what are we going to do?" I ask them.

Merle's eyes go downcast. Meredith gives me a defeated shrug. *Doomed.*

Alvin has been draped over the end of the bed, mumbling as if reciting a mantra and drawing figures in the air with his finger. "It's simple," he says.

The rest of us wait for him to speak. He doesn't.

"Alvin!" half of the students chorus chipmunk-style.

He sighs and sits up, a bemused scowl on his face, as if he cannot believe he must deal with such lesser minds. "Just because something's invented doesn't mean that genetic engineering will stop, does it?"

I see his point. There will always be lab work. Testing. Research and development.

"Okay," I tell them. "If you are asked about some genetic-engineering development in the future, then every now and then try to include a line or phrase that pulls lab stuff into the picture. Something like, 'Since there is sure to be ongoing research concerning X' . . . X being the product or process created through genetic engineering. Got that?"

Everyone nods except Romie.

"Putting phrases in like that will probably put us over the two-hour limit," Meredith says.

"You're going to have to write faster." I gaze around at them. "Understand?"

No one objects. They realize the gravity of the situation. But Romie still looks confused.

"Romie?"

"I'll explain it, Dad," Meredith says with a smile. "Go to bed. We can handle it. Kid talk."

We agree that everyone will spend an hour testing each other, to see how the new phraseology might be worked into the material they already have. As I shut the door, Meredith and Romie are lying on the bed, Meredith mumbling to Romie in English and Siberian Yupik.

In the morning everyone gathers in the lounge, slurping down orange juice from little cartons. The kids look exhausted, but I know their nervousness will carry them for the next few hours. After the two-hour test, there are two hours to prepare for the skit, which we are just going to walk through rather than try for a trophy. Then the two or three hours the skits will take, and they're done until the next day's awards ceremony.

"Everyone have pencils?"

Each produces two, all sharpened.

"Carefully read the whole thing," I remind them. "I've heard that sometimes the judges will add a sentence right at the end that changes what the test asks. Decide what the test is saying, decide how you will attack the problem, and determine which of your ideas will fit, what you'll have to throw out, what you'll need to brainstorm on the spot. Got that?"

Everyone except Romie nods, bright-eyed.

Her eyes are downcast.

"Understand?" I ask again, edging close to her.

The eyes remain down.

Now I'm worried. Do I need to replace her with Bess at literally the last moment?

"Understand?" I ask a third time.

She points to her forehead, and grins.

"Read my brows!"

They're lifted.

Everyone laughs and huddles together, hands touching.

"You won state," I say, "not only for the people of Gambell but for Eskimos everywhere. This time, play for yourselves. Win this, and you will have beaten some of the best and brightest that America has to offer. You understand that? Now go kick some ass!"

They laugh at my language, together shout, *"Do it!"* and off they run to the test, taking my heart with them.

50

The kids return two hours later, exhausted but eager to tell me about the problem and how they attacked it.

"The situation involved a genetically engineered serum called Polyvac that can inoculate against twelve common childhood diseases at once," Meredith says breathlessly.

"Like mumps, measles, and chicken pox," Romie says.

"There was a whole list of problems the judges said cannot be used," Marshall adds. "Like refrigeration of the serum, and outcries against using the serum."

"The test said there have been no adverse effects from the inoculations," Boone says.

"Did you argue that there would still need to be research and development?" I ask.

"We tried," Merle says. "But it was difficult, you know? Everything about the serum was so positive. There wasn't any mention about lab activity at all." He looks up at me from his position on the floor. "You think they'll accept our argument?"

"I don't know. It's chancy." I look over at Meredith. "Did your team finish?"

Fear abruptly displaces the excitement in their eyes.

"Sort of," she says after a moment.

Their fear infects me. "*Sort of?*"

"We had so much material. We would discuss how this and that fit the situation, how something else would fit if we changed it—you know, if we used our information in a different way—and . . ."

"*Did you finish the problem?*"

She nods tentatively, eyes downcast not as an Eskimo would but as if she is about to be scolded. "We finished," she says finally, "but . . ."

"We had to leave a lot of stuff out," Kasha says, the fear in her voice evident.

"You did your best?" I ask.

Meredith nods.

"That's all anyone can ask," I say.

But we all know that I'm voicing the Big Lie. How many times have I told them that doing "your best" isn't good enough? How many times have I said there is no room for error in the modern world, that in a way we are all out on the ice? This is the world of the atom bomb, I have reminded them. This is the world of crises in the Middle East. The margin of error is so negligible, I have told them, as to be nil.

"We didn't finish either," Boone says quietly.

"Not the way we wanted to," Merle adds. "We ran out of time."

Time. If only we had more time. If only our days lasted a week, our lives twice as long.

I know I should be reassuring the kids, for they worked incredibly hard to be where they are. But I want them to emerge from the airplane and give a trophy to the people of Gambell—something to remind everyone that here is a group of kids who identified a goal and let nothing stop them from trying to attain it.

I don't want them to go home empty-handed.

"Maybe the judges will concentrate more on the overall booklet and not so much on what we wrote down in each step," Meredith says hopefully.

I shake my head. "Every part of the test counts. You know that."

"Whatever the case, it's too late to do anything about it," Bruce says.

His words cause me to glance at my watch.

Not too late!

"We have an hour and fifty minutes before the skit competition!" I tell everyone. "We can win *that.*"

"Aren't we just going to walk through the skit?" Marshall asks, almost a wail.

"You want a trophy . . . or not!"

He shrinks back.

"There's no way we can prepare two great skits in two hours," Meredith says.

My mind is racing. "We could do one skit. Both teams, one skit. It's in the rules."

The kids go silent, mulling the possibility.

"Well?" I ask.

"Let's do it!" Romie says, looking up.

"One skit!" Kasha says.

Everyone else soon agrees.

"No Eskimo shyness," I say. "Everyone participates to the fullest!"

"What kind of skit?" Meredith asks.

"A dance." I'm developing ideas as I speak. "Eskimo dance. Meredith, you mime. And Alvin—break-dance." He lifts his head as if to protest, but Londa and Allana glare at him, and his features change to a look of reluctant acceptance.

"Just dance?" Bruce says. "The skit has to act out the main solution."

"We'll use the high school's solution," I say. A look around tells me that the junior high team members agree. To Merle: "Did you use the stuff on Crick in your final solution?" He nods, and looking around at the kids, I continue, "I minored in dance in college. We'll do a statue dance." The kids frown in confusion. "Like this."

I show them. Move. Freeze. Move. Freeze. Move.

"You girls will Eskimo dance and let your hands act out the skit. Meredith and Alvin—you'll use your whole bodies. Every time you stop and freeze, you'll draw the audience's attention to the information the skit is supposed to convey."

"Just read the solution as everyone dances?" Boone asks.

"Londa will read the solution before the skit. Just like you're supposed to. We'll need a narrative that will accompany the dance. Also, someone will have to read it. Someone with a strong, sure voice."

"I will," Boone says.

"Merle and Marshall, can you both drum?"

"No problem," Marshall says. "But we didn't bring our drums."

"The competition says that you can only use the materials they give you—sacks and cardboard and yardsticks. You'll have to make drums out of that. The stuff's in my room." I give the boys my key, and they run down the hall.

"Bruce, you help Boone compose the narrative. The rest of us will practice as you two write. Meredith and Alvin, move back these chairs. Then Alvin, you've got about three minutes to teach Meredith how to moonwalk. The rest of you girls climb into your *qiipaghaat.*"

"What'll we use the garbage sacks for?" Merle asks, running back in with the materials.

"I'll need one to throw up in, if this doesn't work," I tell him.

51

"Five minutes, ten seconds!" I announce after the kids have gone through the dance routine for the fifth or sixth time.

"We've got to be in the auditorium in seven minutes," Bruce says, agitated.

"The skit can't go over five minutes, or you're disqualified," I remind the kids again. "Five minutes." I hold up a hand, fingers spread. *"Five!"*

We agree to several small cuts in the routine, and enact it again.

"Four minutes fifty-one seconds!" I announce.

"Let's go!" Bruce says. "Two minutes to be at the auditorium!"

"Run!" I tell everyone.

We sprint down the stairs and across the lawn, arrive out of breath and draw our skit number from the box near the door. Thirtieth—third from last. *Good.* That means Boone will be able to read over the narrative several more times, and everyone else can practice their movements in their minds, for at least two hours before it's our kids' turn to perform.

Team after team ascends to the stage. Some of the performances are humorous, some serious; some amateurish, some exhibiting the polished professionalism of students with acting experience. As many of the teams finish, they exit the auditorium, a practice that I find rude, for the audience grows smaller as each team competes.

Before each performance, one member reads part of the Step 6 essay that elaborates on the team's best solution. Most are insightful, with excellent science. Several teams, perhaps trying the "shot in the dark" approach we successfully used during the state competition, are ill-prepared for a question about medicine. "We realize the test situation involved Polyvac, a medicine for children," one girl says, trying to cover her embarrassment with a look of confidence, "but we decided that looking at the role of genetic engineering in plant life would be a more interesting application of the problem-solving process."

303

How, I wonder, are such students, from a school for the gifted, going to be prepared for adulthood? They are competing for the *national championship,* yet they cannot make the transition to a situation they did not expect? What will happen when life throws them a curve?

"Boone, study the script," I whisper.

"I'm ready."

"Study it again."

Finally it is our team's turn to enter the ready area. I give them a thumbs-up and cross my fingers.

When at last the kids reach the stage and a visibly nervous Londa steps forward to read the senior team's main solution, the audience has been reduced to three or four teams and their coaches in the first rows of seats in the massive auditorium, and the judges in the last rows.

The first axe falls.

Londa begins stumbling through the words—and I realize that, in my zeal to assure that Boone was prepared, I overlooked that Londa, the alternate, has never read the main solution. As the competition requires, Merle had copied the main solution and brought it back to the dorm, but I did not give it to Londa until we were crossing the lawn.

Her unfamiliarity with the material, combined with her nervousness at standing in front of an albeit nearly empty auditorium, exacerbates her weak reading skills.

"According to James Watson, discoverer of the double helix," she says, her face ruddy with fear, "conscious thought may be the result of a chemical reaction. We feel that it is reasonable to assume, therefore, that thoughts are energy and can thus be transmitted. We should thus have a shaman and para . . . parapsycholo-ogists," I see kids in the front row eye each other, "train microbiologists to project their con . . . consciousnesses"—she reads 'consciences,' to the small audience's even greater bemusement—"into the host cell. They will thus be able to see the structure of the DNA strand. This knowledge will help them put the introduced gene into the strand at the proper lo . . . locust."

One of the front-row kids puts his forehead in his hand and

snorts his humor. Londa glances toward the back curtain and then toward the door. *She's going to run,* I think fearfully, *or she's going to demand that another team member read the solution.*

But instead of running, she grips the podium and presses on.

"To help our microbiologists even better see the structure of the DNA strand, we will develop computer simulation models of the structure of the types of strands in question during ongoing research involving the Polyvac serum. To help in the thought projection, we will include a model of each scientist's aura, obtained through Kirlian photography studies.

"Our microbiologists will train other scientists in thought projection. They will also help the general public understand that plants, animals, and humans have thought-energy in common and, ultimately, Truth in common. The microbiologists involved in Polyvac serum research may serve as a spearhead to deepen our understanding of our environment."

She sighs with relief and disappears behind the curtain.

Moments later, the stage curtain swings open. From backstage, Boone's voice comes strong and clear through the main microphone.

We are Yupiks. Siberian Yupiks. From a blizzard-swept island in the Bering Sea.

Onstage, Merle and Marshall softly beat their cardboard drums, their low chanting wafting through the auditorium. Romie, Kasha, Londa, and Bess slowly rise from a crouched, heads-down position, hips and arms swaying with Hawaiian-like fluidity, the brocade of their *qiipaghaat* looking rich in the lights.

For over 2,000 years we have lived on the island. For over 2,000 years we have not resisted change, but rather have accepted change as natural to the natural world, accepted it and ameliorated its impact.

I can't keep from smiling. "Ameliorate," which I taught to Boone over a year ago, is his favorite word. He works it into almost every Problem Solving piece he writes.

As I listen to the words and watch the kids drum and dance, something breaks within me. For two years, the love and admiration I have for the kids has been building, and now it is as if a dam collapses. I put my head in my hands. My face is contorted with emotion, and tears come.

"What's wrong?" Bruce says quietly, and puts a consoling hand on my shoulder.

I can only shake my head and wave him off.

In the not-distant past, our island has witnessed the greatest change since our ancestors first crossed from Siberia. Our grandparents and even some of our parents have witnessed the change. Because of that we understand history not as the past, preserved as if in amber, but as the present. For us, history is *now*. Change is *now*. Change is ongoing— and dramatic. We have witnessed the coming of the whites, and the progress they bring.

On cue, Meredith rises from a tiny, huddled position and mimes the climbing of a rope. She is all in white. Even her face is white, apparently from chalk in the classrooms that served as the ready area behind the stage. The humiliations she endured with white chalk on erasers have had some benefit after all.

Some of the things the whites brought, we found to be good. Guns for hunting, outboard motors for boating. 'These are good things,' our grandparents said. 'They will help us feed our families.'

But some of the things the white men brought were not good.

The other dancers halt, frozen in pose, as Meredith moonwalks across the stage, in front of them, a motion meant to symbolize the opposite of progress.

There was alcohol. And there was slaughter instead of harvest. The whites slaughtered our walruses for ivory and sport, clubbed seals for fur hats, harpooned whales for lamp oil and perfume—all in the name of fashion. Our people, meanwhile, starved.

'We should fight them,' some of our people said. 'We should fight the whites.' But they knew they would die in the effort. 'We should join them,' others said. 'Act as they do.' But our people knew that would be impossible. They knew that in the end they would lose more than their physical bodies. They would lose their culture. They would lose their souls.

The killing of animals, though, the killing of our spiritual brothers, was not the worst thing. For with the coming of Western ways there came disease.

Alvin emerges from the wings, face devoid of expression, his motions robot-like, arms akimbo, meant to symbolize the industrialized world.

Our grandmothers wept as babies died in their arms. Our grandfathers cried to the heavens for comfort and for eternal justice. Measles and mumps, chicken pox and cholera—and worst of all, influenza. Our people fought the fevers, they lay in their huts that white people would mistake for igloos, and fought the fevers. They died from the fevers.

Boone pauses, and there is an almost preternatural hush in the auditorium. It is as if the place has held its breath.

The first ones to die were the lucky ones. The others buried them beneath rocks on our mountain overlooking the sea. Buried them beneath rocks because the ground was too frozen for digging, too cold for the soul to free itself.

The girls are again dancing, simulating the placement of rocks, as, hands on hips, Meredith faces the audience—a picture of cold, of uncaring. Alvin sinks down into a ball that continues to move. Unlike the break-dancing we saw in Tacoma, there is no beauty here, no energy, only ugliness—a cog in a machine.

Those few who survived were perhaps immune to the illnesses. Those few who survived put their grief and their anger behind them. Years later, when the first serums were developed, our grandparents and our parents were inoculated as other Americans were inoculated, and they prayed that the serums would protect them—would save our culture.

Now there is a new serum. One created through the god-like power of genetic engineering. One created through processes that have enormous potential—and enormous potential prob. . . .

The microphone goes out. There is a squawk, and I hear *Polyv* . . . and the mike again dies before Boone can finish the word. The girls gradually stop dancing and look toward the wings.

Boone's voice comes through in static bursts.

We need to train scientists in . . . to . . .

Romie starts dancing, putting on as straight a face as possible. Kasha is also dancing again, yet also whispering to Boone, who is offstage and apparently does not hear or realize that the mike isn't working.

"I've got to do something!" I tell Bruce.

I start to rise but he pulls me down. "Interrupt, and they'll be disqualified."

"They're going to be disqualified for someone informing Boone that the mike isn't working?"

"You want to risk it?"

"What else am I supposed to do! Just sit here?"

The assistant to Dr. Anne Crabbe, the national head of the program, walks toward the stage. The second hand of my watch continues its remorseless sweep.

"Even if they correct the problem, we'll be overtime," I whisper to Bruce.

"They'll put more time on the clock," Bruce reassures me. "You'll see. It's not the kids' fault."

Boone emerges from the curtain, apparently having at last realized the problem. He blows into the mike, and there's sound again. He goes back behind the curtain.

Train them in thought projection. In the shaman tradition of . . .

The assistant to Dr. Crabbe stops walking and looks toward the stage, clearly relieved that the mike is again functioning.

Another squawk, and the mike goes out again. I hear Boone thump it with a finger.

Merle leaves his drum and rushes behind the curtain. When he returns to the stage, the mike is working, though so weakly that I am unsure whether the judges, in the back row, can hear.

Merle and Marshall start drumming and chanting again, and Alvin and the girls finish the dance routine, but the spell of the performance is broken. The kids bow and trudge off the stage.

Teams from the front row rise, applauding.

A standing ovation.

When the last of the Gambell team has exited the stage, Dr. Crabbe's assistant comes to the podium. "Five minutes, fifteen seconds," he announces. "No scoring."

At first I am too stunned to speak. Their microphone malfunctions, and my kids must suffer for it?

"There's nothing you can do," Bruce says, taking hold of my wrist as I rise to walk toward Dr. Crabbe's assistant.

"The hell there isn't!"

When I approach the assistant, he seems irritated that I could be upset about his decision regarding disqualification. "You'll have to take it up with Dr. Crabbe," he says, and turns his attention to the stage as the next team enters from the wings. "I really don't have time to talk about it right now."

"Right now," I tell him, "is when the judges do the scoring."

"I'm sorry. I cannot reverse the decision. Your team was fifteen seconds over."

"You made the decision, and you can't reverse it?"

"It's out of my hands."

He walks away.

I tell the kids to stay and watch the rest of the performances. As Bruce and I exit, bound for the competition's command center, an elderly woman emerges from the auditorium and hurries after us, wobbling in her high heels.

"Hold up there, young man!" she calls out to me.

We hasten back to her, and her hands go up to her cheeks as she tries to catch her breath.

"I've come to nationals for every one of the program's ten years of existence," she finally manages to say. "My teams have only made the finals once, but I come every year anyway." She looks at me with eyes filled with a kind of awe. "It's the skits that I love. It amazes me, what kids can do."

She takes my hand as if to shake it but instead holds it between hers. Her hands are warm, her fingers laden with rings. "That was the most moving performance I have ever witnessed." She squeezes my fingers. "Thank you. Thank you so very much."

52

That night I lie looking at the ribs of light on the ceiling. All our hopes for a trophy ride on whether Dr. Crabbe and the other administrators accept our protest. The protests lodged in almost every Olympics—how far have they ever gotten most athletes?

There is a knock on the door.

I bound from bed so fast that I get tangled in the covers and fall on my face. I pull on my robe, swearing under my breath, my heart pounding with the irrational hope that someone has come in the middle of the night with good news.

It's Alvin, holding his stomach. "I don't feel so good," he says.

Bruce rises, and together we help Alvin to a chair. "I was up all last night studying," he says. "And tonight I couldn't sleep. So I took No Doz."

"You took No Doz to sleep?" I ask.

"A whole box."

We haul him to the hospital. Fighting exhaustion, I sit in the waiting room while Bruce takes him into emergency. I do not dare go in, for fear the doctors might not let me out again.

It's 2 A.M. by the time we arrive back, put a contrite Alvin to bed, and collapse onto our own beds. When I awaken it is morning, and I am still in my clothes.

We breakfast in the college cafeteria, but I am too nervous to eat. In a couple hours we will know if our protest prevailed.

Everyone is silent as we thread toward the auditorium, which proves packed. Parents and educators have filled the seats not reserved for the teams and are standing in the back and in the aisles. A young, thin woman, Dr. Crabbe announces that the awards ceremony will be video-taped, with the tape going to Dr. Paul Torrance, the international "guru" of gifted education and the program's founder. Elderly, he is too ill to attend. There is a round of applause.

Dr. Crabbe and several other speakers give short talks about the value of the Future Problem Solving Program for education and for the trials of life. The crowd hushes as the curtains are pulled open, revealing tables full of trophies, the three main ones—the team trophies—three feet tall.

"The first awards are for the skit competition," Dr. Crabbe says. "This event combines a flair for drama with the ability to act out complex ideas with only a handful of props. You all remember the garbage bags and yardsticks, don't you?"

Everyone chuckles, and I can see kids explaining the reference to their parents.

She runs through the various winners in the elementary and junior high divisions, kids screaming with delight and coming forward amid polite applause to receive their awards. Finally she comes to the high school group.

"In fifth place . . . ," she begins.

I clench my fists in hope as I wait for the fifth through second place winners to ascend the stage. *Our skit was powerful. Even that lady said so.* "And this year's winner of the skit competition, senior high division . . . from a school that, with finalists in two divisions here at nationals, elected to combine both teams for a single skit . . ."

Meredith grins at me and I grip her hand as we prepare to rise.

"Salinas, California," Dr. Crabbe says.

Most of the Gambell kids are halfway out of their seats. They slump back, faces flush with disappointment. I give them a look of reassurance, but I know that my regret shows in my features. I keep looking toward the stage, afraid of making eye contact with the kids, feeling hollow as the Salinas team waltzes from the stage with the coveted trophy.

Fifteen seconds, I tell myself. *A malfunctioning microphone and fifteen seconds.*

So upset am I that I barely listen as Dr. Crabbe announces the short-story awards. Since the winners hail from all parts of the globe, no one walks to the stage to accept a trophy. There is polite applause for the absentee honorees.

"And this year's international champion in the junior high division," Dr. Crabbe says, "Meredith Guthridge, Gambell, Alaska."

Meredith sits stunned, hands clasped over her mouth.

"Go! Go!" I whisper, and she gives me a big hug before climbing over the other kids, who congratulate her as she heads to the stage.

"Way to go, Mere!" I hear Romie tell her.

"Not going home empty-handed," I mutter to Bruce.

But in the back of my mind I am thinking, *the white child is not going home empty-handed.*

After Meredith sits down, everyone piling around her to admire the trophy, Dr. Crabbe announces the high school short-story winners.

"The fifth runner-up . . . the fourth runner-up . . ."

I see Merle blink as she says, "The first runner-up, Merle Apassingok, Gambell, Alaska."

Oh my god. Inside I am crying with joy. *A story he dictated in two hours, up against over 2,000 entries from throughout the world . . .*

Merle and I shake hands, and he heads to the stage for his trophy. "Now we really aren't going home empty-handed," Bruce whispers to me, as if reading my thoughts.

Next come the individual competition winners, a contest that we elected not to enter at nationals, though any student who wins on either the individual or team level at state is eligible. We give an Alaskan standing ovation as Dillingham's Jennifer Hill wins the junior high trophy.

"*Three* trophies for Alaska," Bruce whispers.

"Combining difficult research, essay writing, creative thinking, and intense verbal interaction in a timed event," Dr. Crabbe says, "Future Problem Solving is played by 200,000 students in over fourteen countries. Here in Cedar Rapids are teams from Canada, Mexico, and over thirty states in America."

She steps to the edge of the stage, microphone in hand, and speaks directly to the kids. "You are indeed the best and the brightest your states have to offer. We, as educators and parents, offer you our sincerest appreciation." She begins to applaud and the other adults throughout the auditorium quickly follow suit. Bruce and I turn and clap for our kids, and I pound Meredith on the back.

"While all of you have engaged in intense and often prolonged study to be here this morning," Dr. Crabbe continues as the applause dies down, "I think you will agree that you could not have made it this far without the untiring efforts of those teachers who coached you. We wish we could thank each coach individually, not only those coaches of the teams here, but also those who coach academics everywhere. Obviously, there is no way to show our appreciation to all the coaches for their efforts, but we can, try," her voice abruptly rises a couple of octaves, "can't we, kids?"

Now it's the kids' turn—clapping, hooting, hollering, my team shaking Bruce's and my hands, and Merle leaning over Meredith and Romie to swat us each on the backs of our necks. Eskimo style.

Gradually the furor lessens, and Dr. Crabbe continues. "Since the national office has no way to honor each coach individually, each year we honor one or two who have demonstrated an ability to lead students into a realm of academics that others might have considered impossible.

"The year's first honoree is Detroit's Sandra Lee Wong, who taught Problem Solving to a group of the learning-disabled. Sandra Lee cannot be with us today, but a representative from her school district has made the trip." A man wearing a red tie goes onstage to accept the award.

"The second honoree," Dr. Crabbe says, "is George Guthridge."

My students cry out with delight, and Bruce shakes my hand as I walk to the stage as though in a dream. "George is from the tiny Bering Sea village of Gambell, Alaska," Dr. Crabbe goes on. "Many of you have met his wonderful students. We are naming George as this year's cowinner of the award—for the Outstanding Academic Coach because of what Alaska's Future Problem Solving office wrote to us the day after his teams won the junior high *and* high school divisions of that state." From the table she takes a letter, which she unfolds. "'He taught Eskimo students not only that they could compete,'" she reads, "'he taught them that they could win.'"

After accepting the award while the audience gives me a standing ovation, I make it back up the aisle, walking on rubbery legs. I collapse into my seat and pass the plaque around as the kids clap me on the shoulders and Bruce, smiling broadly, pumps my hand.

"And now," Dr. Crabbe says, with the authority of a ringmaster as a drum roll sounds from backstage, "the main event!" The auditorium rings with the students' cheers and applause, for this is what the kids have studied for all year. This is what some teams have prepared for, and hoped for, for years.

She lifts up one of the smaller trophies still left on the table. "In fifth place, elementary school division, Cordova, Alaska!"

The Southeast Alaska students jump around with joy, and we other Alaskans give them a standing ovation as they head to the stage.

The applause continues as the other elementary division winners wend their way up for the trophies. There's a pause as Dr. Crabbe lifts the fifth-place trophy for the junior high division.

"You think our junior high team could have gotten fifth?" Bruce asks me. "You think?"

We look down the row to where Sharon Green, the head of our state's program, is seated at the end of the Alaskan contingent. Her face is forward, but there is a tight smile on her lips.

"You think she knows the results already?" Bruce asks.

My mind's too shot to think. Could a fifth place be possible?

But it is not to be. Fifth place on the junior high level goes to a Colorado team. Fourth is announced, and third. By the time the second-place winners head to the stage, I am barely listening. I am thinking of the good fortune that already has befallen us.

"This year's junior high national team champions," Dr. Crabbe says, holding the big trophy as high as she can, "Gambell, Alaska!"

The kids fall over themselves like puppies, hugging, crying, clapping. Bruce and I stare at each other in amazement as we step into the aisle to allow the kids out. They trundle down the aisle, arms around each other, laughing.

"I don't believe it," I tell him under my breath as we follow the kids forward.

"Believe it," he says.

No sooner have we returned to our seats than Dr. Crabbe begins announcing the high school team winners. I am admiring the trophy, which Romie is hugging and rocking back and forth as if it's a child, when Bruce clutches my shoulder.

"It's Sharon Green," he whispers. "She's still got that smile."

I jerk up my head, eyeing her. "Not possible," I tell him.

"Anything's possible," he says.

"No school has ever won two Problem Solving national championships in the same year," I remind him. *"No one."*

"I doubt if there are more than half a dozen schools that have ever won two national academic team championships in anything in the same year," Bruce says.

"And this year's high school national champions," Dr. Crabbe announces, "with a record-breaking score of 237.5 points, Gambell, Alaska!"

More squealing and yelling, Marshall holding the sides of his head as if shaking himself awake and saying, "Oh man, oh man, oh man." Merle gives Boone a high-five.

As we stand and the kids exit the row, Londa holds back. "I can't go up too, can I?" she whispers desperately. "I'm just the alternate."

"It was a team effort, and you were part of it," I tell her.

She is weeping openly as she follows the others to the stage, the rest of the audience on their feet, giving us an ovation that goes on and on and on.

A photographer takes pictures of our teams standing on campus in front of the college bell, and then the kids disperse to the dorms, except for Meredith and Romie. Meredith tugs on my arm. "Can Romie go traveling with us this summer," she asks, "if it's okay with her dad?"

Romie grins and her brows go up when I look at her.

"If it's okay with her parents."

Somehow the grin broadens and brows lift even higher.

"Can Meredith come back with me before school starts?" Romie asks. "I want her to see our Fourth of July celebration."

"We'll have to ask your mom," I tell her. "But I'm sure it will be fine."

The girls giggle and, holding hands, run off to the dorm. Bruce too walks away, arms laden with trophies. I stay behind to arrange with the photographer for copies of the photos. I am more exhausted, and yet more exultant, than any other time in my life. It is a serene day in June. The grass is opulent green, the buildings a burnt red against an azure sky.

53

"Welcome to three-wheeler capital of the world," Jones says, when all of us—less Meredith and Romie, who stayed in Seattle with Mary and Gretchen—get off the plane. He shakes my hand. "Welcome home."

Around us is an array of red and yellow ATVs, many with drivers revving the engines, several sporting American and Alaskan flags. I mount up behind Romie's dad, and we serpentine through the village, some of the people blowing party horns. Children run out of houses to shake our hands and to wave sparklers. Fireworks spew into the sunny sky as we near the school, where we dine on walrus liver and whale roast and seafood from the beach. I feign being full when the Eskimo ice cream comes around.

Afterward, I go for a walk down by the ocean. The water is putty gray from the glacial melt in the rivers that empty into the Bering Sea, the sky so clear that the mountains of Siberia seem a stone's throw away. The wavelets *shush* against the black-gravel beach, then draw under themselves like some primordial animal secreting treasure. The breeze blows my hair and chills my cheeks. I feel alive, here at the edge of the world, and I realize a terrible truth. My heart belongs here, where I can never remain forever, for my people are of another place, my ancestors and relatives scattered and ultimately unknowable.

When I walk back over the slight hill that separates the village from the sea, I find Jones among the skin boats, as usual upside down on their racks, the wood bleached and peeling. His hand rests on the nearest boat, and he gazes out to sea.

"Ever wonder what's there, on Siberian side?" He speaks as much to the breeze as to me.

"I'm not sure what's on *this* side."

"I wonder that too, I guess." Wistfully he adds, "I can't boating no more. Doctor said, and my boat captain he agree. Too much tendonsnitis." He windmills an arm and exhales with a huff as though to indicate the pain. "I don't know I stand it next season, when I watch them go. I can't imagine no world without whaling."

We walk back into the village, crunching through gravel, he with one hand on my shoulder. "You a good man, but you troubled," he says. "You know what your trouble is?"

I do not reply. I know it is not the kind of question one answers.

"You half Eskimo, George. Somebody forget to tell you that." He grins toothlessly.

"My trouble, Jonesie," I say, looking toward my shack with its awful turquoise color that we painted during our first fall, "is that I'm a man without a culture."

He laughs and pats me on the back. It feels good—somehow makes me feel *whole*. "I like the thing you do with the boys and girls," he says.

"I hope others like it," I say.

"Some will, some won't, I guess."

He leaves me to do his maintenance work at the elementary school, so I wander over to my place to pack a few more things we have forgotten for the summer, and then to wait for the evening plane.

Merle and Boone, coming from the store, approach between the Old Village houses. I unlock my flimsy door and we go inside for coffee. We talk about the trip and about the primly dressed *Alaska News* television reporter who met the team at the Anchorage airport. "'And what did the national problem involve?'" Boone mimics, for she tried to interview him.

Merle takes hold of Boone's wrist—Boone making a fist to indicate a microphone—and plays the part of his cousin. "'There was a genetically engineered serum for children, called Polyvac,'" Merle says, mimicking Boone. "'We were worried about the efficiency of placing a new gene exactly at the proper locus on the helix. We therefore postulated . . .'"

Boone, playing the reporter's part, pulls away, looking confused but trying to maintain a smile as the camera rolls. "'Anyway, out in Gambell they study a lot about genetics. And other science *stuff*,'" he adds, using her words verbatim.

We laugh so much that I can hardly pour the coffee. Then I see Boone's smile wane, and a deep sadness seems to seize him. His shoulders sag. He gazes down into his coffee.

"When we were at the store," he says, "Chester—you know Chester?" I nod; he is one of the older men. "Chester asked me, 'What's a tate?' I said, 'A what?' You know, he has that heavy accent when he speaks English. 'A tate,' he says. 'You mean, Tate Solomon?' I asked. 'No,' he says, 'a tate. What a baby suckles.' Then he laughs at me. 'You kids didn't learn nothing in that contest,' he says." Boone lifts his head, a troubled look to his eyes. "He thought it was some kind of vocabulary competition."

"Some people will never understand," I say, feeling a haunting sense of déjà vu from my talk with Jones. "I'm not sure you kids understand. I'm not sure that I do. I'm not sure that any of us truly understands the enormity of what you accomplished."

"It hurts, you know?" Boone says.

There are footsteps in the arctic entry, a knock at the door, and Kasha and Bunnie enter. "There's going to be a dance," Kasha says, in that lovely, lilting voice of hers. She takes hold of Boone's hand and pulls him to his feet. Bunnie stands back, looking at Merle through eyes filled with love. He rises and hands me his cup. "Guess I better take a rain check," he says, laughing lightly. "We'll wait for rain next year, then meet you on the mountain."

"Before you go away to college?" I ask.

"Yeah," he says. "Before I go away."

"You can handle being away from here?" I ask. "Away from hunting?"

"There will always be whales," he says as he steps into the arctic entry, Boone and Kasha and Bunnie already out the door. "But if some of us don't get the education we need to compete in the white man's world, there might not be whales. At least, there might not be hunting." He grins slyly. *"Harvesting,"* he says, his laughter tinged with irony and anger. "Have to remain politically correct."

He stops, a hand on the doorknob. "They expect that of us, you know," he says. "The whales, I mean. They expect us not only to hunt them but to protect them."

Then they all are out the door, out into the evening sunlight, and though they beg me to come dancing, I decline. "I'm going to catch the late flight back to Nome," I tell them. "I need to get back to Seattle as soon as I can," thinking of the hospital. "Don't come see me off. And please tell everyone else not to. I want . . . I just want to be alone."

We shake hands, share farewells, and they walk away, two couples hand-in-hand, very much in love. I watch them until they disappear among the weathered buildings, and go inside to wash the cups and make sure the stove is off, and to finish packing.

Two hours later Jones shows up with his three-wheeler and rickety cart, and takes me to the runway. Patches of ice gleam on the mountain, where the coffins lie. The lake looks deeply blue despite being so shallow, and the slap of the sea on the other side of the isthmus sounds strangely like applause. As I board, the village's boxy houses huddle in the distance.

The pilot is my favorite. He has added an old-fashioned leather pilot's cap and airline sunglasses to his ensemble. There being only the two of us, I sit in the copilot's seat.

"You want to fly this thing?" he asks.

"I'll leave that up to you."

"I was afraid you'd say that."

He grins and starts the engine, which sputters and kicks into life, the props beginning to spin. As he taxis, I wonder where the takeoff will lead. I know I will be back in the fall, but I sense that the teaching will be different—easier, the adventure over. What I do not yet know is that the trophies will remain in my classroom, for Mr. Dan will take a district office job, hoping to wrestle with the devils. The new principal, who will install a beautiful trophy case in the hall, will decide that there is room in the case only for athletic awards, not academic ones.

As the pilot and I wing toward the diamond-shaped sun and bank toward the east, heading toward Nome, I have no feel for what the future holds. I do not realize that when I leave the island four years from now, the trophies will be relegated to the attic. Though they represent the dreams and dedication and extraordinary achievement of ten students who overcame adversity and intolerance and seemingly impossible odds—the principal, without a second thought concerning what those golden Lamps of Knowledge might mean, will stash them away to gather dust.

But they will not be forgotten. For when that principal leaves, a new administrator—one who has lived in the village for years, has in fact married into it—will step in. He will bring down the trophies from upstairs and, with the help of students in the home economics classes he used to teach, will oversee the sewing of a beautiful banner that will hang in the gym and celebrate the national championships.

His name and title? *Lars Lumbreck. Principal. Gambell Schools.*

"Going home for the summer?" the pilot asks.

"*Leaving* home for the summer," I say.

epilogue

I went to Saint Lawrence Island to make money and acquired wealth beyond measure. It's not in a bank, not in the usual way we think of banks, anyway; nor do I carry it in my wallet. It rides in a secret place in my heart, so much a part of me that even now, over two decades later, I do not know where my love ends for those kids and for that village and its tiny school, and where the rest of my life begins. I could have retired years ago, but each year I return to the classroom, often teaching year-round rather than taking summers off, and despite the headaches and occasional heartaches I fall in love all over again.

And what became of my kids from Gambell—almost certainly the only team of Native Americans ever to win a national championship in academics? Kasha, writing in Siberian Yupik and then translating her work into English, as a senior won a national award as an essayist. She and Boone married; they live in a suburb an hour from Anchorage. He was a junior in college when they hit financial bottom—so poor that on their daughter's birthday, Kasha had to use water instead of milk on the girl's cereal. Desperate, Boone went to the house of a friend, a carver from Gambell, and begged to use the man's carving tools and a piece of ivory. Given a walrus rib, Boone waited until his friend left, got down on his knees and, holding the piece of ivory, prayed to the Lord for focus. He then saw a single line he could work within the ivory, a line that would be his focal point. In four hours—an extraordinary feat even for an expert—he carved his first piece, a seal, which he sold to a gift shop. He bought presents for his daughter and his friend, and began carving in earnest. Today, he is one of Alaska's most famous artists, one of the few Native carvers to work in such diverse mediums as marble and bronze. His work is highly sought: Arnold Palmer and Jewel are steady customers. Some of his pieces are in the Smithsonian.

After an unsuccessful attempt at becoming a rock star, Alvin devoted himself to drawing, and is now famous for using pointillism in scrimshaw: drawing on ivory with India ink, with myriad dots depicting a single animal. Allana and Bess live in Gambell and help run the Native corporation. When he is not hunting polar bears, Marshall also works for the Native corporation. He often makes trips Outside to help generate markets for village crafts. Romie also works for the corporation, though she lives in Nome. Her brother, who helped her to harness her fierce drive and overcome her reading deficiency to emerge as a national champion, died in a snowstorm while snowmachining. Londa is a housewife, and lives in Anchorage.

Merle, who was not so much my student as my mentor, attended three years of college, majoring in rural development. Married and with three children (he and Bunnie now have five), he ran out of money and returned to Gambell. The Alaska State Troopers wanted him to attend the academy, and he was literally at the door, his bag packed, when he changed his mind. Looking out at the village, he realized that if he became a trooper, who in rural areas travel constantly, he would have little time for his family and for living a subsistence lifestyle. Today he is a hunter, basketball coach, ivory carver, and grant writer, and attends college part-time, via distance delivery. In 2000, he and Bunnie were honored as the Alaska Native Parents of the Year.

Five years after the events of this book, Gretchen and three other eighth-grade girls from the mainland Inupiat/Central Yup'ik village of Elim won the state Future Problem Solving championship, after scoring 310 points on the qualifying problem, a new national record. She and three other girls then dominated Alaska's Battle of the Books, a reading competition, for the next four years. After earning a master's in education, for several years she taught at-risk kids on the Army base outside Anchorage. She now teaches English at Anchorage's East High School.

After Meredith graduated from college in Asian studies and earned a master's in business, she became the supervisor of technical writers at a pharmaceutical company. Then, in one of those amazing ironies that life offers, she took a job as a quality-assurance manager for a corporation that produces materials for genetic engineering firms, including the main one she studied on the Iowa trip.

Clearly, living in a cross-cultural situation affected my family in very deep ways. Mary recently retired from teaching for Bering Straits, and is married to an Inupiat. I am married to a Thai, Meredith to an African American, the son of a well-known Civil Rights leader, Gretchen to a Filipino. When we and our children go out to dinner, it's the Rainbow Coalition trooping between the tables.

I taught in Alaska villages for eight years until, worn down by frustration with the administration, which worsened after the kids won, I returned to teaching college. Not until I was on sabbatical, working on a doctorate, did I start to understand what the kids and I had done, what Merle calls the welding together of two ladders of learning. We married Western culture's syllogistic, abstract, linear thinking to the holistic, nonlinear, realistic reasoning of indigenous culture. The result is a communicator who addresses the world in a new way.

The educational techniques that I developed on the island remain the basis of my teaching. During the school year, I teach the methods to business people, teachers, and other professors; and each summer I teach the core classes of a rigorous college-prep program to fifty Native American high school seniors, most of whom come from remote villages. Students from Greenland, British Columbia, and from 95 percent of Alaska's communities, some with fewer than twenty-five people, have gone through the program.

Over 240 of those students have graduated from college, and more are currently enrolled. They have graduated not only from all of Alaska's colleges and trade schools but also from such places as Dartmouth, Harvard, MIT, Syracuse, and Stanford. In a single month we had a graduate from West Point, another from Yale Law School, another from the University of Washington Medical School. I teach them the lessons I learned from "The Kids from Nowhere," then watch in awe as they shed the safe, self-absorbed cocoon of adolescence and, emerging into adulthood, spread those iridescent wings of intellect.

And so the wonder continues.

about the author

George Guthridge has been nationally honored four times as an educator for his work with Alaska Native youth. Using his methods, his rural Alaska students have graduated from many of the top universities in the country. A former technical writer and science magazine editor-in-chief, he has published five novels and more than seventy short stories and novelettes, and has been a three-time finalist for the Hugo and Nebula Awards for science fiction and fantasy. In 1998, he and coauthor Janet Berliner won the prestigious Bram Stoker Award for *Children of the Dusk*, which critics compared to *Lord of the Flies* and to Conrad's *Heart of Darkness*. George is now Professor of English at the University of Alaska Fairbanks, Bristol Bay, where he is creating a DVD and workbook series about his revolutionary approaches to teaching writing and grammar. The royalties he receives from this book will go toward building a school in a poverty-stricken area overseas. The school will be dedicated to the Kids from Nowhere.

Other books by George Guthridge

The Bloodletter

With Janet Berliner:
Child of the Light
Child of the Journey
Children of the Dusk
The Madagascar Manifesto

With Carol Gaskins:
Death Mask of Pancho Villa